Desktop
Publishing

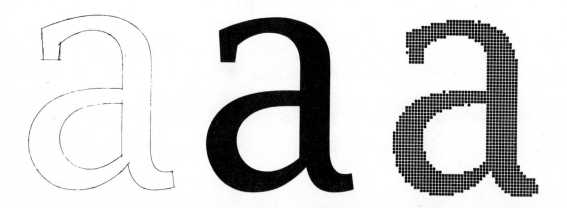

How digital type is formed in a desktop publishing output device: creating and filling an outline to make a letter.

Three representations of *a*.

Three stages of a digital letter design.

Left: Original outline design of Lucida® lowercase *a*.

Center: Solid letterform showing the relationship of black letter to white counterform.

Right: Scan conversion of digital outline to a bit map for use on a laser printer or digital phototypesetter.

Lucida is a registered trademark of Bigelow & Holmes, San Francisco.

Desktop Publishing

Frederic E. Davis
Executive editor of A+ Magazine and a specialist in information technology

John A. Barry
Writer, editor, and etymologist

Michael Wiesenberg
Technical writing specialist and free-lance writer

EVA LANGFELDT
Contributing writer and editor

DOW JONES-IRWIN
Homewood, Illinois 60430

This publication is designed to provide accurate and
authoritative information in regard to the subject matter
covered. It is sold with the understanding that the
copyright holder is not engaged in rendering legal, accounting,
or other professional service. If legal advice or other expert
assistance is required, the services of a competent
professional person should be sought.

*From a Declaration of Principles jointly adopted by a Committee
of the American Bar Association and a Committee of Publishers.*

ISBN 0-87094-766-4

Library of Congress Catalog Card No. 86-70718

Printed in the United States of America

2 3 4 5 6 7 8 9 0 ML 3 2 1 0 9 8 7 6

Introduction

This book is for people who want to publish their own newsletters, reports, books—whatever—and save time and money in the process. *Desktop Publishing* examines one of the most promising and exciting new areas of computer technology: the use of personal computers to produce printed materials. If you already own a computer, you may want to use it as a publishing tool. Knowing that a personal computer can be the foundation of a publishing system may spur you to go out and buy one to put a publishing system on your desk.

Desktop publishing. We hear and see the term a lot these days. What exactly is it? What does it mean? This book answers these questions and others. We define *desktop publishing* as the use of a personal computer, writing and graphics software, and page layout software to produce printed material. We suggest the best systems for certain applications, including business publishing, which we believe is currently the most promising arena for desktop publishing.

Here is a brief road map to the book:

Initially, we briefly discuss publishing—how it originated and evolved and the state of publishing today. Then we go into the main part of the book: applications for and tools of desktop publishing.

Applications. Here, we explore the realm of desktop publishing. We explain what comprises a desktop publishing system, what you can use it for, and how. We provide an overview of the primary components of a system:

- personal computer
- word processing software
- graphics software
- page layout software

and the secondary components:

- communications software
- database and information management software
- spreadsheets and number processing software

We then go on to categorize publishing. We have identified three areas for which desktop publishing technology is best suited:

- business publishing, the most fertile ground for the new technology
- periodical publishing, including newsletters—an area we believe is ripe with opportunities
- book publishing, an embryonic area of desktop publishing whose potential is only beginning to be explored

Throughout our discussion of these three publishing categories, we have interspersed profiles of people and organizations that are putting desktop publishing to work for them.

A fourth publishing category is personal publishing, and we offer some hints about personal desktop publishing in the "Money-Making Ideas" appendix.

Having your own publishing system automatically gives you access to page formatting software, a gallery of electronic art, a range of type sizes and styles, and many other resources. With all these tools at your disposal, you may be tempted to become an overnight publication designer. As we explain in chapter 3, however, effective design takes time, study, and effort, so we give you rules of thumb about good design and how to best achieve it. As in other chapters, we steer you toward other, more detailed sources of information on the subject.

Since we believe that desktop publishing represents a fine opportunity for current and would-be newsletter publishers (the United States alone accounts for more than 100,000 newsletters), we have devoted an entire chapter to desktop newsletter publishing.

Tools. The second major part of the book covers the tools of desktop publishing. Two computer systems—Apple's Macintosh and the IBM PC series of computers and "compatibles"—are the systems of desktop publishing, and we give extensive coverage to each system. We show you what products have emerged to fulfill the needs of desktop publishers and how to put them together to form the system that's best for you. We also examine, in less detail, desktop publishing systems based on high-performance—and high-cost—workstations.

Before we delve into laser printers and typesetting machines—the output devices that bring your creations into print—we discuss the page layout software and typesetting languages that give form to your creations.

Finally, we examine scanners and digitizers, with which you can incorporate photographic and video images into your publications.

Although we have made no attempt to provide a comprehensive source of products, we have endeavored to describe all the major products and product categories in the text and have included a resource guide in the back of the book that will help you locate many other products. Since companies announce new products continuously and make upgrades to previous products, you should consult with manufacturers and dealers and read magazines before you make a purchase, just to ensure that you get the most up-to-date information.

Appendixes give you:

- money-making ideas to help you recoup some of those costs
- a resource guide listing products, companies, and services
- a selected bibliography to point you to more information on desktop publishing
- a glossary of terms found in the book, as well as general publishing terminology

HOW TO USE THIS BOOK

Because *Desktop Publishing* covers a lot of territory, we've arranged it in a modular format to make the information you need easy to find. The road map above shows you the various sections. This arrangement not only makes information you need easy to locate, but it also allows you to skim areas about which you're already knowledgeable, or that don't particularly relate to your needs.

For example, say you publish a small newsletter about coin collecting, and your current method of production involves typing its contents on an IBM Selectric typewriter, pasting the typescript onto art boards, and having the printing done at an instant print shop. You want to computerize your operations, but you're not sure what to do. In such a case, you'd probably want to concentrate on the tools and resources section, although the chapters on newsletters and design might give you some fresh ideas for your existing publication.

If you already own a personal computer and decide you want to start a newsletter, the first place to look is the newsletter chapter. Next, you'll likely look at the tools section to discover what products are best for you.

Say you're a manager in charge of acquiring computer systems for your company or setting up an in-house publishing system. Businesses have tended to select IBM PCs, although the Macintosh is making strides as a business computer system. You're likely to be in a situation that requires you to integrate PCs and Macintoshes into a cohesive system whose purpose is to produce publications of some sort. By reading the chapter on the Macintosh and that on the PC series, you'll be ready to develop a functional system that exploits the best of both worlds.

In short, we believe this book is your essential guide to the realm of desktop publishing.

A WORD OF ADVICE ABOUT BUYING

Something to keep in mind when selecting hardware and software for a desktop publishing system is to pay more attention to the difference between good enough and not good enough than to the difference between good enough and the best. Desktop publishing has established itself as a major area of personal computing and is supported by a wide variety of hardware and software. Before considering equipment purchases, it's a wise idea to determine what your needs are. Sometimes it's handy to write down a needs analysis listing what your desktop publishing system must do, what you would like it to do, what is nice but not necessary, and so forth. Knowing clearly what your needs are will help you avoid making purchasing mistakes.

Once you've decided what your needs are for your particular application, you can then start to look at hardware and software products. You will probably find that some products are not good enough, others are good enough, and yet others are considered the best. It is easy to be dazzled by the best and be tempted to purchase these products. Your application may not demand the best, however; it may only need something that is good enough, and you may end up spending a lot more money than you need to if you purchase something that offers advanced capabilities that you will seldom, if ever, use.

By carefully considering what you need, you will avoid two common pitfalls in purchasing microcomputer products: first, not buying equipment that is capable of performing your task and, second, being oversold and spending much more than you need to accomplish your task.

DESKTOP PUBLISHING IN ACTION: HOW THIS BOOK WAS BUILT

The authors used desktop publishing tools to produce this book. The majority of the writing was done on Macintoshes with Microsoft Word, although some of the text was generated on a CP/M-based system using Spellbinder and sent by modem to the Macintoshes. The authors used Dayna Communications' MacCharlie to convert the Macintosh files to IBM PC format. Author Wiesenberg formatted the files on an IBM PC/AT-compatible Hewlett-Packard Vectra computer with PCTEX from Personal TEX; he used Word Perfect 4.1 to insert the formatting commands. Page proofs were printed on The Desktop Printshop (LP300) laser printer from Corona Data Systems. The authors then mailed PCTEX device-independent files to Textset of Ann Arbor, Michigan, which produced camera-ready copy on an Autologic Micro-5 phototypesetter and sent the copy to Dow Jones-Irwin's production department.

ACKNOWLEDGMENTS

The authors would like to thank the following people for their invaluable assistance and support: Bruce Baker, Etel Barborka, Stuart Beatty, John Bintz, Bruce Blumberg, Paul Brainerd, Colleen Byram, Maggie Canon, Chip Carman, Lance Carnes, Jean Craig, Ben Davis, Robin Davis, Valerie Devonish, Vince Dorn, Kip Farmer, Matt Foley, William Gladstone, Susan Glinert, Mark Hall, Amanda Hixson, Kris Holmes, Bob Hoskins, Virginia L. S. Joe, John Johnson, Steve Kanzler, Ajit Kapoor, Jerrold Kazdoy, Judi Kidwell, Nancy Long, Susanna Michaela, Carol Person, Ann Robinson, and Craig Webb.

Contents

Part One

Publishing Overview

Chapter 1

What Is Publishing?

Publishing is the distribution of printed materials, but the publishing process also encompasses various other areas such as art, language, and marketing. Because of this broader scope, a broader definition of publishing is *the technology of written communication.* Desktop publishing, the latest step in the evolution of that technology, is a new use of personal computer systems as an aid in the preparation of printed material.

HISTORY OF PUBLISHING TECHNOLOGY

The history of publishing coincided with the development of written languages. Paper, which was originally made from mashed papyrus, became a primary vehicle for printed material. Early publications were hand-copied on pieces of paper and sometimes bound to make books. The first forms of printing involved carving a message, usually on a piece of stone or wood, coating it with some type of ink, and pressing that plate against a piece of paper to make an impression. Very early publishers used this process more for reproducing artwork than for printing characters, since images had to be carved in reverse, and it was difficult and tedious to carve written characters for text.

A major milestone in publishing technology was movable type. The best-known movable-type pioneer was Johann Gutenberg (ca. 1390–1468), who combined the concepts of movable type and printing presses to create one of the first practical publication systems.

Movable type works on a letterpress, which pushes a piece of paper against solid pieces of movable type, and the resulting piece of paper has slight indentations where the type has made contact with the paper. If you look carefully at the paper in a letterpress document, you can see that the type has made an impression in the paper.

Movable type remained the primary means of forming printed materials until the invention of the Linotype machine in 1888. With the Linotype machine, an entire line, usually 20 to 80 characters, of text could be assembled automatically into a mold filled with molten lead. It created a line of type, hence the name *Linotype.* These lead blocks of type were assembled into columns and used to print pages. This typesetting device marked the beginning of automated typography. Although Linotype machines marked a significant evolution in publishing technology, they also had many drawbacks. Printers had to double as metallurgists and melt a great deal of lead to create lines of type.

The Linotype remained the predominant form of typesetting machine until the early 1950s, when CRT typesetters were first developed. A CRT typesetter was based on cathode ray tube technology similar to that of a television set. The development of CRT typesetters marked the beginning of electronic phototypesetting, which has remained the major publishing technology.

PUBLISHING TECHNOLOGY TODAY

CRT typesetters are still prevalent, but laser-driven typesetters capable of resolutions of 1200 dots per inch (*dpi*) or higher are rapidly gaining acceptance. (A 1200-dpi resolution, for example, means that the typesetter can squeeze 1,440,000 individual dots—i.e., 1200 horizontal by 1200 vertical—into a square inch.) These laser devices will probably overtake CRT typesetters in popularity within the next couple of years.

Both laser typesetters and CRT typesetters are digital devices. Digital systems store characters as numeric codes. The characters are re-created from these numeric codes on a CRT screen that is an internal part of the typesetting machine, in CRT typesetters, or re-created by a laser beam, in laser typesetters.

Despite these advances in technology, a popular, inexpensive method of do-it-yourself typesetting and page layout still persists. This "typesetting" consists of using a typewriter or computer printer to print the text, which is then laid out by hand and pasted up on a sheet of paper, along with perhaps some press type for headlines and possibly some graphics. A photocopy machine takes care of the printing.

Some small publishing houses still use letterpresses because this technology yields finely crafted printing that is desirable for certain art books, but movable type and letterpresses will probably remain only as a specialized craft.

Today, most typesetting professionals use digital typesetting machines. With the hardware and software to support them, digital typesetters are currently very expensive. A complete system can cost anywhere from $30,000 to $100,000 and up. One reason for this high cost is that the typesetting device requires custom equipment to drive it. Desktop publishing technology, which deals primarily with digital typesetting machines, will reduce the cost of producing typeset materials because it makes the text entry and formatting system independent of the typesetting device. A general purpose personal computer, such as the IBM PC or Apple Macintosh, can control much of the typesetting process. When true phototypesetting is not necessary, a personal computer system with an advanced printer, such as an Apple LaserWriter Plus or Hewlett-Packard LaserJet PLUS, can produce acceptable final copy.

Part Two

Applications

Chapter 2

The Realm of
Desktop Publishing

Desktop publishing is one of the most promising and exciting applications of personal computer technology today. It is called "desktop publishing" because most of the tools it requires can fit on top of a desk. In fact, anyone who has a personal computer such as a Macintosh or IBM PC has the potential to become a desktop publisher. This book will show you how you can put your computer system to work to publish reports, catalogs, newsletters, magazines—even books. If you plan to turn your computer into a desktop publishing system, or if you're planning to buy a personal computer for that purpose, what do you need to effectively set yourself up to produce professional looking publications?

DESKTOP PUBLISHING SYSTEMS

A basic desktop publishing system consists of a personal computer such as an Apple Macintosh or IBM PC, page layout software, and a page printer, such as a laser printer, or a typesetting machine. You can own all the elements of a system, or you can own only a personal computer and take formatted files to a service bureau that will do typesetting from your files. If you use such a service bureau approach, you can set yourself up as a publisher for less than $3000.

A desktop publishing system based on the Apple Macintosh Plus and LaserWriter.

A desktop publishing system involves more than the production of publication-quality material, however. A well-rounded system exploits all the technological advances that have made "personal computing" personal. When you have a computer on your desk, you have the potential to write and format documents, create and incorporate graphics, prepare camera-ready copy for printing, obtain a wealth of information from on-line news and information services, keep databases of mailing and subscription lists, create your own advertising fliers and brochures, and keep all the financial records relating to your publishing endeavor—no matter how large or small it is.

The following is a brief look at the major components of a desktop publishing system.

Personal Computers

Two families of personal computers, Apple's Macintosh and the IBM PC series and compatible computers, have emerged as the main computing cores of a desktop publishing system. Chapters 5 and 6 give you an in-depth look at these computer systems. UNIX-based workstations, which we examine in chapter 7, also play a role in desktop publishing, although these more powerful systems are too expensive to be considered "personal" computers.

Software

Software gives you the applications that turn your computer into a desktop publishing system. Within the realm of desktop publishing and in this book, we have established six software categories. We've further classified these six kinds of software into two camps: primary and secondary software.

Primary Software

The three kinds of primary software are word processing, graphics, and page layout software. They are fundamental to the creation of the words and images that become pages in your publication.

Word Processing. This is where your publication starts—with the writing of text. Numerous word processing programs are available for personal computers. The leading word processing programs for the Macintosh are MacWrite and Microsoft Word; the IBM PC series offers a wider choice, including Microsoft Word, MultiMate, Word-Star, PFS:Write, and DisplayWrite. All of them allow you to do on-screen editing, and some are more complex and feature-laden than others. We, for example, used Word, Spellbinder, and WordPerfect to write and edit this book. Outline processing programs such as ThinkTank for the IBM PC and Macintosh help in the preparation of outlines and can serve as useful adjuncts to word processing programs.

Graphics. Graphics software varies in sophistication and capabilities. Most graphics packages not only let you create your own artwork, but most also have canned graphics called clip art. Some examples of graphics software for the Macintosh computer are Mac-Paint, MacDraw, and MacDraft. For the IBM PC series, important graphics programs include Microsoft Chart, Harvard Presentation Graphics, and PC Paint.

Page Layout. These packages allow you to take the text and graphics you've fashioned with packages in the previous two categories and turn them into finished pages. Most of the programs replicate, on the screen, an artist's layout board. The difference is that you lay out the pages electronically. PageMaker and MacPublisher for the Macintosh and DO-IT and SuperPage for the IBM PC series are examples of page layout programs.

We cover primary software in depth later in the book.

Secondary Software

Communications, database and information management, and spreadsheets and other number processing packages comprise secondary software applications. Once you have your desktop publishing system set up and operating smoothly, you can exploit programs in these categories to obtain information, maintain mailing lists, and keep financial records, among other tasks.

Communications. No computer is an island, or at least it shouldn't be. The capabilities of an individual computer are limited by the software that you have on hand to use with that computer. If you hook it up to other systems, however, using communications software with a telephone line or a local area network, you can have virtually unlimited information resources at your disposal, with information as diverse as the Library of Congress card catalog, abstracts of medical journals, current stock prices, movie reviews, and local news. Since desktop publishing is a communications technology, it can exploit data communications to send electronically prepared data to another computer for typesetting or to receive information from large computer systems such as that of Dialog or from other individual computers for the purpose of page design, typesetting, and the like.

For example, you can gather specialized information from on-line services and then edit and design it and sell it as a report. Another application is to prepare a newsletter for which you gather information or abstracts of articles on a specific topic. Yet another use is to search a database for a specific set of financial or statistical information that you can translate into graphic form with software in your desktop computer and incorporate into a publication. Since bibliographic retrieval services now index thousands of publications from all over the world, you can also use a modem and an information service such as Dialog, Nexis, or Dow Jones/News Retrieval to obtain excellent bibliographies for specific areas of interest. Modems and their accompanying software are the tools that put your computer in touch with other personal computers and with mainframe computers and information services. A modem is an important part of a complete desktop publishing system, not only for the exchange of documents but also for the retrieval of information that you can incorporate into published materials.

Database and Information Management. The on-line databases we alluded to in the communications software category are only some of the information services that have sprung up to provide data to information-hungry personal computer users. Other on-line services are listed in the Resource Guide. You can also put personal databases such as dBASE III or Omnis 3 to work for you and your publishing operations. Databases can not only be used to compile and organize information resources, but they are also ideal for keeping track of mailings, subscriber lists, and other publishing-related chores.

Spreadsheets and Number Processing. Popular spreadsheet programs such as Lotus 1-2-3 or Excel can serve you in financial record keeping and budget forecasting and also have the ability to create charts and graphs. As with data you can create and obtain with other types of software, you can use spreadsheets to incorporate numeric information into your publication, if appropriate. For example, if you published a financial newsletter, you could take such data and use it to create a chart full of projections for placement in a story about trends in a given area.

Page Printers

In many ways, inexpensive laser printers are the stars of desktop publishing. These devices allow you to get typeset-quality output that is indistinguishable from typesetting machine output to the untrained eye. We refer to laser printers as "page printers," meaning that you can produce pages of publication quality with them (a dot matrix printer such as the Apple ImageWriter can also be a page printer, since it can replicate typesetting—although at a low resolution). The most popular laser printer for its price and capabilities is Apple's LaserWriter. Other laser printers are the LaserJet from Hewlett-Packard and the Lasergrafix series from QMS.

At the high end of the page printer spectrum are high-resolution typesetting machines. Although ownership of one of these machines may elude your budget, you still have the possibility of setting type on them at service bureaus from the files you've created with page layout software.

The first part of this chapter has outlined what a desktop publishing system is—both in terms of hardware and software—and how you can use it for more than the primary applications of publishing. Publishing itself is the focus of the rest of the chapter. Other software that you can use in secondary desktop publishing applications is listed in the Resource Guide at the end of this book.

PUBLISHING CATEGORIZED

This book divides publishing into four distinct areas: business publishing, periodical publishing, book publishing, and personal publishing. These categories and other information in this book were derived from a model of publishing described by author Davis as part of his Ph.D. research in the area of computer-assisted publishing. All four areas can benefit from desktop publishing technology.

Business publishing involves the printing and distribution of company materials. It includes business reports, brochures, catalogs, product documentation, forms, letterheads, and corporate communications such as internal memos, advertising and promotional materials, and other items.

Periodical publishing is the printing and distribution of materials on a regular basis. The materials are usually distributed to the same group of individuals or a similar group at an interval that can be

- daily, as in the case of newspapers
- weekly, as in the case of newsletters and magazines (see chapter 4 for an examination of using desktop publishing systems to produce newsletters)
- monthly, as in the case of magazines and journals
- or even annually, as is the case with some journals and reviews

Periodical publishing also involves a coherent content and usually similar look from issue to issue.

What distinguishes book publishing from other types of publishing is that it involves the printing and distribution of a single, cohesive work. Book publishing's production time is usually longer than that of other types of publications.

Personal publishing is the printing and distribution of materials by individuals. The materials can include poetry, free-lance writing, essays, reports, humor, school papers, greeting cards, wedding and birth announcements, party invitations, personalized calendars, and so on. Personal publishing also encompasses artistic uses of publishing such as the publication of poetry. Often personal publishing overlaps with another type of publishing, as in the case of people who publish a book on their own or who send a periodical such as a newsletter to friends, members of an organization, or people with a common interest. The production of essays, reports, and other such documents, is another area of personal publishing that benefits from desktop publishing technology. The option of publishing your own reports can be an excellent method for dissemination of scientific information, especially in the publish-or-perish academic world. People in the personal category of publishing usually publish for their own benefit—financial gain and commercial success are not usually the prime motivations.

Since most desktop publishing systems are currently too expensive for personal use, and because personal applications are often similar to other uses, we do not include detailed coverage of personal publishing in this book. Although most laser printers are now too costly for casual use, Apple Computer and other manufacturers are developing lower-cost personal laser printers that should be available soon. These next-generation personal laser printers will help make personal publishing more affordable. QMS makes a $2000 laser printer now (see chapter 9). Personal publishing systems will help further freedom of speech, since, as the saying goes, freedom of the press is guaranteed only to those who own one. (For more on personal publishing prospects, see Appendix A, "Money-Making Ideas.")

BUSINESS PUBLISHING

Businesses, particularly technology businesses, face fierce competition and must move fast to stay ahead—or at least abreast—of their competitors. Corporate use of desktop publishing can not only save money, but it can also cut the time required to get important documents into print. With a desktop publishing system, a business can produce typeset documents and quick-print them. Newsletters, product information sheets, and other such corporate material can come out of small in-house publishing operations within companies. Other business applications that fall within the purview of desktop publishing are business reports, brochures, catalogs, letterheads, invoices, purchase orders, and corporate communications such as internal memos, presentation graphics, advertising, and promotional materials.

Business Reports

Business reports take many forms. Companies prepare them for internal use or for distribution to clients. With a desktop publishing system, people can prepare better-looking reports than they would get with a typewriter or letter-quality printer. For example, one person can draft a report. Then another person can take that same information and prepare the report for publication or presentation on overhead transparencies, using desktop publishing tools with charts or graphs of the information the report presents.

Brochures

Brochures are an important marketing tool. You give them to customers when you sell them a product or give them to potential customers, who take the brochure home to be reminded of your business. Brochures fill an important need for a company by communicating something about the company's product or service. They can be small, such as single-page fliers to announce a particular sale or service, or they can be more elaborate, having several pages and colors.

Desktop publishing aids in the publication of brochures. It not only lowers the cost of a brochure, but it also enables you to produce targeted brochures for products or services that may appeal only to a small group of people.

A brochure can contain a prospective customer's name and address, which you merge in from a database and print on a laser printer. A custom brochure will likely catch the recipient's attention, since it contains the person's name or even some information about the person from your database.

A brochure is often the initial printed material a potential customer sees, so it should look good. If you don't have the time and money to spend on typesetters, desktop publishing technology can give you professional-looking brochures, which have more credibility than something you might otherwise hastily throw together with a typewriter or dot matrix printer. You stand a better chance of convincing somebody to buy the product or service that the brochure represents. If you plan to design your own brochure, read chapter 3, "Design for Effective Communication."

Corporate Communications

Businesses run on paper. Memos flood corridors and in-baskets; personnel departments must constantly update their directories; employee handbooks are always up for revision. Although some companies have instituted "electronic mail," the paper mills grind on.

Since no end is in sight for the amount of printed material companies continue to disseminate, it makes increasing sense for firms to have and utilize desktop publishing systems. Think of some of the benefits:

- Memos. Many memos are tossed, unread, into the wastebasket. Many, you can argue, deserve to be. Along with the deserved detritus, unfortunately, are important items. Desktop publishing can help set a standard of memo composition and formatting that may save useful memos from the scrap heap. Employees might take more pride in their memos, and the overall quality of these documents might improve. Good-looking memos are also better candidates for filing, they can communicate ideas more effectively, and they carry an air of authority and credibility.
- Employee Handbooks. Picture the average such document: cranked out on a dot matrix printer and photocopied; sandwiched between bland covers. A typeset handbook, revised at reasonable intervals, might boost morale by giving employees a sense of increased self worth and company spirit.

- Other uses for desktop publishing in businesses:
  - Overheads. Overhead transparencies for presentations are much more effective if they're neat and professional looking.
  - Employee forms. Crisp, clean forms are more likely to receive prompt attention than hazy, typewritten, xerographic forms.
  - Outside materials. Correspondence, memos, reports, and other documents that go to outside suppliers, associates, auditors, and others, can only reflect favorably on your business. They might even help increase business.

Saving Time and Money

Steelcase, Inc., of Grand Rapids, Michigan, is a one-billion-dollar-a-year company that employs more than 10,000 people and manufactures office furniture. The company also produces its own forms, everything from invoices and expense reports to letterheads and memo pads. Until the advent of the LaserWriter, Steelcase created all of these forms by hand, using typewriters, press type, and stock logos. After evaluating several typesetting systems to help relieve the workload of hand making all the forms, Justin Corby, forms design and control manager for Steelcase, bought two Macintoshes and a LaserWriter, for approximately $15,000, along with MacWrite, MacDraw, and PageMaker. According to Corby, the staff members learned the system faster than he'd imagined possible. Before he bought the system, they required 167 hours within a week to produce 197 forms, but with the system in place, they needed only 144 hours to produce 198 forms. At this rate, Corby figures, the system will pay for itself in about six months.

Advertising and Promotion

Desktop publishing applies to many phases of advertising and promotion. Electronic page layout and design systems are a boon to the production of press releases, promotional materials, and advertisements for newspapers, magazines, or trade journals. By using selective information contained in a database and merging sections aimed at the specific audience into a typeset document, you can create fliers, press releases, and promotional materials that are aimed at the person who receives them. For example, you can personalize form letters for custom mailings that include special paragraphs and personal messages. Another type of promotion is a calendar with the recipient's birthday, anniversary, hiring date, or other information incorporated into the calendar. Such a personalized calendar will stand out from other calendars.

The ability to incorporate information into a promotion that is specific to a particular client makes that promotion much more effective. Desktop publishing can create highly targeted, customized promotions while lowering the cost of creating various kinds of promotional materials.

Many companies send press releases describing their latest products to the media. Often they give the information to public relations firms, which then produce the press release on their own equipment or charge top dollar for having the material typeset, sometimes with quality illustrations, also costing a premium and usually produced by a design studio. If the PR firm produces the information itself, it is usually typewritten on the company's letterhead. Small companies may elect to produce their own press releases to keep costs down, typically typing them on their own stationery or, worse, producing them on a low-resolution dot matrix printer.

The media receive hundreds of such press releases each month. Editors are used to seeing typeset material, so if you want their full attention, you cannot afford to send out releases that appear cheaply produced. (Of course, you must also write the release coherently.)

The description of a superlative product on a page of lined computer paper in dot matrix print may go into the wastebasket in favor of a description of a mediocre product on a carefully laid out, typeset page that incorporates striking graphics. A desktop publishing system will give your release the professional look that is more likely to catch an editor's eye. It also bypasses the high costs of outside publishing services and gives you more control over the content of your message. As with any desktop publishing application, you can tailor and update the release up to the last minute.

A Typical Scenario

Imagine that your company is announcing a new product and needs a data sheet and press release in a hurry. After interviewing the appropriate product designers, the product manager for the given item produces a rough draft or an outline of the data sheet and release, with suggestions for promotable features, and sends the diskette or transfers it electronically to the editorial services department. There, a writer turns the rough copy into a draft that circulates to the appropriate reviewers for approval.

When the necessary people have marked up the approval draft, they return it to the copywriter, who incorporates the changes and formats the document. Then a graphics designer adds the appropriate logos, address blocks, and the like, and sends the laser-printer-created, camera-ready document to a quick-print shop, which turns out thousands of copies in a matter of days.

Desktop publishing is ideal for documents of this type—those that emerge under time constraints, yet do not warrant a large production expenditure.

Catalogs

Desktop publishing technology reduces expenses, allowing you to produce catalogs for specific groups of people, personalized catalogs, and catalogs that you might not have considered publishing otherwise because of the high cost. A catalog constructed from a database, produced with electronic page layout software on a computer, and printed on a laser printer can have the look of an expensive catalog, in spite of its much lower cost. A company can produce special catalogs and catalog supplements targeted to a specific group of people by searching a database to find people with a common interest.

Company Uses Its Own Products to Publish

One company that is using desktop publishing technology to produce documents is Sun Microsystems of Mountain View, California. Sun manufactures technical workstations that run Interleaf publishing software (see chapter 7, "Workstations").

Like most high-technology companies, Sun creates an immense amount of printed material about its products. The marketing department alone has an annual budget of hundreds of thousands of dollars for the writing and printing of this material.

Although Sun spares little expense in producing glossy "high level" brochures and data sheets, the company's marketing department has increasingly relied on Interleaf and the UNIX typesetting language *troff* to print lower level and interim materials—particularly when production speed is a critical factor.

From time to time, Sun uses its desktop publishing tools to expeditiously print data sheets on recently announced and released products. This approach has the advantage of getting some documentation out the door faster than would be possible with traditional publishing methods. While Sun is using up its stock of these interim documents, the company can prepare, if appropriate, to produce slicker versions of the documents.

As an example, consider companies that produce time-sensitive catalogs with information on scores of products. If vendors are late in delivering product information to the company, the catalog may be inaccurate or incomplete as the printing deadline approaches. If the catalog is on line, an electronic publishing system can log and update product information at the last minute, giving the company better control over what is ordinarily a chaotic process.

Product Documentation

Many high-tech companies produce their own product documentation. Typically, it is written by an engineer, run off on a line printer, photocopied, three-hole-punched, and thrown into a binder. The documents are of the engineers, by the engineers, and for the engineers. Such documents usually look terrible and are virtually incomprehensible to nonengineers.

This practice still exists at some companies, but with desktop publishing, companies can have better editorial and production control over their own documentation and impart to it a professional look that helps clarify the information. Clear, easy-to-read, and easy-to-understand product documentation enhances the usefulness of products and cuts down on the number of phone queries from baffled customers. Companies can alter the documentation more easily and cheaply than an outside production house can. Even if your product changes only slightly, the documentation must reflect changing instructions for its use. Using desktop publishing equipment makes revisions much faster and cheaper.

Traditional Documentation Production Methods. Traditionally, businesses have handled product documentation in one of two ways, depending on the size of the business. Large corporations can often afford in-house production departments, and small companies frequently buy the services of graphic artists, typesetters, and layout and pasteup people. The steps are usually the same in both kinds of companies. (Generally, the procedures we describe here apply to most traditional methods of producing any publication.)

Say you're a technical writer and have produced a document. Early drafts go out for review by the developers of the product and the marketing department. If your company is large enough, others interested in the development of the documentation, such as support personnel (those who answer the phone when customers call with questions); sales engineers; installation personnel; and, often, prospective users, review the draft. These early drafts are frequently written on a computer or a word processing system—word processing is often the only concession many companies make to computerizing their documentation production methods—and printed on a high-speed dot matrix printer or a daisywheel printer.

After you've incorporated all input from reviewers, you submit a printed copy (hard copy) of the document for typesetting. On this hard copy, you add formatting instructions, usually in colored pencil or pen, to help the typesetter. You identify different textual elements, such as the levels of headings, font changes, and the arrangement of tabular material, in this fashion. In a large company, the typesetting department is in house, and you get back galleys within days or a week or so. Typically, a large corporation has one typesetting group, with several documentation groups clamoring for its services, so the turnaround time for typesetting can easily exceed a week. In a small company, you give the printed version of the final draft to an outside typesetting service and wait a week to a month or more for galleys.

In both cases, you carefully review the typeset galleys and find mistakes, both in the transcription of the text and in the formatting. You then return the galleys to the typesetter for corrections. Sometimes the corrected material itself has more mistakes, necessitating another wait for further corrections and the additional expense of creating new typeset galleys.

While this is going on, you also make separate arrangements for illustrations. Black and white photographs must be halftoned, color separations of photos and art must be made, and all artwork must be sized to fit on the allotted space on the page. The halftone process simulates different levels of gray with different dot patterns, closer together for darker shades and further apart for lighter shades. Color printing is even more complex, requiring the mixing on the page of dots of different colors. Photographs must be transformed into color separations before printing. Each color is then laid down on a separate pass in the printing process. Illustrations are another element that further lengthens the production time.

Often the product continues under development during all stages of the writing process, and the developers come to you at this point with urgent last-minute changes that must go into the documentation. Some companies do not permit changes to documentation at this stage, planning instead to handle them "at the next update." Other firms believe it is more important to give correct information to their customers, however, and they insist on your making changes even while the documentation is in the galley stage. This approach produces yet more delays.

After the galleys are approved, they must be pasted up. What exists now is not pages of text, but long strips of unpaginated material, with no "running heads," "running feet," or page numbers. A layout person cuts these long strips into page-size blocks, leaves room for the illustrations, and then pastes the text down onto layout boards. At the top of each board, he adds a running head. At the bottom he adds page numbers, and, if they are used, running feet.

He adds the illustrations and callouts to each illustration. (A *callout* is a word or phrase at the edge of the illustration that explains one of its elements.)

After the layout person pastes up the entire document, he returns it to you for review, and you find mistakes. A callout might be in the wrong place or point to the wrong element. Sometimes a block of text is mislaid, and you have to redo the whole job, an expensive undertaking. If the layout is done in house, the corrections may take hours. If the mistake is something as major as a dropped paragraph or illustration early in the document, the corrections may take days. When an outside contractor does the layout, the corrections usually take one or more days.

Not until the main part of the document has been correctly pasted up can you determine the proper page numbers for the table of contents and index. This delay means more work for the typesetter, who may have set all the titles for the table of contents in place, without page numbers. Now the typesetter has to enter the numbers, and you must again carefully check the results, which sometimes still have errors.

After the project team determines that the whole job has been correctly coordinated and everything is properly in place, you can finally send the document to the printer. Even the largest corporations hardly ever do their own printing; printing typically takes one to six weeks.

Product Documentation with Desktop Publishing.   Now say you're a technical writer with a desktop publishing system. You can skip all or most of the steps, right up to the point of sending the document off to the printer. Using a desktop publishing system, you can continually lay out the document while writing it. You can inexpensively print drafts for review, and reviewers can critique not only the content, but also the format.

You can use the graphics capabilities of your system to produce line art and other illustrations, and you can incorporate text and graphics with page makeup software. Many of these page layout programs permit automatic insertion of running heads and feet and page numbers. Some also automatically generate tables of contents and indexes.

The majority of errors caused when a typesetter reenters all the text do not occur. Formatting problems resulting from misunderstandings between you and the typesetter are also minimized, and dropped paragraphs or misplaced illustrations take seconds, not hours and days, to move. Since you have been interactively laying out the document from the start, the final draft can be ready to go within minutes of your entering the last piece of text. If you have any last-minute changes, you enter them, and the software automatically reformats the document.

More and more companies will find it cost- and time-effective to use the methods of desktop publishing for product documentation.

PERIODICAL PUBLISHING

Periodical publishing is the production and distribution of information with a similar theme and/or design that is distributed on a regular, or periodic, basis. It includes newsletters, newspapers, magazines, journals, and reviews. Newsletters are usually relatively short publications that deal with a specific area of interest. Newspapers are general interest periodicals issued daily or weekly. Magazines are generally more elaborate publications that come out weekly, bi-weekly, monthly, quarterly, or even annually. Journals and scholarly reviews are published monthly, quarterly, annually, or irregularly and cover specific areas such as science, literature, or art.

How Periodical Publishers Use Desktop Publishing

Desktop publishing can benefit any of these enterprises but will probably be the biggest boon to publishers of newsletters and journals. Newsletter publishing and journal publishing are alike in many ways. Both newsletters and journals usually focus on a specific subject matter. Since newsletter and journal publishers usually run smaller organizations than those of newspapers and magazines, they are in a better position to change their methods to adapt more easily to desktop publishing technology. Newsletter and journal publishers frequently have less money to work with, so the cost savings of desktop publishing will attract their attention.

For larger publishers, such as those whose products are newspapers or magazines, adopting a new technology can be very expensive, since changing existing methods may involve hiring and firing employees and changing operations. Switching to desktop publishing technology may necessitate many other changes, and the cost of making these additional changes may offset the money an organization saves by adopting this technology for the creation of the entire newspaper or magazine. Larger publishers that already have systems in place can adopt parts of desktop publishing technology initially, however; reap a savings immediately; and then avail themselves of other areas of the technology as desktop publishing develops and as they are able to gradually change their organizations' internal systems.

An example of how a magazine can adopt only a portion of desktop publishing illustrates this point. Let's say you're a large publisher, and the current system at your magazine involves receiving manuscripts on paper, editing them, and indicating type specifications on the manuscripts. Typesetters then enter the text, with its editing changes, into a typesetting device and use it to run off galley proofs. The art and production people use the proofread galleys as dummy type to create mockups of the final product by hand, after which the typesetting machine produces the final type for the camera-ready copy.

Adopting desktop publishing technology for such an operation need not require that editing, typesetting, and layout all involve the computer, even though you can do them all with a desktop publishing computer system. By starting with only a portion of what desktop publishing offers, you can continue to receive manuscripts and edit them on paper. Instead of entering the manuscript into a typesetting machine and running typeset galleys, however, the staff can enter the manuscript, with its corrections, into a desktop publishing system and create galley proofs on a page printer—a much less expensive method than running them out on a typesetting machine. After the production people receive these proofs, they can continue to do the layout by hand, and a typesetting machine or service that offers use of such a machine can create the final typeset output for the camera-ready copy. Adopting the desktop publishing system only as a way to produce type and galley proofs allows you to recoup the investment for the equipment from just a single capability of the computer system, with little disruption of existing procedures.

After you have made these initial changes, you may want to inspect other parts of the system to see how additional areas of desktop publishing can help. Eventually, you can institute on-screen manuscript editing, a process that lets you accept authors' manuscripts in an electronically readable form. Then you or your staff can read the manuscript directly into the computer and edit it on the screen. You run the type out on a page printer for galley proofs, and the rest of the process relies on the existing system of manual layout and pasteup. As you alter your system or as the technology changes to meet your needs, you may be able to do some of the page layout with desktop publishing tools.

For example, with current desktop publishing systems that use the IBM PC or Macintosh, you cannot view an entire $8\frac{1}{2} \times 11$ inch page on the screen at full size. Since this size is standard, some people may hesitate to rely on desktop publishing technology for a page layout system. Within a year, however, full-page displays for the Macintosh and IBM PC series computers will make the page layout aspect of desktop publishing more attractive. Several companies, such as Interleaf, make electronic publishing software that can display a full page on the large screen of a UNIX workstation, such as those from Sun and Apollo. Although these systems are considerably more expensive than desktop publishing systems for the IBM PC or Macintosh, they allow you to do more.

A newspaper publisher who wants to adopt desktop publishing technology incrementally may be able to use personal computers initially for creating graphics, eventually add the production of galley proofs, and ultimately employ the system for page layout, on-screen editing, and collection of information from reporters.

Desktop Newspaper Publishing

Newspaper producers have a reputation for being resistant to the use of advances in publishing technology. According to a survey conducted by the Society of Newspaper Design, though, 47 percent of the newspapers that responded to the survey were using Macintoshes in their graphics departments. Some examples of Macintoshes in use at newspapers:

- Peter Morales, owner of the newspaper in Rogue River, Oregon, creates graphics with MacDraft and prints them on a LaserWriter. He formerly used the traditional method of making graphics with drafting tape and a knife.
- The Dallas-based *Texas Women's News* is written and partially laid out on a Macintosh.
- The *San Francisco Chronicle* and *San Francisco Examiner* both use the Macintosh to produce graphics.

- In the small town of Hopkinsville, Kentucky, the *New Era*'s David Riley uses a Macintosh to create charts showing the auction price of tobacco. He changes the bars on the graphs into symbolic representations of cigarettes. He sends charts that show statewide sales over the Associated Press photo network.

These examples come from Craig Webb, an editor on the Foreign Desk at United Press International in Washington, D.C. The UPI graphics department also uses Macintoshes to make up news graphics.

Another large news organization that employs the Macintosh is the picture periodical *USA Today*. According to Webb, *USA Today* started using Macintoshes as "electronic sketch pads." The newspaper now has several dozen Macintoshes that it has assembled for the "nuts and bolts of graphics work."

When *USA Today* started publication in 1982, says Webb, 19th century techniques predominated in the production of newspaper graphics. Artists drew charts by hand and had to start over again if they miscalculated. Maps were traced from atlases or pictures of a globe. As a result, most newspapers were relatively light on graphics.

USA Today helped change that situation with its heavy emphasis on graphics. Initially, Webb says, the newspaper's voluminous graphics production was a result of a huge staff that would be out of reach of most newspaper publishers.

What became a boon to a journalistic giant such as *USA Today* is, perhaps, more beneficial to shoestring and medium-size newspaper operations, since graphics production is relatively fast with a desktop publishing system, and "even the clumsiest of artists can produce decent charts."

Webb says the newspaper industry is split, roughly according to the size of newspapers, on the approach to using the Macintosh. Smaller newspapers, he indicates, make heavier use of the computer and are inclined to overlook page layout problems. Webb believes that, for the most part, innovation in newspapers' use of desktop publishing comes from the bottom up. Larger papers, typified by *USA Today*, are more worried about on-screen resolution and are thus more sparing in their use of the Macintosh.

A long-term prospect for the use of desktop publishing in newspapers may be exemplified by the 28 Knight-Ridder newspapers. Knight-Ridder has set up Press-Link, which relies in part on use of the Macintosh, to allow the papers to incorporate more high quality maps, charts, graphs, and line drawings into breaking news stories and to share those graphics from paper to paper. Newsroom artists use Apple's MacDraw and Microsoft Chart software to create original drawings for storage in a computerized graphics library, which is available to each paper through an electronic mail and bulletin board system. The papers can download artwork and print it in camera-ready form on Apple's LaserWriter printer or modify it before printing to fit local requirements. Roger Fidler, Knight-Ridder's director of graphics and newsroom technology, credits the LaserWriter. The closest competitors that can provide similar abilities offer only systems that cost at least $120,000 for a single workstation, he says.

Small newspapers with limited budgets probably have the most to gain by investing in a desktop publishing sytem. One of the main reasons, Webb points out, is that the personal computer—a Macintosh, for example—a small newspaper uses in its publishing operations can also serve to produce mailing lists, maintain spreadsheets, do billings, and assist in many other overall functions of a newspaper.

In determining what portions of desktop publishing technology your organization might consider adopting, first study the system you're currently using, how expensive it would be to change each component of that system, and what organizational disruption—personnel changes, for example—would result from instituting each area of the technology. Then you will be able to weigh the pros and cons of each element of desktop publishing technology for use in your publication.

The three major benefits of this technology are editing text with a word processing program, laying out and designing pages with page layout software, and creating type with a page printer or typesetting machine. By studying your existing system and determining cost and

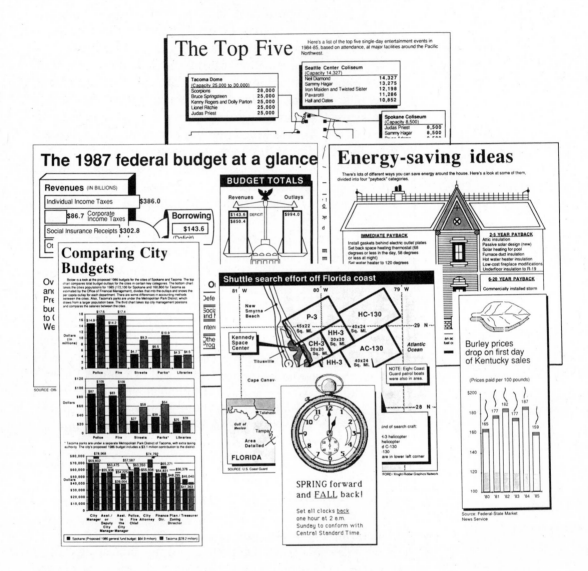

Macintosh graphics (energy, top five, city budgets) courtesy of *The Chronicle and Spokesman-Review*, Spokane, Washington.

Newspaper graphics (clock, tobacco) created on a 128K Macintosh. Courtesy of *The Kentucky New Era*, Hopkinsville, Kentucky.

MacDraw graphics (shuttle search, federal budget) from a Macintosh Plus. Courtesy of Knight-Ridder Graphics Network.

personnel requirements in each area, you will be able to calculate how much adopting each portion of this technology can save your business. Magazines and newspapers that are just starting and do not have an existing system in place may be able to use desktop publishing technology from the outset, however, and reap savings from its various areas.

BOOK PUBLISHING

Desktop publishing can comprise part of the operations of nearly any book publisher. Small and medium-size houses will probably use it to best advantage, but even large book publishing conglomerates will be able to employ it to some extent.

Typical Book Production Scenario

Traditionally, a publisher coordinates a book's editing, printing, and distribution. A book starts with the author. Publishers wring it through their editorial cycle, and third parties typeset and print it. Frequently, the publisher's production department pastes up the camera-ready art that goes to the printer, but often outside contractors perform even pasteup tasks.

Typesetting costs can be staggering, particularly when author and publisher make changes on galley proofs. The typesetter charges the publisher for every change that did not result from a typesetter error. The nature of book publishing—with its long lead times and frequent publisher/author battles—is such that *acs* (author corrections) or *aes* (author errors) on galleys are plentiful, and costly. Typesetters like to joke that *acs* keep half of them employed.

The profit margins on books are small, and most books do well to break even. Large publishers, at least, rely on blockbusters to keep them in the black. Most small book publishers must struggle just to stay alive. Desktop publishing technology can help keep costs down.

Desktop Technology for Book Publishers

For a total investment of $7000 to $15,000, a publisher can purchase a desktop publishing system that can greatly aid in the production of books. With a personal computer, page makeup software, and a 300-dot-per-inch (dpi) laser printer, a publisher can get inexpensive page proofs that eliminate the long and costly galley proof stage. An outside service bureau can produce final typeset copy.

In some circumstances, producing a book entirely with a laser printer is appropriate, either at the standard 300-dpi resolution or at an artificially increased resolution. To increase the resolution of the type to beyond 300 dpi, you can use photo reduction to increase pixel density. For example, you can laser-print the type at 14 point, increase the horizontal and vertical margins, and then photographically reduce the output by 29 percent to end up with 10-point type. The photoreduction process squeezes the dots that form each character together to produce characters with crisper resolution and fewer jagged edges. The effective resolution becomes 420 dpi. This particular example is feasible, however, only if the printer accepts A-size paper.

The main drawbacks of this approach are that, because it requires extra steps, it is more time consuming and that photoreduction adds significantly to overall costs. For a strictly utilitarian presentation of information, however, 300-dpi type will suffice. Books that need to convey a sense of immediacy may even profit from the slightly rough profile of 300-dpi type. A publisher's ability to exercise the control over typesetting that desktop publishing technology allows means bringing the product to market faster than is possible with traditional publishing methods.

The appropriateness of 300-dpi type depends on various factors:

- The subject matter of the book
- The book's audience
- The book's content
- Perceptions of the book

In short, a book publishing operation using a personal computer and medium-resolution laser printer to produce camera-ready type is acceptable—even desirable—depending on the book and its audience.

For interim publishing operations, larger publishers can also benefit from desktop publishing technology. The bane of ac's accentuates how larger book publishers can cash in on a personal computer/laser printer scenario.

Before even taking a manuscript to a typesetter, a publisher can use a desktop publishing system in proofreading, copy-fitting, indexing, and other pretypesetting tasks. Using the output from a laser printer as galley proofs, a proofreader can ascertain that the typesetter gets a nearly pristine manuscript from which to work.

The proofreader can use the laser printer output not only to find typos, but also to make sure that informational content is correct and to check page layouts. These interim "galleys" are a perfect place for fact checking. Furthermore, at this stage, even wholesale rewriting is possible.

This desktop publishing scenario is more compelling if the publisher works with a typesetter who can accept the publisher's manuscript electronically. Assured that the files are nearly perfect, the publisher sends them to the typesetter, who runs out type from computer files.

An inexpensive laser printer is suitable for a small publisher with few titles. Such printers have a recommended duty cycle of approximately 3000 pages per month. For larger-scale publishing operations, a more expensive laser printer with a higher duty cycle becomes a virtual necessity. Such printers can produce 30,000 pages per month and can cost $30,000 and more. If a publishing house is putting out more than 30,000 pages per month, purchase of a typesetting system may be appropriate.

Although full-blown typesetting systems are expensive, Linotype Company offers a typesetting machine, the Series 100 Linotronic 100, which lists for about the same amount as a top-of-the-line laser printer. The Linotronic typesetter, however, gives about four times the resolution of the average laser printer, which is about 300 dpi.

In addition to providing high-resolution camera-ready type at a much lower cost than that of traditional typesetting scenarios, in-house typesetting equipment allows publishers to exercise much greater control over the production of their books than they can by using outside services, which often charge more than $20 per page. In time-sensitive areas, such as computer technology, in which fast turnaround is crucial, in-house typesetting gives a publisher an edge over the competition.

In very large publishing houses, an in-house typesetting system probably makes sense only for one or two divisions—unless each division so equips itself.

Using Desktop Tools to Produce Books

Desktop publishing techniques played a role in the production of six books the computer magazine *InfoWorld* did for Harper & Row Publishers. Although *InfoWorld* used fairly expensive desktop publishing tools, the principles involved are generally applicable to many book publishing scenarios.

In 1983, *InfoWorld* obtained a contract with Harper & Row to write the text and produce camera-ready mechanicals for six computer-related books for the publisher. After some debate, the magazine decided to use its own typesetting equipment to set the type for the books. At that time, *InfoWorld* had just purchased a Bit Blaster laser printer from Autologic.

To minimize the costs of typesetting film and to avoid conflicts with the magazine's weekly production schedule, the *InfoWorld* book editors produced all galley proofs on the laser printer. For example, they sent laser printer galleys to proofreaders. They sent other copies to product reviewers and software vendors to verify factual information such as addresses. When they had all comments and corrections back from these sources, they incorporated them, and only then did they run the actual typeset copy for pasteup.

Since they had produced formatted pages individually on the laser printer, they had merely to cut the pages apart on the photo galleys and paste them up as complete pages. They left holes for illustrations, which they positioned on the boards after pasteup.

After *InfoWorld* had completed the books, the magazine's system administrator estimated that use of the laser printer to produce page proofs had saved the magazine $10,000 or more in film costs. *InfoWorld* had the advantage of having at its disposal an expensive text processing system and a relatively expensive laser printer. The *InfoWorld* book production scenario is applicable to desktop publishing in principle, however, because a smaller publishing company could have saved even more in typesetting costs.

Depending on the desired quality of the finished product, a smaller outfit could even have used the final laser printer output as camera-ready copy for its books.

Currently, desktop publishing is naturally suited to producing small publications such as newsletters, but, as evidenced by the book you are holding in your hands, this technology works for even more ambitious publishing endeavors.

Chapter 3

Design for Effective Communication

A desktop publishing system is more than a compatible combination of hardware and software. Sophisticated hardware and software are of marginal value if what you produce with them doesn't look good. Just as the Macintosh MacPaint program is said to have created a lot of amateur artists, desktop publishing technology has the potential problem of creating a lot of amateur design and layout artists. For your publications to look good, you have to give consideration to their design, particularly with long documents, in which many pieces must work together to form the whole.

Any publication is an organic entity. To achieve good design, keep in mind that design, type, illustrations, white space, callouts, and the other elements in your publication must complement each other.

Many books on design are available, some of which we've listed in the bibliography. As a quick guide to design, we've included some rules of thumb in the following section. These rules of thumb appear in a box, followed by a brief elaboration of the rule. They are meant to give you some general concepts that will help you get the most out of the appearance of your publication.

When you're deciding how to design a publication, make sure the design reflects the aim of what you're producing.

A flier has different goals than a periodical has, and a catalog has different goals from those of an annual report, and so forth, so it's important to use design and type to coincide with the character and content of the document. The design and type should convey to the readers visually what the important areas of the document are.

Before you start, establish some ground rules.

If you work in an organization in which different people write and design documents, try to get all of the people together for a meeting. If the designers clearly understand the concepts a document is supposed to present and the people who write the document understand the tools and resources of the designers, a more cohesive product will result. If the concepts in your document are related to complex processes or sophisticated technological products, you might want to bring the product's designer or someone else familiar with the material into the meeting as well. The more communication about the various elements that a publication is synthesizing, the better your publication will be, whether it's a one-page advertising flier, a catalog, an annual report, a periodical, or a book. The more information you can bring together about the content of the document and the way you'll implement its design, the more legible the final document will be and the more effectively it will communicate its content to its readers.

As a first step, design in miniature.

If you are planning a complex document, such as a long report, newsletter, magazine, or book, use a preprinted form with properly proportioned rectangles that represent the total number of pages of your document. With such a form, you can plan the document's layout and design before you actually work with the computer software that will carry out that design. You can draw up these preprinted forms by hand and photocopy them or create them with a computer graphics program such as MacDraw for the Macintosh. One method that works well is to create an $8\frac{1}{2} \times 11$ inch sheet of paper with four sets of two pages each (i.e., eight pages) in miniature. Each of these small-scale representations of the page can be further subdivided into the columnar format you will use for your published document.

Using this technique, you can establish the text and graphic elements of your document in a rough form, during the design stage, and see an overview of the finished product's appearance. You can use these sheets as scratch pads to try out various combinations of text, graphics, and white space to achieve a consistent style or desired effect.

By representing the entire publication in miniature in a schematic form and planning what goes where, you will achieve a design consistency in a rough fashion, which will help you specify exactly which commands you need to give to the computer software to shape the design. It is often hard to visualize the final product when you're working solely with computer software.

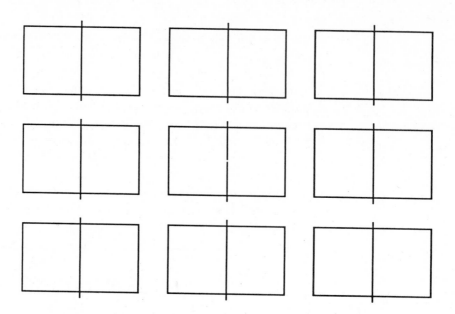

For designing in miniature: a preprinted form representing pages.

As you plan the design, think of the main body of the text as a train of thought or flow of an argument that starts at the top left corner of a page and ends diagonally opposite it, no matter how many columns you are using. Illustrations should enter into the flow of the text in their logical, supportive sequence. When considering how to fill the publication with the body of the text and the illustrations, decide whether you want to aim for a set number of pages for convenience of printing and reproducing the material. Are you limited to a certain number of pages of photographic material because of the type of paper stock you are using? Take such design restrictions into account in advance; then consider how many pages you need to fill. Find out how many column-inches or column-lines of text you have to work with. These figures will be useful when you plan the sizes of the illustrations, white space, headlines, and other design elements.

By working with a miniature version of the document in a rough format, you'll have an easier time changing the sequence or distribution of illustrations within the text. On these miniature schematic representations of the pages, you can also mark specifications, such as the distance between headlines and the body of the text and between captions and illustrations. Other specifications to note are the exact typeface, typestyle, and type size you're using for each section, headline, subhead, caption, and other element. This method lets you duplicate specifications consistently throughout the publication and also create future publications with a similar cohesive look, which is especially important in periodical publishing.

If your document will have numerous pages bound together along a center spine, think in terms of horizontal spreads representing two facing pages, instead of thinking of single, vertical pages. The single, vertical page is often the way desktop publishing software represents a page, but if you first look at opposing pages in miniature, you'll have an easier time designing in terms of the actual look of your publication. A design element that flows from one page to the other in a spread helps readers move from one page to the next. Think of a two-page spread as one large, horizontal block, rather than as two smaller, vertical blocks that represent the individual pages. Remember, however, that you have to contend with the gutter between the two pages and that certain design techniques help readers' eyes move across the gutter, aiding the flow of illustrations and text from one page to the other. Since, for example, the columnar formatting of text encourages vertical representations of information, try to emphasize horizontal shapes whenever possible and appropriate.

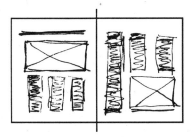 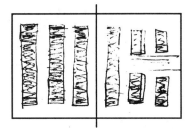

A rough mockup of two spreads (created with MacDraw).

Think about columns in your design.

Usually, in desktop publishing systems, pages are considered to be $8\frac{1}{2} \times 11$ inches, which is the standard size of paper for office correspondence and many publications. Given the $8\frac{1}{2} \times 11$ inch page size as a standard, a typical "live matter page"—i.e., the area of actual text and graphics on the page—is usually 7×10 inches, which leaves a $\frac{1}{2}$-inch margin on each side of the page and a $\frac{3}{4}$-inch margin at the top and bottom.

You can break a 7×10 inch live matter page into numerous columns, margins, and other elements, but three predominant sizes have emerged for one-, two- and three-column layouts. With a single column, you have one 7-inch-wide column, which is equivalent to a 42-pica width (6 picas equal approximately an inch). A two-column format has two 20-pica columns with a 2-pica gutter, or valley, between the columns. A three-column format generally yields three 13-pica columns with two $1\frac{1}{2}$-pica valleys on either side of the center column.

Use standard column sizes.

Good rules of thumb are five columns for classified ads; three or four columns for a newspaper or newsy look; two or three columns for magazines; and one, two, or three columns for reports, papers, and other similar documents.

Although these formats predominate in publications, you can arrange various amounts of columns in innumerable ways on a page. Deviating by design from the standard formats can help you achieve a distinctive look for your document or publication.

Avoid narrow, justified columns.

This format usually adds too much spacing between words, wasting space, adding unsightly holes, and making the columns hard to read.

To remedy the problems narrow columns cause, you can either set the column flush left with a ragged right margin or make the column wider; usually a minimum of 30 characters per line produces acceptable letterspacing.

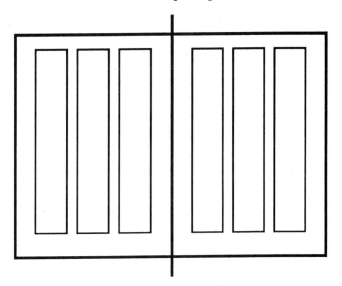

A three-column format.

Use ragged right columns when you want your document to look informal or when you regularly need to change items in a document such as a product catalog. It's easier to substitute for sections of text that are ragged right than it is with justified text, since you have more flexibility in deciding where lines end and in determining column length, which is important if you're plugging new elements into an existing document.

> **Note these rules of thumb about rules.**

Rules are straight lines, either individual or in a group, of either the same or varying lengths, that you use to delineate areas on a page. A thin rule can run vertically between or beside columns of type. Heavy rules run horizontally across a column or a page to split segments of a document from one another or delineate components of a page or a two-page spread. Borders are ornamental rules; be careful not to overuse them. Elaborate borders are most appropriate on certificates or forms.

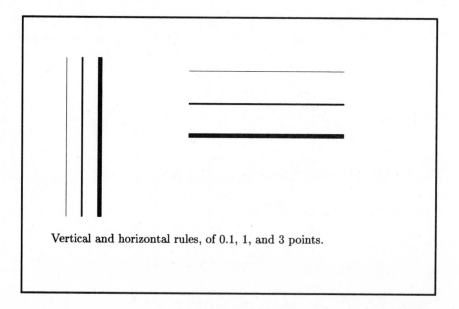

Vertical and horizontal rules, of 0.1, 1, and 3 points.

You can create boxes with simple lines or with ornate borders. They help set off blocks of text, or text and graphics, that can stand by themselves, separate from the main body of the text. Boxes can also frame different types of illustrations, such as schematics and photographs, to give them a consistent look, which is important if you are producing a catalog or another publication or document that draws material from a wide variety of sources. A similar type of box around each instance of a certain type of graphic element can help tie these elements together.

> **Think of graphic tools and illustrations, such as charts, graphs, and photographs, that you can use to help communicate key concepts and ideas.**

Just as you edit text for grammar and style, you can also edit illustrations by selecting appropriate materials and organizing them to support the organization and logical flow of the text. Also, the placement, size, and emphasis of illustrations should conform to the relative importance of the textual materials the illustrations accompany. Don't add illustrations for their own sake. Use them only when they aid effective communication and help reinforce concepts that are part of the main body of the text.

Charts, graphs, and tables can complement text in communicating information clearly. When you have information, such as numeric values, that is especially suited for presentation in charts or graphs, don't overlook the opportunity to use it as a graphic element in your document. Avoid using charts, graphs, or tables as mere adornments, however. They can confuse your readers, who may attach extra importance to them and wonder why they are there if the need for them is not apparent.

Make them as simple as possible. Try not to compare more than three different elements with each other. Even three can be too many if the elements are indistinct and are not far enough apart from each other on the graph. For example, in a line graph, lines that overlap often can make the graph visually confusing, so you might be better off breaking your graph into several separate graphs to illustrate individual points.

To present a chart or a graph in its simplest form, remove as many of the background grid lines as you can without affecting the meaning. If some background grid lines are necessary for interpretation of the chart, retain them but remove all the unnecessary ones.

Try to use horizontal and vertical rules to divide the different elements, without making the result look too crowded and crosshatched. If you don't use rules, use wide white spaces and margins. Coloring the rules and varying their thickness are other ways to separate different groups of items. You can delineate more important categories with thicker rules and less important groups with thinner ones.

Victory Sportshoe
Department Budgets

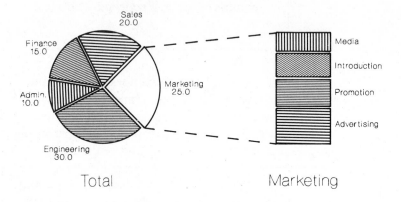

Bar and pie charts created with Harvard Presentation Graphics from Software Publishing Corp.

Your chart, graph, or table should provide clear labels and captions that explain the significance of the material. The meaning should be evident on first glance. If you decide that your chart is not clear enough, try a different kind. Sometimes a pie chart can present information more simply and clearly than a bar chart can, and sometimes a bar chart is the better choice.

When you are preparing tables or charts that contain a lot of text, be sure to give them enough space to be easily legible. Too often, tables are crammed into a tight space, which makes sorting one item out from another too difficult. Readers become confused when they try to read across a crowded table that doesn't leave enough room between individual elements. A general rule is to add 25 percent to the size you think a table will require—then you can put some space between the elements to segregate them into logical groups.

One of the advantages of desktop publishing technology is that when you have made a rough design of your document and actually start to create it, you can experiment inexpensively with several different types of charts and graphs. For example, with the Macintosh you can use Microsoft's Excel program. Excel creates a gallery of different types of charts and graphs the program prepares automatically. Adjunct graphics programs for Lotus 1-2-3 on the IBM PC can also create charts and graphs from materials in spreadsheets. Since personal computers give you a lot of flexibility in the preparation of

1985 Sales Results

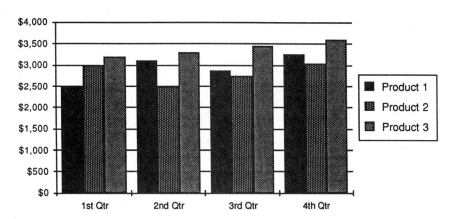

Bar chart created with Excel from Microsoft.

different types of charts and graphs, you should experiment with a few different kinds to see which are the clearest and most effective.

In order to make charts and graphs easy to understand, try to avoid using complicated keys and labeling systems. Whenever possible, use the actual information in the chart, rather than symbols that represent that information. If you have to employ symbols, try to keep the system simple, make it easy to decode visually, and provide the key in an obvious and easy-to-read format.

You can dress up charts and graphs with graphic images, especially with the Macintosh, with which you can use images from clip art libraries or from video digitizers. Using visual images as part of a chart or graph can aid you in communicating the point you are trying to make. Headlines can effectively draw attention to charts, or a long headline can tie together a series of charts.

Use contrasting elements for visual appeal and reading ease.

You can break up a page of text attractively by dropping in a thought-provoking statement or quote from the main body of text that you set apart somehow—either in a box, within rules, or surrounded by white space—to catch the readers' attention. For someone who is skimming through a document, these free-floating phrases, which are called *callouts* or *pull quotes*, can highlight important material.

These free-floating phrases are called *callouts* or *pull quotes.*

Another technique that satisfies the needs of readers who skim is using large type in combination with smaller type on the same page. The smaller type indicates relative unimportance and lets readers know that they can skip over that material if they don't have time to read everything on the page. It also informs them that more detail is available to explain the text in larger type. The smaller type is often set in relatively narrow columns underneath wider columns. For example, you can set a single, large column of large type to emphasize an important point and have two columns of smaller type underneath it in a two-column page layout. In a four-column page layout, you might have a double-width column of larger type with narrow columns underneath.

Sometimes natural contrasts between two distinct elements in the text, such as questions and answers in an interview, vie for your attention. When you have two clearly delineated dialogues within the main body of the text, you can set one in italic, boldface, or a larger typeface to distinguish it from the other.

We've used the principle of contrasting elements in this design section by calling attention to our rules of thumb in boxes. Elaborations of the rules follow in roman type.

Break up long passages of text with subheads to help organize and summarize the document for readers and to draw their attention to specific points.

Be careful not to overdo the use of subheads, however, or the document will be too choppy and hard to read.

Using boldface for headlines is more important than using a large type size. It is also important to write headlines that are long enough to be meaningful. Often, a small, bold headline can be as effective as a long one. If you use a short headline, a blurb after the headline can further explain the subject matter. Headlines can span the entire width of a page, or they can be narrow within a column—boldface words stacked on top of each other. Keep in mind that a small headline surrounded by white space can be more effective than that same space filled to capacity with giant characters.

DOROTHY lived in the midst of the great Kansas prairies, with Uncle Henry, who was a farmer, and Aunt Em, who was the farmer's wife. Their house was small, for the lumber to build it had to be carried by wagon many miles. There were four walls, a floor and a roof, which made one room; and this room contained a rusty-looking cooking stove, a cupboard for the dishes, a table, three or four chairs, and the beds. Uncle Henry and Aunt Em had a big bed in one corner and Dorothy a little bed in another corner.

Example of an initial cap; in this instance the rest of the first word is also capitalized, smaller.
Courtesy of Magna Computer Systems.

If you break up a column with an element such as a subhead or large initial cap that interrupts the text, try not to allow fewer than three lines of text at the top or bottom of a column that is either above or below the element. If you follow this guideline, you can isolate the subhead or other element and tie it to the running text. Readers won't mistakenly think you are beginning or ending a separate section of text.

Chou Remains Cremated

Journal Star (Peoria, IL), Jan. 12, 1976

Saigon, Thieu look venerable to attack

Montana Standard (Butte), March 31, 1975

Man Robs, Then Kills Himself

The Washington Post, Dec. 19, 1975

War Dims Hopes for Peace

Wisconsin State Journal, Dec. 27, 1965

MBA STUDIES MUSHROOM

SBA News (Youngstown, OH), Fall, 1975

Various types of headlines.

Don't capitalize every word in a headline. It's better to use a bold typestyle and a large type size to set apart the headline from the main text.

Use all capital letters only for lines that are very short—a short headline or subhead, for example. Since long lines of capital letters are hard to read, they are usually a drawback. You can use them to advantage, however, if you want to slow readers down to add impact to a statement. Employ this technique only sparingly, though.

Use white space effectively.

Just as the margins of the page help organize the area of text and graphics, white space can facilitate the organization of information within a document. White space, or air, is most effective when it has a clearly defined shape and does not look like a leftover area. For example, don't allow a short last line of a paragraph to appear as the first line at the beginning of a column. These short last lines of paragraphs are called *orphans* if they top a column, *widows* if they appear within a column.

What's your type?

The most crucial aspect of your publication is the type. Although the field of typography is complex and requires a great deal of study, some general guidelines about the selection and use of type will help you make your publication not only look good, but also read well.

Typography is the art of using printed characters. The vocabulary of typography is often confusing. Various people sometimes use the same terms with different intended meanings. Most of the confusion in terminology centers on the distinctions between typeface, typestyle, and font. In this book, typeface refers to the general design (e.g., Times Roman, Helvetica, Palatino) of a group of characters; typestyle refers to a particular design of or design enhancement to the typeface, such as a plain typestyle, a bold typestyle, or an italic typestyle; and font refers to an individual set of characters of a typestyle and size. Therefore, a typeface is the entire group of fonts in all the various typestyles and sizes. The typestyle is a collection of fonts of various sizes, with a unified style.

Other people have not been as careful in their use of this terminology, a prime example being the documenters of the Macintosh computer, who use the word *font* to describe a general character design, such as Times Roman, in a range of sizes and styles. What we call a typeface, therefore, is labeled a font in Macintosh terminology.

Computer Modern is a typeface.

Computer Modern italic is a typestyle.

14-point Computer Modern italic is a font.

**Use as few fonts as possible—about three or four
per document. Generally, use the same typeface for
headlines and subheads as for the text.**

The most important general guideline for using type effectively
is to use the smallest possible number of typestyles, typefaces, and
type sizes. Desktop publishing systems, especially those on the Macintosh, offer an array of styles, faces, and sizes that are easy to use
in a document. Easy access to rich typographic resources allows a
great deal of creativity and flexibility in expressing the contents of
a document, but the use of too many of these elements in a single
document creates a disjointed publication and dilutes the power of
special typography as an attention-grabbing tool for major concepts
or important ideas.

The rule of thumb of using the smallest number of typestyles, typefaces, and type sizes applies to virtually any document, whether it's
a single magazine page or a book. Typography should emphasize the
specific contents of a document. By varying type size and weight,
you can effectively control the degree of importance that readers attach to any specific area of the text. A judicious use of type elements
can help focus readers' attention on major points and can help break
up the text into digestible segments. An overuse of typefaces, typestyles, and type sizes can distract and confuse readers. It is a good
idea, for example, to use the same typeface for headlines and subheads as you use for the main body of the text. Using a consistent
typeface results in a better-looking, more cohesive publication.

> **Beware of point sizes.**

Because of the design of typefaces, 12-point type in one typeface is not necessarily the same size as 12-point type in another typeface. For example:

> This typeface is 12-point Computer Modern Roman.
>
> This one is 12-point Dunhill.
>
> This one is 12-point Typewriter Type.

Take a look at a sample paragraph set in a specific typeface, typestyle, and type size before deciding on the exact point size you will use.

Font sizing is even more confusing because different suppliers of a particular typeface make slight variations in the design and placement of characters within that typeface. For example, Helvetica from different suppliers may vary in actual size, even though you might expect 12-point Helvetica characters from different sources to be the same. It is a good idea to check samples of type from various suppliers when you're making estimates and comparisons. If you're using a desktop publishing system that includes page layout and font specification software that remains the same for various output devices, you may be able to obtain fonts of the same size from different devices. In other words, a 12-point Helvetica produced on a PostScript-compatible laser printer should produce the same character placement and size as a 12-point Helvetica from a PostScript-compatible typesetting device from Linotype Company, for example. Still, typefaces, typestyles, and point sizes from various suppliers do vary.

> **Highly stylized typefaces are better for use as graphic
> elements than as typesetting elements.**

Numerous specialty typefaces are available, particularly for the
Macintosh computer. Such typefaces are useful for headlines in the
main body of the text under certain circumstances, if you use them
carefully and sparingly. Too many specialty typefaces can clutter up
a page, and one unusual typeface can clash with another one.

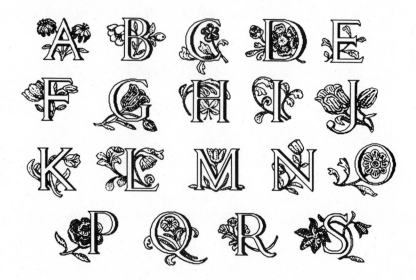

A stylized typeface called "French Manuscript."

Specialty typefaces can work to good advantage as graphic elements, however. For example, certain of these typefaces—Saigon
for the Macintosh or German, Greek, Chinese, Russian, and so on—
connote a geographical area. Specialty typefaces sometimes connote
times gone by and can be helpful in setting a historical tone. You
can also find fonts that look modernistic.

> **Use light, small type for captions.**

Captions should supplement an illustration, rather than compete with it for attention. If you are using a serif typeface such as Times Roman for the body of your text, consider using a sans serif typeface such as Helvetica for the captions, or perhaps a smaller size of the Times Roman. If a smaller size is difficult to read, consider using italics. An exception to these suggestions is advertising copy, where large headlines can work as captions for illustrations of products.

Be consistent in the placement and spacing of elements throughout your document.

An overall rule of thumb when you're designing your publication or document: Standardize the placement of all elements such as the space between headlines and text, spacing around subheads, and the space between pictures or graphic elements and captions.

Write down in a safe place the exact typeface, typestyle, and type size you're using for each separate component of your document.

Keeping records of typographical specifications allows you to update your document or create future documents with the same specifications.

We hope you will find these guidelines helpful in designing your publication. A good design will not only make it look good, but it may also be a factor in its success.

Chapter 4

Newsletters: a
Golden Opportunity
for Desktop
Publishers

Newsletter publishing is a fast-growing business. More than 100,000 different newsletters are published in the United States alone, by organizations ranging from large corporations to local civic groups. These newsletters cost from nothing to hundreds of dollars per year and have circulations from less than a hundred to hundreds of thousands of recipients. Newsletters are one of the main communications media for special-interest topics. Almost all of us receive newsletters from some sources—our local schools, our congresspeople, etc. Some companies publish newsletters for corporate communications, sales relations, public relations, shareholder information, employee information, and so forth. Trade unions and nonprofit groups publish newsletters for their membership. Newsletters are perceived as timely, reliable sources of information, and their publishers are often quoted as experts in their field. At least 5000 major U.S. newsletters require paid subscriptions, which range from a dollar to several thousand dollars per year.

Newsletter publishing is the area of publishing for which desktop publishing is probably best suited. Newsletters are almost always confined to an $8\frac{1}{2} \times 11$ inch format, the size of publication today's desktop publishing systems based on the Macintosh and IBM PC series computers are best at creating. Another factor that makes newsletter publishing and desktop publishing such a perfect match is that newsletters usually have very small staffs, sometimes only one or two people. Whether these publishers are independent or groups within a large organization, they can easily change their methods to use desktop publishing technology effectively. Also, a single person using a desktop publishing system can easily perform all stages of publishing, including editing, type creation, typesetting, and page layout.

Yet another reason makes newsletters prime candidates for desktop publishing: Typeset materials are easier and more pleasing to read than typewritten materials, and typesetting also takes up less space than typescript does, which means more information per page and lower printing and mailing costs, as well as a higher-quality yet less expensive final product. Not only does typeset text help make your newsletter more readable and convey more information, but desktop publishing also lets you use typography creatively to add special impact to certain ideas (see chapter 3).

An amateur appearance can detract from a newsletter's credibility, but a newsletter you create with desktop publishing technology can look superb, even though you can produce it at a relatively small cost. In fact, you need only a partial desktop publishing system to put out a newsletter. Simply having a personal computer means you can write text you can transmit over the phone by modem to a typesetter—a less expensive process than keying the information in by hand. Such transmission is possible with any personal computer or word processing machine that uses telecommunications software and equipment. Also, you can create a document, edit it, and specify typography and page layout. You can then use a service bureau to print the final laser-printed or typeset copy. This system works especially well with the Macintosh, since you can see an on-screen representation of what the final product will look like.

By using a service bureau, which gives you the use of a page printer, you need only a single computer, without the additional cost of a page printer or typesetting machine, and you have a low-cost entrée to desktop publishing. With the Macintosh system, an inexpensive dot matrix printer such as the ImageWriter II can serve as a page proofing device. This printer gives you a fairly close representation of what a laser-printed or typeset page will look like.

Furthermore, a desktop publishing system based on a general purpose computer such as the Macintosh or an IBM PC series computer has uses beyond the actual publication of documents. An example is employing the computer and a modem to get information from on-line databases. A main value of newsletters is that they provide specific information about a subject and summarize information about that particular topic. Retrieval of information related to your newsletter from on-line databases turns your desktop publishing system into a research tool as well as a typesetting and page layout device.

NEWSLETTERS CATEGORIZED

Most newsletters share several common characteristics. They are usually $8\frac{1}{2} \times 11$ inches in size, and they do not contain advertising, except for perhaps small classified ads. Newsletters do not have glossy covers and rarely have more than 24 pages; most provide specialized information in a summary form.

newsletters According to Howard Hudson, publisher of *The Newsletter on Newsletters*, there are four primary categories of newsletters: subscription newsletters, the main type that entrepreneurial desktop publishers will be interested in; organizational newsletters; franchise newsletters; and public relations newsletters.

Five main categories of *subscription newsletters* exist: investment newsletters, aimed at investors and the financial community; business newsletters, which convey diverse business-related information;

consumer newsletters, which are aimed at a large general audience; affinity newsletters, which distribute information to a group of people with a common interest; and instructional newsletters.

The next three categories of newsletters are related to business publishing. *Organizational newsletters* are published by nonprofit organizations and government agencies for their membership or by companies for their employees. Most organizational newsletters are free. *Franchise newsletters*, also known as syndicated or third-party publications, are preprepared newsletters of interest in certain fields. A given company can purchase the newsletter, print its name in the heading, and provide the document to its customers. The newsletters in the final category, *public relations*, are usually product descriptions or sales pitches disguised to look like newsletters so they will appear to impart more valuable information and seem less like direct sales pitches.

Business newsletters are the type of subscription newsletters that usually command the highest price, since businesses are willing to pay a premium for valuable information, from late-breaking technical data to details about government actions that may affect their operations. Another reason that business newsletters are the most expensive is that they usually have a small, targeted audience whose members place a higher value on information received in newsletters than do other recipients. Also, because businesses usually have to deal with vast amounts of information, the ability of a newsletter publisher to summarize that information and provide it in an easy-to-digest form helps save businesspeople time. Most often, a business purchases a newsletter based on the perceived importance of the information, rather than on the price.

Affinity newsletters are targeted at groups of people with common interests. To be successful, an affinity newsletter must generally provide specialized information that is not easily available elsewhere. *Organizational newsletters* are similar to affinity newsletters in that they serve groups of people with common interests, but organizational newsletters are usually free, since they frequently discuss the group rather than provide information necessary for a special interest. In order to make money publishing an organizational newsletter with a desktop publishing system, you should sell the newsletter as a service to the management of the organization, rather than as a product for the membership of the group that that organization is reaching.

Consumer newsletters have the largest target audience, but it is difficult to charge much for such a newsletter. Whereas a business might not bat an eyelash at spending $50 or much more a year for a good newsletter, consumers may think a price of $15 a year too high, since they are used to subscribing to glossy, advertiser-supported magazines for a similar price. One of the difficulties in marketing consumer newsletters is that since the price the readers are usually willing to pay for a newsletter is low, you'll have a hard time justifying the expense of obtaining subscribers, producing the publication, and mailing it. Because newsletters are most effective at communicating specialized information, it's wiser, and often more profitable, to publish a higher-priced newsletter with a limited market than a low-priced newsletter for a broad market.

NEWSLETTERS FROM YOUR DESKTOP

To create a successful newsletter, especially if you're doing it to make money, make sure you clearly understand what market your newsletter will address, why the people in that market need the information your newsletter provides, and why they can't get that information elsewhere.

To help understand your market, ask yourself some preliminary questions. For example, will your proposed newsletter match the personality of its audience? Does it reflect the information needs of that audience? What are the major types of information the prospective audience is looking for? If the audience has other ways to get this information, how much does it cost? Who are the potential readers who will find your newsletter indispensable, and how many are there? How many other people might have a secondary interest in it? Are the members of the target audience individuals who will have to pay for the newsletter out of their own pocket, or are they working in a company that will pay for the newsletter? Are they in a position to buy more than one subscription? Does any direct competitor provide this information to the audience? Will you be able to use your desktop publishing computer system to retrieve valuable information from databases and market this information to your target audience? Why will someone want to buy the newsletter? If other newsletters already serve this market, does your newsletter take a different enough approach to provide unique information worth paying for? If you can answer these types of questions, you will be prepared to start a successful newsletter.

After you've determined the target market and positioning of your newsletter, you need to choose a name. It is especially important for it to describe either its subject matter or its target audience. For

---

How to Spot Newsletter Opportunities

If you're interested in using a desktop publishing system to publish newsletters and you're trying to find some good opportunities, a few telltale signs in any special interest group will tell you if a newsletter has a good chance of succeeding in that group. For example, if the interest is broad and served by many periodicals, but those publications lag too long between the time that articles are written and when they're published, interested people may be willing to subscribe to a newsletter to get more-current information. If the special interest is narrow and few or no periodicals are serving it, you may be able to corner the market with necessary information in a newsletter. A special interest related to a business or profession that requires generally unavailable information may be a ripe opportunity for a newsletter. If it is a business special interest and the business is in a fast-moving market in which conditions change from day to day or week to week, publishing a newsletter will let you get a jump on traditional magazines. Highly specialized business markets are one of the best bets for newsletters. The computer and electronics fields, for instance, have many specialized newsletters that command a respectable subscription price.

---

example, a newsletter entitled *The Smith Letter* does not reveal anything about the publication. If it were called *The Electronic Publishing Newsletter*, no one would have any doubt about the subject matter. Newsletter titles can be clever while still being descriptive, such as the successful *Moneysworth* newsletter, which eventually became a magazine when its subscription base grew to more than half a million (the tabloid now has a circulation of 900,000). Although a clever title can make your publication more memorable, if you can't think of anything that is both clever and descriptive, opt for a name that is descriptive.

Once you've decided what market you will focus on, what unique approach you will use to provide information to that market, and what you will name your newsletter, you still need to determine how to identify the members of your target market. If you cannot think of a good way to get actual names and addresses of the people in your audience, your newsletter will not succeed, no matter how good the quality of the editorial product.

SELLING YOUR NEWSLETTER

The major expense in your newsletter's publication will not be design, since the economies of desktop publishing will save you money, and it will not be printing, since the per copy price is inexpensive. Your major expense will be obtaining subscribers, so be sure to budget accordingly.

Two main avenues are open for selling your newsletter: advertising it and marketing it with direct marketing. Advertising consists primarily of print media and broadcast advertising. Examples of print media advertising are newspapers, magazines, and perhaps even other newsletters. Examples of direct marketing are direct mail and telemarketing. For telemarketing, you need to obtain names, phone numbers, and information about people whom you will call with a subscription solicitation. With direct mail, you will have to pay for mailing lists and prepare mailings to solicit subscribers in select groups. In addition to the direct costs of obtaining subscribers, large newsletter publishers may also incur the expense of hiring a public relations company or using publicity techniques such as traveling to give speeches or to be on panels.

Advertising

Print media advertising is generally more appropriate for obtaining subscribers for a newsletter than is broadcast advertising such as radio and TV. It is hard to know anything about the audience that your message will reach via the latter media. Their audience is broad, but you will be paying for people who will certainly not be interested to receive your message. Likewise, print advertising in general interest publications such as national magazines is a rather haphazard way of obtaining qualified subscribers. If you do use a national publication, a classified ad may more effectively catch people's attention than a more expensive display ad will. Use a national magazine for a display ad only if your newsletter focuses on a topic

Are You an Editor or a Publisher?

If you are contemplating starting a newsletter, ask yourself several questions to help focus your efforts.

Are you a journalist or a marketer? In other words, is your area of expertise as an editor of a newsletter (a journalist) or as a publisher (a marketer)? Perhaps you'll decide that you're knowledgeable in both areas. Most people tend to be one or the other, however.

Journalists generally pick a topic that they know well and determine how to develop it into a newsletter that will serve a specific market segment. Marketers mainly first identify a target market segment that may welcome the opportunity to pay for information in a newsletter, and develop a newsletter for that market segment. Problems can arise because many marketers do not understand the craft of writing and editing, and many journalists disdain marketing and do not pay proper attention to business details. If you fall into one of these categories, you should consider finding a partner with complementary skills or locating people to perform the functions that are outside your area of expertise.

The production of a newsletter involves a clear division of labor and responsibilities. The editorial side concerns itself with creating documents and using desktop publishing technology to print them, and the marketing side includes circulation and business management, as well as marketing proper. If you do not feel comfortable with or competent in all of these duties, decide what you can do best and find outside services or employees to take care of the tasks that you don't plan to tackle yourself.

of interest to a large portion of the general population.

Look instead for a publication that serves an audience similar to the one that you are targeting. For example, if you have a newsletter on desktop publishing technology, consider advertising in a magazine that goes to art directors or to people in the printing business. A trade publication serving any of your target groups can deliver your ad to an audience that may be interested in paying for your publication.

One way to help people get acquainted with your newsletter at a lower cost than a full subscription is to offer a sample copy of the newsletter for a small fee. You can make an offer like this along with a regular subscription offer, and it may encourage uncertain recipients to take a sample copy and decide whether or not they want to subscribe. Whenever people do accept a sample copy, be sure to follow up with a letter seeking a subscription if they haven't responded to your offer within a short time.

A technique for determining which publications are drawing the best response is to list your address slightly differently in each ad. Some companies do so by using a different department letter or number that corresponds to each publication in which the ad appears. Keeping track of your responses' origins allows you to determine the cost per response to each publication—valuable information in deciding where to spend your advertising money.

If you plan to advertise your newsletter, several reference books tell you what publications accept advertising and how much it costs. Good places to start checking are *Business Publication Rates and Data* and *Consumer Magazine Rates and Data* from Standard Rate & Data Service, Inc. These guides list publications according to subject matter or industry. Once you've determined the target areas, you can contact each publication's advertising manager and request a rate card and media kit, which may include research material on the publication's audience. If they don't provide this material, ask a sales representative about some characteristics of the target audience. For a large advertising campaign, you may want to retain a reputable advertising agency to assist you in planning and developing effective advertising.

Direct Marketing

The two primary direct marketing tools for delivering your subscription pitch are telemarketing and direct mail. Although telemarketing is an effective technique, it is often more effective for obtaining renewals than for getting initial subscribers. People sometimes wish to continue subscribing but never get around to sending in their renewal form. Having a telemarketer call them to ask for a renewal is less of an intrusion than if they receive a phone call from a company they know nothing about. One of the best ways to use telemarketing for subscription renewals is to let the subscribers charge the subscription to a credit card, which enables you to collect money over the telephone.

Using telemarketing for initial subscribers can be costly, since you are not sure how well qualified the audience is, but if you obtain the telephone numbers of a highly select group of people, telemarketing may get you new subscribers. If you cannot get names, phone numbers, and information about a select group, direct mail will probably be the most appropriate direct marketing technique.

The most important aspect of using direct mail is obtaining the right mailing lists. Next most important is to present a mailing that entices people to subscribe and makes it easy for them to do so.

Mailing Lists

There are three types of mailing lists:

- your own in-house lists
- direct mail response lists
- lists compiled from various sources

Your own in-house lists are usually the best ones, since the people on them are familiar with your organization or publication. If you're just getting started, however, you probably don't have such a list. Your in-house list will comprise your subscribers, both those who renew and those who don't, and other people who inquire about your newsletter as a result of an advertisement or word of mouth.

Direct mail response lists, the second-best bet, are composed of people with a proven likelihood of ordering something by direct mail. These people are better targets than the general population.

The last, and least effective, type of list is compiled from the telephone book, a membership directory, or other source.

Many mailing list services sell numerous and varied mailing lists, with a wide price range from company to company and list to list. A publication called *Direct Mail List Rates and Data* from Standard Rate and Data Service contains descriptions of more than 70,000 mailing lists available for rent. Another good source of information on lists is *Direct Marketing Magazine*, which carries advertisements from list compilers and list management companies.

Yet another list source is a reputable mailing list broker or list management company. A list broker finds lists that are appropriate for your audience and receives a commission from the lists' owners. A good list broker should have a fair idea of what kind of results various lists produce. When looking for a list broker, try to find one who has some experience in the newsletter business.

Other possible sources of mailing lists are trade associations or other nonprofit organizations whose membership may be particularly interested in your subject area. The *Encyclopedia of Associations*, published by Gale Research Company, is an excellent guide that lists thousands of nonprofit associations. Some of these groups do not release their membership lists, but others offer them at low prices to keep their members abreast of developments in their field. The policy varies from organization to organization, so query the groups that are related to your subject matter.

The computer system with which you're producing your newsletter is also an excellent tool for maintaining your mailing lists. Both the Macintosh and IBM PC series computers have good database programs available that can handle mailing list maintenance. Some of these database programs also merge names and addresses into letters to produce customized letters. Sophisticated programs can even select specific passages of text for certain names on the list. Thus, if you have particular information about somebody on the list, you can either refer to that specific information and insert the reference into the letter or construct the letter from various paragraphs, depending on the interests or other qualifying factors of each person on the list.

Another advantage of using a computer is that you can check the names you already have against the names you acquire from other lists. When you get lists from scattered sources, you often end up with duplicate names. Searching through lists and taking out duplicate names is known as merge/purge.

Yet another consideration of using mailing lists is keeping them "clean," which means removing names of people who are no longer at the same address or who have retired or died. The best way to keep a mailing list clean is to mail to it frequently and keep track of returned letters. Be sure to print the words *Address Correction Requested* on everything you mail out.

Direct Mail Results

It's important to track the results of your mailings, another task your computer system can perform, using a spreadsheet program such as Lotus 1-2-3 on the IBM PC, or Excel on the Macintosh. You can also use a spreadsheet to estimate the cost of your direct mail effort.

Direct mail marketing gives you a way to measure the success of the marketing effort by rating the response to your mailings. A response of less than 1 percent is considered poor; a good response is 1–2 percent. Anything more than just a few percentage points is considered phenomenal and is highly unlikely with a long list, although it may be possible with a short list of targeted potential subscribers. When you're determining how much you should pay per name for a mailing list, do not expect more than 1 or 2 percent of your mailings to result in paid subscribers. Thus, for every 1000 mailings, you might expect 10 to 20 paid subscribers.

You can also use a spreadsheet to estimate the cost of a mailing. You should be sure to keep track of factors such as the cost of the typesetting, page layout, artwork, photography, and so forth, related to creating the direct mail materials; the cost of purchasing names from mailing lists; and the printing costs, which include the price of a letter, other sales material, and a preprinted business reply card or envelope. You should also estimate the cost of folding any of the materials, labeling and stuffing the envelopes, and transporting them to the post office. When you estimate the price of postage, keep in mind that people tend to read first-class mail first but that it costs more to send. Third-class mail is less expensive but doesn't receive as much attention. Standardize your costs based on the number of responses you get per thousand names compared with the cost per thousand names.

Depending on whether you mail your piece via first or third class and how expensive the enclosed materials are, your costs will usually range from $300 to $1000 per thousand pieces you send out. Estimating what your response will be helps you figure out if you will receive enough money in subscriptions to pay for the cost of your mailing, which will be a factor when you determine what price to charge for your newsletter. For example, if the cost of mailing 1000 pieces is $500 and you plan to mail 10,000 pieces, that particular direct mail campaign will cost you $5000. If you receive a 1 percent response from 10,000 solicitations, you will get 100 orders. If your newsletter costs only $10, you will get only a $1000 return on a mailing that cost you $5000.

Of course, if you increase the number of pieces you mail, you can achieve a certain economy of scale, especially if you can live with using third-class mail. Large mailings with low response rates can be quite expensive, however, which is why it's critically important to obtain good sources for names.

The high cost of obtaining orders is one of the main reasons that the price of newsletters is higher than what you might expect. If you are providing important information in your newsletter, $100 a year for a subscription is not too much to ask, especially if it is a weekly publication.

Eventually, you will build your own in-house mailing list that will produce much higher response rates than will rented, purchased, or compiled lists. These in-house names will be less expensive per response to mail to and will therefore enable you to make a profit on your newsletter.

Careful tracking of responses to mailings and costs per response can mean the difference between success and failure for your newsletter. The electronic spreadsheet programs available for personal computers are an effective tool for keeping track of this type of information.

HOW TO DO DIRECT MAIL

If you're going to send a direct mail piece to many people, it's an excellent idea to contact a company that specializes in direct mail marketing. You may decide, however, to use your desktop publishing system to create your direct mail package. The basic direct mail package consists of an envelope; a personal-style letter; a descriptive brochure, flier, pamphlet, sample issue, or pages from an issue; an order form; and a return envelope, which can either be postage paid or without postage. In light of the high cost of mailings, our recommendation is to send it without postage, since people who are willing to order your newsletter should be willing to put a stamp on the return envelope. You can obtain return envelopes inexpensively from business form printers such as Nebs. You may be tempted to include other items in your direct mail package, but remember that they may drive up production and postage costs.

If you can think of ways to get direct mail pieces to their recipients without paying for postage, do so. For example, if you can obtain a list of people attending a conference or trade show, enter their names into your database, and prepare a personalized letter for each attendee, you can place it in an envelope, along with your direct mail piece, for distribution with the registration materials for the show or conference.

Use a #10 envelope, preferably without a window, with the person's name and address typed on the outside. In light of the volume of unsolicited mail people receive, your envelope must grab enough attention to get opened. People usually open first-class mail first, especially if the name and address are typed or look typed. Some kind of teaser or other information on the outside of the envelope may encourage recipients to open it, although it adds to the cost of the envelope. If you do put a message on the envelope, repeat its theme at the beginning of the enclosed letter.

Your letter, which should be no longer than four pages, points out the benefits of subscribing to your newsletter. A postscript at the end is an especially effective attention grabber. The flier, brochure, or other enclosures should reinforce the benefits you've pointed out in your letter or elaborate on any special offers you have made.

You'll be sending two types of mailings: one to attract new subscribers and the other to seek subscription renewals. Renewal mailings should have a success rate of 50–75 percent, in contrast to the 1–2 percent you can expect from mailings to potential new subscribers. If you are getting less than a 50 percent renewal rate, you should question the content and quality of your newsletter, the performance of your direct mail piece, or your definition of your target audience. After people have renewed once, the chances that they will renew again go up, so you can expect a 60–90 percent renewal rate for the next couple of years. Since the costs of obtaining renewals are much lower than those of attracting new subscribers, renewals are where you will make your biggest profits. Direct mail techniques are more appropriate than telephone solicitations for renewals, because the latter method is more expensive.

FILLING ORDERS

When you attract subscribers, you must fulfill their orders, a natural job for a personal computer with a database program. In addition to tracking orders and billing information and compiling subscription statistics, the computer can help you prepare order acknowledgments, track expiration dates and subscription terms, and calculate sales tax. Your database program should be flexible enough that you can change the format of your database after you've started.

STATE YOUR PURPOSE

After you've targeted your audience and determined how you're going to entice them into subscribing, you will need to stake out the territory your newsletter will cover and decide on your approach to providing information. The first step is to write a short statement of purpose of about 20 to 30 words. If you can't describe the newsletter succinctly without going over that limit, the idea may not be well focused enough to become a successful publication. The description can change as your needs and ideas change after you discover more about your market or talk with experts in the field. When you've finished your research and pinpointed your market, though, a single statement of purpose should communicate the newsletter's purpose to the people who are in charge of your marketing, circulation, editing, writing, and so forth. This statement can be a guideline to help everyone involved produce a uniform, targeted publication that will be successful with its intended audience.

TIPS ON FINDING DATA FOR YOUR NEWSLETTER

To put out a newsletter, you need a regular supply of information. If you plan to obtain data from on-line databases on a weekly or monthly basis for use as source material, look at the dates associated with the data you're retrieving and make sure you'll have enough to fill the intended size of your publication. Don't plan a ten-page weekly newsletter compiled from on-line database information if only two pages a week of information are available. Make sure you investigate the database searches to ascertain how much information you can get. Systems such as Dialog tell you how much information a particular search yields. Viewing some of these entries will inform you of the appropriateness of the subject matter and give you an idea of the length of the entries, so you can determine how much material you will use in assembling this information into a newsletter or other publication.

Any information you obtain from government publications bears no copyright and can be quoted from freely and used without fear of reprisal. When you employ copyrighted information in a newsletter, check with the publisher. You can sometimes use material from other publications, but you cannot infringe on copyrighted material.

One of the main concepts of copyright law is that information itself cannot be copyrighted; only the manner in which that information is presented can be. So if you find out about something by reading copyrighted publications and you write about this information in your own style and own words, you won't be violating the copyright. With this caution in mind, try to read a lot of publications that might have information of interest to your target market to find ideas that you can put into your newsletter.

Another good idea is to write to companies and other organizations involved in your area of interest and ask to be put on their press release lists. By sending an item to PR newsletters that describe your subject area, you may be able to receive additional press releases from other companies and organizations.

You may be able to find a clipping service that extracts material from newspapers, magazines, and so forth, according to your specified areas of interest. These services are available in most major cities, and you should be able to find one in the telephone book. The more information you can assemble and the better your information resources, the more informative your publication will be.

Information-Gathering Tools

Personal computer software can assist you in obtaining information from on-line databases. An example of such software for the Macintosh is Dow Jones Spreadsheet Link. This program works with the Dow Jones Straight Talk communications program to retrieve a wealth of information—stock prices, historical averages, and so forth—from the on-line databases in the Dow Jones News/Retrieval service and transfers it to the Excel, Multiplan, or Microsoft Works spreadsheet for particular stocks and for other types of specific information. Whenever you want the information updated, you instruct your computer to retrieve the information from the database, and that information transfers to the spreadsheet automatically. When you use a program such as Excel on the Macintosh, you can not only obtain spreadsheet data but can also create excellent-looking charts and graphs to cut and paste into a desktop publishing document with any of the Macintosh page layout software programs. You're then ready to reproduce the document on the Apple LaserWriter or any other PostScript-compatible printer.

An example of software for the IBM PC that you can use in conjunction with an on-line database is the Pro-Search program from Menlo Corporation. Pro-Search is a program that helps you construct an appropriate search strategy for on-line databases such as those provided on Dialog, without your having to actually log onto the Dialog system itself. This procedure can save you time and money, since charges for Dialog accrue by the minute as you are logged onto the database, not necessarily as you are making a search.

Database companies such as Dialog and BRS provide personal computer users with immediate access to abstracts, titles, and, in some cases, the full text of millions of different articles, spanning tens of thousands of publications in virtually every major language.

Besides bibliographic information, on-line databases contain stock quotes, business data, government statistics, economic models, scientific data, and so on. The list of resources available on line is growing rapidly. Refer to the Resource Guide for a list of the major on-line services.

The potential of using the same computer system for gathering information as you do for publishing that information may well be the most significant impact that desktop publishing has on our society. Desktop publishing technology holds the promise of inexpensively producing publications derived from inexpensively obtained information.

Here is an example of how effective on-line searching for information can be, compared with hand searching for that same information: One of the authors was an on-line search consultant for fellow students while attending graduate school. A client was investigating the use of myth and magic in television commercials and advertising. She had been searching through libraries by hand for six months and had not been able to find a single published reference on the subject. After spending 20 minutes on-line with Dialog, at a cost of about $15, the author obtained more than 20 published references to the subject matter, including several papers published as parts of conference proceedings and two Ph.D. theses listed as dissertation abstracts.

MORE TIPS

Your computer may be able to assist you with other sources of information. For example, use your readers as news sources. Send them a questionnaire you've designed with your desktop publishing system and use their responses as the basis for various stories. You can compile the results of a questionnaire with a spreadsheet and use a graphics program that can take the spreadsheet data and automatically convert it into a graph of the responses. You can then write a story about your questionnaire's findings.

Most database programs can help you prepare a database with different output formats. One of the formats can be a questionnaire, and the database program can keep track of the results.

Another way to gather information with your computer is to use teleconferencing or bulletin board software to assemble a group of people electronically to "discuss" an issue. You may be able to reprint transcripts of the participants' commentary about the issue as part of your newsletter. This technique is especially effective if the commentators are experts in the field. The Source and CompuServe are two information services you can use.

Don't forget the government, either. Government, at all levels from federal to state to local, has a tremendous amount of information in the public domain—i.e., not protected by copyright—so you can quote freely from it and reuse it as you choose. Much of this information is free. (Write or call the Government Printing Office in Washington, D.C., for more information.) Many research reports and other materials that are prepared at universities and even by private companies may be in the public domain if their preparation was funded by the government.

HOW TO SUCCEED IN NEWSLETTER PUBLISHING

If you are just getting started in the newsletter business, look at some of the books about newsletters listed in the bibliography and study some successful newsletters to get an idea of what it takes to succeed.

One requirement for success is a unique editorial style. The style can be straightforward and factual; argumentative; personal; controversial; predictive, to forecast trends in your area; intimate, to look inside a particular subject area; interpretive, to explain complex material; or humorous. In any case, the style should fit the audience. If you have more than one writer, strive for stylistic consistency. See the bibliography for reference materials on good writing style and grammar, both of which are essential to your publication's credibility and professional impression. If you are covering a field that employs a lot of jargon, you can develop an in-house style sheet to standardize its usage.

If you're uncertain about your editing and proofreading skills, hiring a trained copy editor/proofreader is worth the money. You can also find software to check spelling and grammar, which can be useful in identifying and correcting some problems, but these programs are not infallible. A human proofreader is still your best bet.

Like any other publication, a newsletter must have a timetable on which you plan all tasks necessary for the creation of each issue. You may be able to use CPM (critical path management) or PERT (program evaluation and review technique) software if you have a particularly complex publication or group of publications. Plan all the publication dates of the year on a calendar, taking account of holidays. Then get calendars of events that relate to your newsletter's subject area, transferring them to your master calendar and seeing if they will affect your schedule. If you anticipate adjusting publication dates because of such events—especially if you will be at the events yourself—make all the necessary arrangements to change your production schedule accordingly.

To get an idea of what a classic newsletter looks like, observe the *Kiplinger Washington Letter*, which dates back to 1923 and has remained very successful since then. A good newsletter should convey its information in a concise and personal format. Don't attempt to entertain your readers; just try to provide them with as much solid information as possible.

The Look of Your Newsletter

Unless you have design training and experience or have a very limited budget, hire a professional art director who's experienced in producing either magazines or newsletters. If you do decide to design your newsletter yourself, see chapter 3.

Although it is important to carefully consider the recommendations of a designer or art director, you don't have to follow them if you think that they will not work for your market. If you don't like the first design, have someone else give you an alternative, so you'll have a choice. It's well worth the extra money that you might spend to get a design that you're satisfied with.

Before you work with a designer or art director or do the design yourself, you need to consider your logo or nameplate. It is the most important design element of a newsletter, since it is the trademark by which the newsletter will be identified. Coming up with a logo involves two primary considerations: the title of the newsletter and an appropriate design that enforces recognition and recollection of your logo and that has a symbolic tie-in to your subject matter or target audience. A company newsletter usually uses the corporate logo, along with an appropriate title in a distinctive typeface. Other newsletters use only type to create the logo, and yet others use a combination of type and a symbol or other stylized element.

It's especially important to hire a professional designer to create a logo, and often you are better off choosing a different designer from the one who is designing the publication proper. Specialists in logo design understand how symbols and designs communicate different impressions to different people. If you can't afford such a specialist, try to find a good graphic artist with professional experience. You'll have to live with your logo for a long time.

Also keep in mind that your logo will appear in many places besides your newsletter. It will show up on envelopes, letterheads, business cards, subscription order cards, and other items that you may also be creating with your desktop publishing system.

Color can be effective on the pages of your newsletter, and many savvy newsletter publishers have a graphics designer create a color logo that is sometimes preprinted, along with other constant design elements, on a six-month or year's supply of colored paper. Then each edition of the newsletter is designed to fit within the template and is printed on it in black ink.

To complement the logo and the title of your newsletter, write a descriptive phrase or tag line for your title. For example, a newsletter about desktop publishing might have a tag line "The Newsletter for Computer Typesetting and Page Layout" or "Covering Computer Publishing Technology." The tag line is sometimes worked into the logo design and can also appear on the masthead. The masthead is where you put business information about the newsletter, such as the name, address, phone number, date of the issue, volume and issue numbers, copyright notice, personnel involved with the publication, and subscription prices. It's also a good idea to get an ISSN (International Standard Serial Number), which can also appear in the masthead and identify the title of your newsletter, help you with sales to libraries, help you communicate with suppliers, and get you second-class postal rates. Each page should have a page number and a copyright notice, along with the newsletter's title. Many newsletters carry a date and volume number on each page.

Another factor to consider in the design of your newsletter is the page size, the column width, and the placement of the columns on the page. The most important reason you should not deviate from the $8\frac{1}{2} \times 11$ inch page is that it is the standard size of business correspondence, documents, and filing systems. Other sizes are difficult for readers to save and are more expensive to print. Some publishers have tabloid—i.e., 11 × 14 inch—newspaper-size newsletters on newsprint to emulate the look and feel of a newspaper, and this technique can sometimes be used to good advantage. Most newsletters are $8\frac{1}{2}$ × 11 inches, though, and most have a single column of text with generous margins on either side for reader notes. Another reason for wide margins is that a shorter line of text—40–60 characters per line—is more readable. Since short lines are easier to read, you may want to experiment with a two- or even three-column format. A three-column format gives your newsletter the look of a miniature newspaper, but be very careful with layout and design in such a format. It is generally inadvisable to have more than three columns in a newsletter.

When you've established the design elements and have the data that you want to incorporate into your design, such as your logo, page numbering, page headers, and footers, you will need to choose the typefaces for the body of the newsletter. For the main body of the text, the smallest advisable type size is 9 point, and the largest is 12 point. Also keep in mind that a 9-point face in one typeface may not be exactly the same size as 9 point in another. For a detailed discussion of typeface selection and other design factors, see chapter 3, "Design for Effective Communication."

We recommend that you use a serif typeface for the body copy of your newsletter. The small strokes, or serifs, at the top and bottom of the main strokes help the eye move from character to character, making words and lines of text easier to read. The best-known serif typeface is Times Roman, which is highly recommended as a general purpose typeface for the main body of text. If you have no particular preference for another typeface, it's hard to go wrong using Times Roman.

This is a serif typeface.

This is a sans serif typeface.

The most commonly used sans serif typeface is Helvetica, an excellent face for headlines but not recommended for the main body of text in a newsletter. Helvetica Narrow, a Helvetica variant that squeezes more characters onto a line, is primarily for long headlines that won't fit into an allotted space with regular Helvetica.

You'll also need to consider whether you want justified or ragged-right columns. With ragged-right columns, the lines of text end at the end of words or at major word breaks. Justified text generally has a more formal look than ragged right. Your choice should depend on the tone of your newsletter, the style of your communication, and your audience. This paragraph is justified, and the next one is set ragged-right.

Typewriter type gives a newsletter an informal look and also conveys the impression that the information is fresh, having just been typed and sent out to readers. It also suggests a personal letter or correspondence. The best-known typewriter typeface is the serif face Courier. Typewriter type is measured in two main sizes: elite, which equals 12 characters to the inch, and pica, which equals 10 characters to the inch.

PRINTING YOUR NEWSLETTER

The two main options for printing newsletters are photocopying and photo-offset. Reproducing your newsletter with a photocopy machine can yield a good-looking product if you use a high-quality photocopy machine, especially if you have colored paper with a preprinted color logo. Photocopying is best for a small number of newsletters, up to several hundred, but when you get over a thousand copies, it is more economical to use photo-offset printing. Photo-offset produces better quality and is the least expensive method for printing in large quantities. When you select a print shop, be sure to shop around, because photo-offset printing is a very competitive industry, and you may get a wide difference in price quotes from one company to another. Also be sure to look at samples of the printer's work.

You also need to decide what kind of paper to use. A photocopy machine most often uses $8\frac{1}{2} \times 11$ inch sheets, but an offset printer is more likely to be able to print your newsletter on 11×17 inch sheets, which you can fold in half to obtain the standard $8\frac{1}{2} \times 11$ inch size. One sheet printed on both sides and folded over is four $8\frac{1}{2} \times 11$ inch pieces of paper. This method limits your newsletter to multiples of four pages, but you can insert a single double-sided $8\frac{1}{2} \times 11$ inch sheet into the center, for an additional two pages. The

Tips for Newsletter Design

- Words in all uppercase letters are hard to read. If you have only a few headlines in your newsletter, you can use all caps for the headlines, but if you have many headlines or subheads or long ones, use uppercase and lowercase. In fact, some editors and designers suggest that only the first letter in the first word of a headline be capitalized.
- Bar charts and pie charts illustrate quantity better than line graphs do. Charts labeled with numbers are easier to comprehend than charts labeled with color or shading.
- Extra white space between characters gives an open look but does not allow the maximum amount of information per page.
- Typewriter typefaces can be used effectively in newsletters because they reduce the emphasis you have to put on design for the main body of the text.

advantage of printing on folded 11 × 17 inch sheets is that you do not need to staple the pages together. Staples can make the back sides of pages hard to read. If you cannot use the folding technique, it's best to leave the sheets loose, unless you want to punch holes into your newsletter so readers can save it in a three-ring binder.

Desktop publishing technology has more to offer newsletter producers than simply typesetting and page layout. You can use your desktop publishing computer system for gathering information electronically, editing that information, writing new material, cutting and pasting information, merging text with graphics, creating graphics from numeric data, preparing mailing lists, tracking order fulfillment, preparing accounting and financial information, projecting costs, tracking projects, and managing time.

A Newsletter/Desktop Publishing Plan in Action

Amanda Hixson is a journalist who covers the personal computer industry from Mountain View, California. In mid-1985, she started *P.C. Review*, a newsletter evaluating personal computer business software. The production and promotion of Hixson's newsletter demonstrates the many uses of desktop publishing technology. Working with three partners, Hixson writes, lays out, prints, and promotes *P.C. Review*, using readily available desktop publishing tools.

She composes each issue, using Microsoft Word for text and MacPaint for graphics. She sets up graphics as disk files and calls them into PageMaker, with which she lays out the newsletter.

Next, she sends her files by modem to one of her partners, another Macintosh user who produces his own newsletter, which analyzes the personal computing industry. He edits Hixson's material and helps with page layout. When the issue is completed, either she or the partner sends it electronically to their other partners in Los Angeles. These two partners have a LaserWriter, which they use to run off the camera-ready copy that goes to the printer. They set the type in a 10-point serif face.

Hixson says she uses this jointly owned desktop publishing system to design her own business cards and direct mail pieces (from which she notes she's had a 2 percent response rate). She also uses her Macintosh as a database for mailing lists and performs business tasks with the computer.

Her Los Angeles partners have gone even further in their uses of the system. They, too, produce a newsletter, which covers teleconferencing. In addition to the newsletters, they produce books with the Macintosh/LaserWriter combination. They sell the books themselves or market them through other companies.

Hixson and partners are using their desktop publishing system to write, design, and print both newsletters and books; keep their financial records; and maintain databases. They also employ telecomputing to share files and transport them to the LaserWriter. The total investment in the components of this system comes to less than $20,000.

Similar scenarios should become increasingly commonplace among newsletter producers.

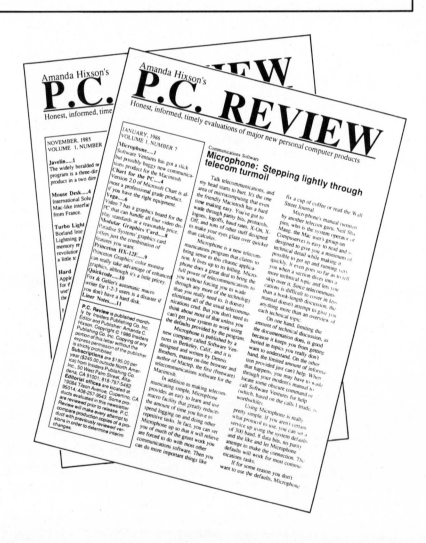

Part Three

The Tools of
Desktop Publishing

A personal computer is the primary component of a desktop publishing system. Although any type of personal computer can play a role, three types of computers (two personal, one not so personal) stand out as the most significant for use in creating a versatile desktop publishing system:

- the Macintosh family from Apple Computer
- the IBM PC series from International Business Machines (this group includes the so-called IBM PC-compatible computers produced by Compaq and many other companies)
- UNIX-based systems from a variety of manufacturers

Of these three types of computer systems, the Macintosh is the best suited to desktop publishing applications. The IBM PC series is next in line in terms of cost-effectiveness and versatility. UNIX systems are generally much more costly than either the Macintosh or IBM PC series computers, and often the issue of whether a UNIX system is truly a desktop computer becomes a factor. UNIX systems are single-user computers or, more often, multiuser host computers. These UNIX multiuser systems fall halfway between the typical definition of a personal computer and that of a minicomputer. Smaller UNIX systems might more accurately be described as supermicros, since they are based on microprocessor technology but offer capabilities equivalent to those of many minicomputers. These supermicros are customarily referred to as workstations. Sun Microsystems and Apollo are two companies whose products exemplify the UNIX supermicro. DEC's MicroVAX is another supermicro that can be used for desktop publishing, and IBM's RT PC is a CAD/CAM (computer-aided design/computer-aided manufacturing) workstation computer that also works as a desktop publishing system. These systems are quite costly, but prices may fall in the next year. Apple is also expected to introduce a less expensive supermicro workstation in late 1986 or early 1987 that will be Macintosh-compatible yet powerful enough to compete with Sun and Apollo workstations and the RT PC.

UNIX systems use software such as *troff*, *ditroff*, *Plot*, and *TEX*. Although you can achieve excellent results with these systems, a considerable investment in hardware, software, and training is necessary. In contrast, desktop publishing systems based on the Macintosh or IBM PC series cost only a fraction of the amount of a UNIX system, yet can achieve similar results.

UNIX supermicro systems use a variety of microprocessors, but the most popular and predominant is the 68000 family from Motorola, which includes the 68000, the 68010, and the 68020. The 68000 series is a family of 32-bit processors, meaning that the mathematical units used for computation and processing are binary numbers 32 digits long. Although the number of bits of a processor (usually 8, 16, or 32) makes little difference to a person using the computer, the number of bits a processor uses often serves as a gauge of the system's sophistication, 8-bit processors being the least sophisticated, 16-bit representing an intermediate level of sophistication, and 32-bit representing the current state of the art in microprocessor technology. The Macintosh uses a 32-bit 68000 microprocessor chip. The IBM PC series, however, uses the 8088 and 80286 families of 16-bit microprocessor chips.

Chapter 5

The Apple Macintosh

Apple's Macintosh computer and LaserWriter page printer ignited the desktop publishing industry. The Macintosh and LaserWriter were the first *WYSIWYG* (what you see is what you get) page layout workstation and high-resolution page printer combination that sold for less than $10,000. (Although the Macintosh is considered a "personal" computer, we occasionally refer to it as a workstation because it can operate in a network and share files; for more on the characteristics of workstations, see chapter 7.) Before the Macintosh/LaserWriter introduction, a similar workstation and high-resolution output device cost in the range of $40,000 to $100,000. Although the Macintosh has a smaller screen than larger systems do, it is much easier to use for typesetting and page layout because the Macintosh's operating principle is easier to learn.

Apple introduced the Macintosh computer in January 1984. It represented the culmination of a 15-year research effort, started by scientists at Xerox's Palo Alto Research Center (PARC) and developed for the mass market by Apple during the early 1980s. The Macintosh was a lower-cost, more refined version of Apple's Lisa computer, and the Lisa was a lower-cost refinement of Xerox's Star computer, which was a descendent of the Xerox Altos computer, an experimental system never brought to market. All of these computers had the goal of creating a computer that was "people literate" and therefore easier to learn and use than traditional computers that used command line technology and required people to become "computer literate." The Macintosh was the first commercially successful computer to bring people literate technology to the marketplace.

Now that Apple has pioneered this technology for the mass market, other companies are acting quickly to imitate the technology. The low-cost Atari 520 ST, with its Macintosh-like GEM operating system; Microsoft's Windows for the IBM PC and compatible computers; and the IBM TopView product are all attempts to create a more people-literate computer interface. This new software technology has become known as the Macintosh user interface or a Mac-like user interface. (The term *user interface* refers to the method of interaction between a person and a computer—where the two entities come together.) This interface is distinguished from older command line user interfaces by its use of conceptual objects in the operating system, which is why computer scientists call the Mac user interface an "object oriented" operating system.

In a command line interface, by contrast, the computer presents a prompt, and you type a command and press the Return key, after which the computer interprets the command and undertakes the appropriate action. For example, if you want to copy a file from one diskette to another in a two-disk-drive system with a command line user interface such as that of the IBM PC, mainframe computers, and many other types of computers, you might type a command such as *COPY A:MYFILE B:*. This command copies the file named *MYFILE* from one drive called the *A:* volume to the other drive, known as the *B:* volume. When you type this command line, the computer takes no action until you press the Return key. Then it interprets the command and, if the syntax of the command is correct, takes the requested action. If, however, a space is missing, an extra space is inserted, or a word is misspelled, the command will not have the expected result, and either an error message will appear or an inappropriate and sometimes damaging action will occur.

Conversely, an object-oriented operating system represents certain conceptual computer features as graphic objects, and you manipulate them to produce the desired result. To take our previous example, suppose you want to copy a file from one diskette to another in an object-oriented operating system. In such a system, the screen represents a conceptual desktop and files are represented by small, cartoon-like drawings called icons. Often, different types of files have different icons. The icon for a word processing document looks like a typewritten page, that of a spreadsheet document looks like a small spreadsheet, and so forth. The two disk drives are represented by icons of each diskette (see illustration). This object-oriented method of operating the computer has been dubbed "the desktop metaphor."

With this type of interface, you use a device such as a mouse to point to the icon that represents the file you want to copy, and you move that icon into the icon of the destination disk with the mouse. With the mouse, you can control the movement of the cursor and move images from one place on the desktop to the other. By moving a duplicate image from one window to another window, you instruct the computer to copy that file from the source to the target. You type no commands, nor do you have to memorize syntax.

This simplified method of operating a computer greatly reduces the time you have to spend to learn how to use the computer productively. Also, in the case of the Macintosh, Apple has adamantly encouraged third-party software developers to produce software that uses a consistent method of operation. Macintosh software developers have done an excellent job of following Apple's guidelines for software consistency. The result is that if you learn one Macintosh software program, it is much easier to learn another Macintosh program, since almost all of the programs for the Mac operate in a

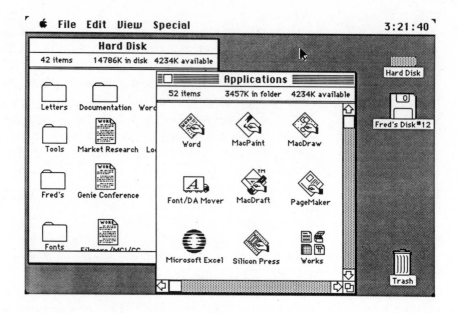

The Macintosh desktop.

similar manner, even though their functions and features may be radically different.

As an example, the word processing program MacWrite operates similarly to the graphics program MacDraw, which operates much like page layout software such as ReadySetGo, MacPublisher, and PageMaker. All the commands in each program are presented in pull-down lists (called menus) that you can select with the mouse. You don't have to remember all the commands for each program— you need only select them from menus that each program presents. The various menus of commands and features are grouped into categories, and every application program lists each category at the top of the screen. Since different applications have different functions, the categories of commands and features change from program to program. Virtually all Macintosh programs are consistent, however, in listing all the categories at the top of the screen. Under each category, you can get a pull-down menu that lists each of the commands and features, any of which you can activate simply by pointing to it with the mouse and pulling it down from the top of the screen.

Because the Macintosh depends on graphic representations of conceptual objects, it features a high-resolution screen that makes it excellent for desktop publishing applications and word processing, since it displays multiple typefaces, typestyles, and type sizes on the screen at the same time. Also, the high-resolution screen's clarity makes it easier to look at for long periods of time than the screens of many other computer systems, reducing eyestrain and headaches.

Another advantage of the Macintosh's display is that it shows black characters on a white background, which is the way printed pages look. This kind of display not only helps you get a good idea of how a final page will appear, because it looks like a printed page, but it is easy on your eyes if you look back and forth between printed pages and the screen. The reduction in eyestrain is due to a phenomenon called positive contrast. It is better to look at a white screen with black characters on it, then at a white piece of paper with black characters, and back again, than it is to look at a black screen with green characters—such as that of the IBM PC and many other computers—and then at a white page with black characters. In the latter case, your eyes have to strain to adjust to the opposite contrasts of the page and the screen.

The Macintosh Series of Computers

When the Macintosh debuted in January 1984, it featured a 32-bit Motorola 68000 microprocessor. The computer had a bit-mapped 9-inch monochrome display, with 512×342 pixels, that was built into a single unit that housed the display, an internal disk drive, and the internal circuitry of the computer. A detachable keyboard with 57 keys and a mouse cursor controller connected to the main system unit. The Macintosh was a compact computer that took a minimum amount of desk space and was easy to transport.

The original computer featured 128K of RAM (random access memory—internal memory work space), 64K of ROM (read only memory, the instructions the computer uses to operate), a built-in floppy disk drive that used single-sided 3.5-inch diskettes capable of storing 400 kilobytes (400K) each (the equivalent of about 215 double-spaced pages), two serial ports, a four-voice sound generator, and a built-in clock calendar with battery backup. The original Macintosh was criticized for its limited internal memory of 128K because the machine's software required a lot of memory to operate, thus leaving little space for applications such as word processing and graphics.

An external disk drive was available, but hard disks were difficult to use with the system since the Macintosh had to be connected via one of the serial ports, which slowed down data transfer. Although the Macintosh represented the most advanced technology available in a general purpose personal computer at that time, the limitations in internal memory and disk storage prevented the Macintosh from gaining acceptance as a business computer. Apple quickly remedied some of these limitations, in late 1984, by introducing the Macintosh 512K. It was identical to the original Macintosh, but the internal memory, or RAM, had quadrupled from 128K to 512K. Apple further stepped up the performance of the Macintosh with the January, 1986, introduction of the Macintosh Plus.

Apple no longer manufactures the 128K Macintosh. The introduction in early 1986 of a new, higher-priced, higher-performance model, the Macintosh Plus, made the Macintosh 512K the low-cost system.

The main differences between the Macintosh 512K and the Macintosh Plus are that the latter features a new keyboard that includes a numeric keypad; twice the internal memory, which has doubled to one megabyte and can be expanded easily to up to four megabytes; a new set of ROM chips, doubled from 64K to 128K and containing internal instructions the computer uses in its operation; and the replacement of the 400K internal disk drive with a double-sided 800K drive, which stores twice the data on a 3.5-inch diskette. The older 400K diskettes were only barely adequate for many Macintosh programs.

Critics of the original Macintosh design also noted the difficulty of connecting hard disks or other mass storage devices, since they connected to the serial ports, which had a maximum speed of 230 kilobits per second. The Macintosh Plus features a Small Computer System Interface (SCSI, pronounced *scuzzy*). This SCSI connector provides a much faster communication channel for the Macintosh and has provision for up to seven devices, such as hard disks, to connect to the single port.

The accompanying chart compares the original Macintosh, the Macintosh 512K, and the Macintosh Plus.

Characteristic	Macintosh	Macintosh 512K	Macintosh Plus
Processor	Motorola 68000, 32-bit internal architecture, 7.8MHz clock frequency	Motorola 68000, 32-bit internal architecture, 7.8MHz clock frequency	Motorola 68000, 32-bit internal architecture, 7.8MHz clock frequency
Memory	128K RAM, 64K ROM	512K RAM, 64K ROM	1Mb RAM, expandable to 4Mb; 128K ROM
Disk capacity	400K, single-sided, 3.5-inch, hard-shell diskette	400K, single-sided, 3.5-inch, hard-shell diskette	800K, double-sided, 3.5-inch, hard-shell diskette
Screen	9-inch diagonal, monochrome, bit-mapped video display; 512 × 342 pixels	9-inch diagonal, monochrome, bit-mapped video display; 512 × 342 pixels	9-inch diagonal, monochrome, bit-mapped video display; 512 × 342 pixels
Interfaces	Synchronous serial keyboard bus, 2 RS-232/RS-422/AppleTalk serial ports; 230.4K bps maximum speed; mouse interface; external disk interface	Synchronous serial keyboard bus, 2 RS-232/RS-422/AppleTalk serial ports; 230.4K bps maximum speed; mouse interface; external disk interface	Synchronous serial keyboard bus, 2 RS-232/RS-422/AppleTalk serial ports; 230.4K bps maximum speed; mouse interface; external disk interface; SCSI interface, 320K bps maximum
Sound generator	4-voice sound with 8-bit digital-to-analog conversion using 22kHz sampling rate	4-voice sound with 8-bit digital-to-analog conversion using 22kHz sampling rate	4-voice sound with 8-bit digital-to-analog conversion using 22kHz sampling rate
Keyboard	57-key, 2-key-rollover, software-mapped detachable keyboard with optional numeric keypad and cursor keys	57-key, 2-key-rollover, software-mapped detachable keyboard with optional numeric keypad and cursor keys	78-key, 2-key-rollover, software-mapped detachable keyboard with built-in numeric keypad and cursor keys
Mouse	Mechanical-tracking, optical-shaft-encoding mouse with .54 pulses per mm of travel (90 pulses per inch)	Mechanical-tracking, optical-shaft-encoding mouse with .54 pulses per mm of travel (90 pulses per inch)	Mechanical-tracking, optical-shaft-encoding mouse with .54 pulses per mm of travel (90 pulses per inch)
Clock calendar	Custom CMOS clock/calendar chip with user-replaceable battery backup	Custom CMOS clock/calendar chip with user-replaceable battery backup	Custom CMOS clock/calendar chip with user-replaceable battery backup

THE MACINTOSH EXAMINED

The Macintosh is a relatively low cost system that is easy to learn and use—and one that enjoys a wealth of excellent adjunct products in all phases of desktop publishing. It is possible to use either of the two currently available models, the Macintosh 512K or the Macintosh Plus, for desktop publishing, but we believe that the Macintosh Plus, although more expensive, is better suited to the creation and production of publications.

The Macintosh Plus

The Macintosh Plus has double the amount of memory in these three key areas: RAM, ROM, and disk storage (see chart for comparison). With the increased internal memory, you can work on larger documents and more-complex graphics, and you can load several programs into the computer's memory with the Switcher Construction Kit program available from Apple. You can have your page layout software, graphics software, and word processing software all active at the same time, so you can easily cut and paste information into your final page layout without having to stop one application program and start a new one each time you shift between programs. The additional ROM provides a faster set of the QuickDraw graphics instructions, which means the computer can create graphics more quickly than its predecessors could. The ROM includes information for several other enhancements to the Macintosh, such as the ability to use double-sided disk drives.

It also includes instructions for using a hierarchical file system—valuable when you are working with many documents for source material in a desktop publishing system and have stored a lot of clip art. A hierarchical file system lets you organize thousands of documents on a large-capacity mass storage device such as a hard disk. By streamlining the job of locating and working with many documents and applications, it not only speeds up the computer's performance but can also save you a lot of headaches.

The ROM also has software that lets you use part of the one

megabyte of RAM for a special type of memory known as RAM cache. A RAM cache is a special area of memory where the computer stores information you are using. Since it is faster to retrieve information from the computer's internal memory than it is to retrieve it from the disk, a RAM cache can speed up your application programs and the computer's general operation by as much as 200 percent. Additionally, the ROM contains a new set of mathematical instructions the computer can use to perform calculations more quickly than the Macintosh and Macintosh 512K can.

The double-sided disk drives not only provide twice as much storage as the single-sided ones of the same size, but they also operate more quickly than the older 400K disk drives. The increased capability you get from twice as much RAM—added to the improved performance and new features of the extra ROM and the doubled storage space per diskette—justifies the extra expense of a Macintosh Plus.

The Macintosh 512K may have a place in desktop publishing, however, if you are using more than one computer system in your business and some of the systems are slated only for simple data entry or other lower-level tasks. You can supply some of your employees with the lower-cost Macintosh 512K and hook the computers together with the inexpensive AppleTalk network. AppleTalk costs only $50 per connection and allows up to 32 devices such as computers and printers to share information. Sharing resources using a network such as AppleTalk can help spread the cost of a laser printer among several computers.

Several AppleTalk options are available for the IBM PC series of computers (see "Local Area Networks" in chapter 6) as well. With these options, IBM PC series computers can easily share information with Macintoshes. The options make it easy and inexpensive to create a functional local area network for use in office automation as well as desktop publishing. If the people in the accounting division of your organization are using IBM PCs with Lotus 1-2-3, for example, they can send 1-2-3 files over the network to a Macintosh. Then the Macintosh can read the files into a program such as Excel, which can create charts and graphs representative of the data and merge them into a document such as a corporate presentation, business report, quarterly report, or annual report.

Since the Macintosh is better suited to desktop publishing applications than the IBM PC is, the Mac has a place as a partner for the IBM PC in organizations whose personal computers are predominantly PCs. The Mac's lower cost (occasionally as low as $1495 for a 512K version) than that of the IBM PC AT with an Enhanced Graphic Adapter Card—required to approximate the Mac's capabilities—makes the Macintosh a cost-effective desktop publishing workstation.

Apple provides several methods for upgrading the Macintosh 512K to become a Macintosh Plus, so if you are strapped for cash, you can start with a Macintosh 512K computer and upgrade it later. In the long run, however, it is usually less expensive to purchase a Macintosh Plus initially, rather than pay the upgrade cost.

In addition to the increased computer memory, the Macintosh Plus's other important advantage over the Macintosh 512K is its SCSI port, into which you can connect low-cost hard disk drives, tape backup devices, and other mass storage systems. Future storage systems such as optical disks and CD-ROMs will doubtless be available with the SCSI interface, an industry standard used by many manufacturers besides Apple.

Cost Saving Example

A 20-megabyte hard disk connected to the Macintosh through the serial port costs more than $2000; Apple's Hard Disk 20, which connects to the disk drive port, costs $1495; and a 20-megabyte SCSI hard disk drive for the Macintosh Plus costs only about $1000. The latter price may drop in the near future.

Another advantage of the SCSI port is that it accommodates up to seven devices. You can connect both a hard disk and a tape backup to the computer. A tape backup is a tape drive, usually containing cassette tape, that holds from 10 to 60 megabytes and onto which you can transfer information from the hard disk to make archival backup copies. Backup copies are important if your hard disk ever fails. If it contains important information that your business depends on, back up your hard disk at least every week. A tape backup system also lets you remove files that you do not use frequently from your hard

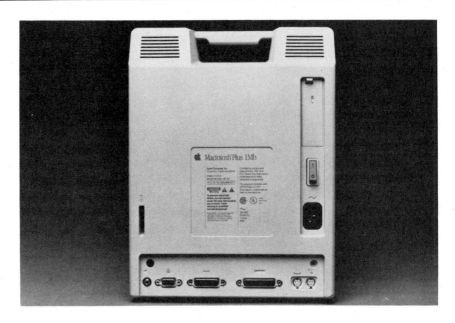

The Macintosh's SCSI port (third from right).

disk and load them only when you need them. This technique keeps your hard disk from filling up.

The SCSI port can accommodate very-large-capacity hard disk drives. For example, the AST-4000 hard disk, which is similar to AST's Colossus line for the IBM PC series, is a large-capacity hard disk with a built-in tape backup system that provides 74 megabytes of hard disk storage you can expand to a full 370 megabytes with optional AST expansion units. The tape backup system can handle 60 megabytes of streaming tape backup, so you can fit most of the contents of the 74-megabyte hard disk onto a single tape, and you can store most of what a 370-megabyte system can hold on as few as six tapes. A large drive such as this is especially useful if you have set up a local area network and are running fileserver software such as the TOPS network (see "Data Transfer" in this chapter). Many users can share a single device, and you can spread the cost of that large hard disk among several users. Each user can share information with other system users. The basic AST-4000 with 74 megabytes and the 60-megabyte tape backup lists for $6995. It features advanced SCSI architecture and a hard disk with a 30-millisecond average disk access time and data transfer rates of 5 megabits per second for the hard disk and 90 kilobytes per second for the tape drive.

Another hardware item you should consider for your desktop publishing system is a modem. You can use a modem to transfer information between your Macintosh and another computer, which can be

Typical Costs for Macintosh Desktop Publishing Systems

Recommended System for Typical Applications:

Macintosh Plus computer: list price, $2599
External disk drive: list price, $499
Apple Personal Modem and Macintosh Plus Connector Kit: list price, $429
ImageWriter II printer: list price, $599

System for More Complex Applications:

Macintosh Plus computer: list price, $2599
SCSI hard disk: list price, $1000 and up
Apple Personal Modem and Macintosh Plus Connector Kit: list price, $429
AppleTalk Connector Kit: list price, $50
LaserWriter Plus printer: list price, $6798

Additional workstations at the same location can be either Macintosh Plus computers or Macintosh 512K computers for lower-level tasks, and an AppleTalk Connector Kit.

The least expensive system that uses a Macintosh computer for desktop publishing applications consists of a Macintosh 512K computer with page layout software. You can construct documents and preview them on the screen, but to print them out, you have to send or take your disk to a service bureau that has a suitable output device, either a laser printer or a typesetting machine. A step up from this system is one that adds an ImageWriter II printer for printing out page proofs before you use the service bureau to produce your final output.

Our recommendation, however, is that you get a Macintosh Plus computer with either an external 800K drive or a SCSI hard disk drive and the LaserWriter Plus printer.

useful if you have offices at different locations that need to transmit information to be printed at the main office, where you have your LaserWriter or other output device. The Macintosh is transportable, so people who travel with it can use a modem to send data back to the home office. If your publication carries news, you may be able to have reporters on the road type stories and transmit them to the home office electronically for printing.

A modem (modulator/demodulator) allows you to use a standard telephone line for data communication with another computer. A computer stores information in binary digits, or bits, which are represented in the computer by tiny on/off "switches" inside the chips. The computer transmits data by changing these on/off switches into fluctuations in voltage. The speed and other characteristics of this fluctuating voltage determine the transmission speed and protocols.

A modem converts the fluctuation in voltage into audible tones that can be transmitted over the phone lines with a process called *mo*dulation. A modem at the other end of the line receives the tones and converts them back into electrical signals by a process called *dem*odulation.

Various transmission speeds and communications protocols are in use for transmitting data among computers. The protocols define common conventions to facilitate data transfer and to regulate telecommunications hardware and software. Transmission speed is measured in bits per second (*bps*), sometimes referred to as *baud*. Examples of communications protocols include error checking schemes, called parity, and conventions for the number of bits, either seven or eight, that transfer a character. Another protocol has to do with the number of start and stop bits that specify the beginning and end of transmitted characters. For communications to work without many errors, both the sending and receiving computer must follow the same protocols and use the same transmission speed.

The three most common transmission speeds that modems use are 300 bps, 1200 bps, and 2400 bps. A rough guideline for converting these speeds into more meaningful values is to divide the transmission speed in bps by 10 to determine the approximate number of characters transmitted per second. Using this formula, you can get a rough idea that a 300-bps modem transmits about 30 characters of data per second, a 1200-bps modem transmits about 120 characters of data per second, and a 2400-bps modem sends about 240 characters per second. Assuming that a page of typewritten manuscript copy contains approximately 25 double-spaced lines of about 60 characters per line, then one manuscript page equals roughly 1500 characters. Using the previously mentioned guideline, we can conclude that transmitting such a page takes about 50 seconds at 300 bps, a little more than 12 seconds at 1200 bps, and a little more than 6 seconds at 2400 bps.

When you're trying to determine what modem to buy, take a look at what you need it for. If you will be transmitting only short documents between two systems or if time is not a consideration, a 300-bps modem may be sufficient. Three-hundred-bps modems are considerably less expensive than 1200- and 2400-bps modems. If your application requires sending and receiving a lot of information, however, or if you are using a remote information service that charges by the minute, then a higher-speed modem may be a better investment, since it will cut down the amount of time it takes to send and receive information.

Although the higher-speed modems can transmit at the slower speeds, so you can transmit at 300 or 1200 bps with a 2400-bps modem, the reverse isn't true—so don't buy more speed than you need. Some of the information services such as The Source, Dow Jones News/Retrieval, Dialog, and CompuServe can work at 2400 bps; others cannot. Check with the information service you plan to use to find out if the service can work with high-speed modems and, if so, the surcharge. At this time, a 1200-bps modem is probably your best bet, since it is less expensive than a 2400-bps modem yet transmits at four times the speed of the 300-bps modem.

We recommend the Apple Personal Modem, Hayes Smartmodem 1200, or the Smartmodem 2400.

MACINTOSH SOFTWARE

In the early days of the Macintosh, critics complained about a lack of software. That problem has vanished. More than 1000 software packages are now available for the computer, a significant number of which have applications in desktop publishing. We have defined six software categories for your desktop publishing system.

- *Page layout software* such as ReadySetGo, MacPublisher, and PageMaker for page composition and layout.

- *Word processing programs* such as MacWrite, Microsoft Word, the word processing features of Microsoft Works and Lotus Jazz, and outline processors such as ThinkTank for writing and editing.

- *Graphics software.* Among the programs in this category are MacPaint, MacDraw, and MacDraft; also included are graphics accessories such as Art Grabber, CheapPaint, FullPaint, and a wide variety of clip art.

Graphics, word processing, and page layout software are the primary software tools of desktop publishing we discussed in chapter 2.

- The other three categories, *communications software, database and information management software,* and *spreadsheet and other number processing software,* are secondary tools for desktop publishing.

PAGE LAYOUT SOFTWARE

Software with which you design and lay out pages is the heart of your Macintosh-based desktop publishing system. After you have conceived and perfected the design of your publication and written it, you are ready to lay out your pages, employing the various elements—typefaces, columns, headlines, and others—of your design. The page layout programs for the Macintosh vary in sophistication and capabilities. The three best-known programs are Page-Maker, MacPublisher, and ReadySetGo; all three of these products are WYSIWYG systems, so you see on the computer screen how the final page will look. Several other, lesser-known page layout products are also available for the Mac, however, including two versions of TEX and products such as MacDraw and MacDraft. TEX is better at formatting text than the three leading page layout programs, but it is much more complicated. It is particularly well suited for creating complex or long documents such as books because it is more adept at such tasks as breaking words for hyphenation, spacing characters and words, and handling mathematical formulas. You can also employ MacDraw, MacDraft, and other graphics programs for page layout as well as for general graphics, drawing, and drafting. These general purpose programs give you some flexibility not found in programs specially tailored to page layout. For example, PageMaker allows a maximum page size of only 11 × 17 inches, whereas MacDraw lets you create pages up to 4 × 8 feet and print them on multiple sheets of paper for assembly into giant documents for presentations, advertising, or other special purposes. As special-purpose page layout software, programs such as MacDraw, MacDraft, and other CAD programs should not be overlooked.

Deciding what page layout software to buy can be confusing. It's a good idea to take a look at the software and try it out before you purchase it. Since everyone's needs and budgets are different, there is no clear choice. If you have a graphic design background, however, you will probably find PageMaker the easiest to work with. The people who created PageMaker based their product on traditional page layout tools, and most graphic artists take to PageMaker quickly. One test conducted by a computer magazine had a graphic artist pit the three leading Macintosh layout programs—PageMaker, MacPublisher, and ReadySetGo—against each other in laying out and printing the same predesigned page. In this test, PageMaker took less than three minutes to lay out the page; MacPublisher took more than twice as long for the same task; and ReadySetGo took even longer. PageMaker was the winner of this formatting race, but the individual designer's work methods may have influenced the results.

Another purchasing consideration is that PageMaker costs almost $500, and the other programs are only about a third of that price. And to further muddy the choice, MacPublisher offers several valuable features not found in the other packages, such as an automatic table of contents and page jump referencing, kerning, built-in telecommunications, and the ability to print in color on the ImageWriter II. The most important of these capabilities is MacPublisher's line justification system, which adjusts interletter spacing to justify lines of type ("letterspace justification"). The other two programs add space between words to justify lines ("word spacing justification"). Letterspace justification can produce better-looking output in some circumstances, especially in narrow columns.

All three of these packages have some similarities. You use on-screen rulers to show you where to place text with the Mac's mouse. All three work with both the ImageWriter and the LaserWriter and PostScript-compatible typesetting machines. You can import text and graphics into these programs from other programs such as Mac-Paint and Microsoft Word. Layout pages have predefinable columns and adjustable column guides and grid blocks into which text automatically flows. For periodicals such as newsletters, you can save layouts and reuse them for subsequent issues.

The results you can get with these products depend on the products' sophistication, their ease of use, and your design talents. As we point out in chapter 3, good design takes a conscious effort and requires some learning. That chapter provides general design suggestions that apply to the use of page layout software.

PageMaker

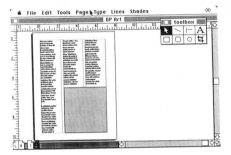

Laying out a page with PageMaker.

PageMaker, widely regarded as the best of the Macintosh page layout programs, costs significantly more than the other two leading page layout programs. A product of Aldus Corporation of Seattle, Washington, PageMaker most closely resembles the traditional layout process that graphic designers are used to. Paul Brainerd, president of Aldus, was a vice president of Atex, Inc., a company that produces dedicated typesetting systems that cost more than $100,000. Brainerd, who is credited with coining the term *desktop publishing*, has utilized experience that he and others at Aldus have in computer typography. According to Brainerd, "We have taken the key functions of $100,000 publishing systems and made them available on a low-cost personal computer. We worked closely with Apple in the development of its laser printer. Apple's product fills the gap between typing and typesetting within office environments." Aldus is developing an IBM PC AT version that will run with Microsoft Windows and promises to offer similar features to those of the Macintosh product, but the Macintosh version will probably remain Aldus's premier product.

With the Macintosh's mouse, you specify the layout of single- or multiple-page documents, using text from a word processing program such as MacWrite, Microsoft Word, Jazz, or Microsoft Works, and integrate it with graphics from MacPaint, MacDraw, Excel, Jazz, Microsoft Works, and other sources. The program can smooth graphics from MacPaint in order to achieve better print quality. Note, however, that the smoothing mechanism actually worsens the print quality in some cases, so test it each way before you decide whether or not to use smoothing. You can produce a typeset camera-ready copy of a page at a variety of resolutions by using a PostScript page printer such as the Apple LaserWriter or a Linotype 100 Series typesetting machine. PageMaker is a professionally designed product that is a good choice if your applications are demanding. If you are on a limited budget, though, you may find it too expensive for casual use. Aldus offers a technical support policy that provides registered users with free telephone support for 45 days after purchasing the product and the option of purchasing an extended support service package for $75 a year.

LIST PRICE • $495

SYSTEM REQUIREMENTS • Macintosh 512K or Macintosh Plus; ImageWriter or LaserWriter

Aldus Corporation
411 First Avenue South, Suite 200
Seattle, WA 98104
(206) 622-5500

MacPublisher

Don't let the low price of MacPublisher fool you. MacPublisher is a unique and useful program that is packed with features and gives you bang for your buck. Although it doesn't have quite the elegance of PageMaker, it is an intriguing program that makes innovative use of the Macintosh graphical user interface. MacPublisher builds a page differently than PageMaker and ReadySetGo do; instead of creating an actual image of the page with all the text and graphics, MacPublisher creates a page mockup that contains only rectangles that represent the location and size of text and graphic elements, and stores the elements as special text and picture files that you edit separately from the page layout. MacPublisher rebuilds a page whenever it changes. The company says it took this approach to allow creation of master pages, repeating elements, and predefined "canned" page layouts; to help prevent data loss on machines with limited memory (MacPublisher can run with as little as 128K RAM); and to facilitate the programming for the automatic table of contents and automatic page jump ("continued on page x") features. Since the page layout is independent of the text and graphic content, you can easily create publication formats you can reuse as you need them. This reusable formats feature can be especially useful for creating catalogs or other publications in which you want the format to remain the same but in which you need to update or replace information on a regular basis.

MacPublisher features either automatic or manual kerning to correct printer spacing idiosyncrasies and to allow a greater amount of control and fine-tuning of character placement and spacing. You can employ manual kerning to create ligatures (letters that touch each other, such as æ, fl, fi, ff, or ffl) and construct a custom table of kerning pairs and save it as a resource file for later use.

Other MacPublisher features include nine different gray-screen overlays; the ability to zoom in on a document up to a 900 percent enlargement to examine details; and document size up to 96 pages, with 256 articles (each with 15 carryovers), and 128 pictures. MacPublisher handles 20 page sizes and even has a French version available.

LIST PRICES • MacPublisher II, $149.95; MacIndex (indexing software for MacWrite and MicroSoft Word), $49.95; Designs for MacPublishing (clip art, etc.), $39.95; Mac-Hy-phen (40,000-word hyphenation dictionary supplied as a desk accessory for use with MacPublisher, PageMaker, and Microsoft Word), $39.95

SYSTEM REQUIREMENTS • Macintosh; ImageWriter or LaserWriter

Boston Software Publishers
1260 Boylston Street
Boston, MA 02215
(617) 267-4747

ReadySetGo

ReadySetGo is up against some stiff competition. It was the first of the three major Macintosh page layout products to get to market, and it seemed like a nice product at the time. When you stack it up against the slick but pricey PageMaker and the inexpensive and clever MacPublisher, however, ReadySetGo doesn't seem to have any strong features that will help it keep a solid place in the market. ReadySetGo has already gone through several revisions that resolved some of the original complaints about the product, and development efforts may add new features that will give it a better market position against MacPublisher and PageMaker. Many people are using the program with good results, and you may want to investigate ReadySetGo, especially to see if any new features are available.

LIST PRICE • $195

SYSTEM REQUIREMENTS • Macintosh, LaserWriter

Manhattan Graphics
163 Varick Street
New York, NY 10013
(212) 989-6442

JustText 1.0

JustText is a combined word processing and page composition system for graphic arts professionals who need the high-quality output from the LaserWriter or Linotype Series 100 typesetters. It creates PostScript files from ordinary text files with embedded typesetting codes without requiring special fonts on the System disk. JustText includes discretionary and automatic hyphenation, user-controlled kerning, hanging indents and bullets, and multiple columns.

The package features three graphics conversion programs—Paint to PostScript, ThunderScan to PostScript, and MacVision to PostScript—collectively called LaserTools. You can position the resultant PostScript image files with the EditArt utility. Other utilities and PostScript files on the disk include Labels, for making standard microfloppy disk labels; Envelopes, for printing addresses directly on envelopes; Icon Collector, which finds icons in any Macintosh program and generates art files of their bit images; and Pattern Library, which contains a large selection of background patterns.

LIST PRICE • $130 (JustText 1.1, slated for release in August 1986, will be $195)

SYSTEM REQUIREMENTS • Macintosh; LaserWriter or Linotype Series 100 typesetter

Knowledge Engineering
G.P.O. Box 2139
New York, NY 10116
(212) 473-0095

Silicon Press

Silicon Press is a program for the ImageWriter II and LaserWriter that facilitates printing on odd-size paper and other materials such as labels and tags. This versatile program offers numerous possible uses, from printing address and packing labels and promotional items to creating price tags, sale labels, and even tiny copyright labels for microchips. Silicon Press can turn your Macintosh desktop publishing system into a specialty printing shop.

LIST PRICE • $79.95

SYSTEM REQUIREMENTS • Macintosh 512K or Macintosh Plus

Silicon Beach Software
P.O. Box 261430
9580 Black Mountain Road, Suite E
San Diego, CA 92126
(619) 695-6956

MacWrite Translator

A handy program developed by Cornell University called MacWrite Translator lets you translate a document from MacWrite into formats used by other computer software. Using the MakeTable command, you can define characters to replace MacWrite's representation of formats such as ruler settings and typestyles. This program could be useful if you wanted to translate MacWrite files into files a typesetting system could utilize. MacWrite Translator is available from DCS, 401 URIS Hall, Cornell University, Ithaca, NY 14853.

LIST PRICE • free (public domain software)

SYSTEM REQUIREMENTS • Macintosh

WORDS AND GRAPHS

Many tools are available to produce the text and illustrations that go into your formatted document or publication. In this section, we provide a brief overview of some of those tools that have proved successful and are well suited for use in desktop publishing applications.

Word, Write, and ThinkTank

Microsoft Word is an excellent word processing program with advanced features such as multiple-column formatting, footnoting, and a built-in spelling checker. This program also lets you edit up to four documents simultaneously and cut and paste among those documents easily. If you need to manage more than four documents at a time, you can use Apple's Switcher program to load two Microsoft

Allotype Typographics PostScript Fonts

Allotype Typographics makes eleven specialized downloadable fonts for publications in classical Greek, modern Greek, and Polish, as well as those that require many scientific symbols and representations of chemical structures. The PostScript fonts work with the Apple LaserWriter and other PostScript-compatible printers and are compatible with programs such as MacWrite, MacDraw, Microsoft Word, and Page-Maker.

The fonts are

- Kadmos—a classical Greek font
- Demotiki—a modern Greek font
- Czasy and Szwajcarskie—Polish fonts
- Czasy small caps and Szwajcarskie small caps—small caps sets for Polish typesetting
- Thomsen and Haber—"convenience" fonts for chemists and other scientists
- Structure—a font containing 100 of the most important chemical structures, bonds, and abbreviations
- Tempora small caps and Helicon small caps—Small caps versions of the Adobe Systems serif and sans serif fonts in the LaserWriter and other PostScript printers

LIST PRICE • $75–$125 each

SYSTEM REQUIREMENTS • Apple LaserWriter or other PostScript printer

Allotype Typographics
1600 Packard Road, Suite 5
Ann Arbor, MI 48104
(313) 577-3035

Word programs into the Macintosh's memory simultaneously and switch between the two programs, each of which can contain up to four open documents, for a total of eight documents that you can work on at once.

MacWrite is a simpler word processing program that is easier to learn and use than Word but does not have as many features. MacWrite, for example, allows you to open only one document at a time.

ThinkTank is an outline processor that helps you create outlines of your topics as an aid to the writing process. You can use the program with either Word or MacWrite.

Excel

We recommend Microsoft Excel for the preparation of graphs and charts. The graphing and charting capabilities of Excel are available separately at a lower cost in the Microsoft Chart software package, but Excel has features that make it worthwhile for many applications. One advantage of using Excel is that it is easier to change a value, if necessary, and obtain the graphics more quickly. Figure changes, updates, and revisions occur rapidly in Excel. By using an Excel macro, you can get a chart or graph immediately (a macro is a command sequence that you can program to automate a series of tasks).

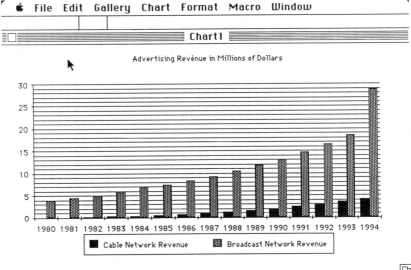

Excel Graph

Another advantage of Excel is that since it reads and writes to and from the Lotus 1-2-3 .WKS format, it lets the Macintosh accept information created with Lotus 1-2-3 on an IBM PC series computer. You create charts and graphs of 1-2-3 data, using Microsoft Excel, and print them on the Apple LaserWriter. Because the graphics capabilities of the Macintosh and the LaserWriter make charts and graphs that look much better than those from an IBM PC series computer, Excel's compatibility with Lotus 1-2-3 makes it a particularly useful and versatile tool for charting and graphing. A gallery of more than 40 types of predesigned charts is possible with Microsoft Excel.

GRAPHICS: MACPAINT, MACDRAW, MACDRAFT

MacPaint is a bit-mapped-graphics program that creates graphics at the resolution of the Macintosh's 9-inch diagonal screen—512 × 342 pixels at a density of about 72 pixels per inch. This resolution is not nearly as crisp as that of the LaserWriter, at 300 dots per inch. MacPaint is an innovative and powerful program, however, with which you fashion numerous types of art and graphics. You can improve the resolution of a graphic image made with MacPaint by using a stat camera to reduce the original. This method, in effect, increases the density of the pixels and brings the image up to a higher resolution. Publications such as *USA Today* employ the technique to improve the quality and resolution of their Macintosh graphics. They draw graphic images in a large size and then reduce them to fit the intended space. This reduction packs the dots closer together to better the image quality. Another advantage of MacPaint is that you can use it with predrawn graphic images such as clip art.

MacPaint can be used for a wide variety of drawing tasks.

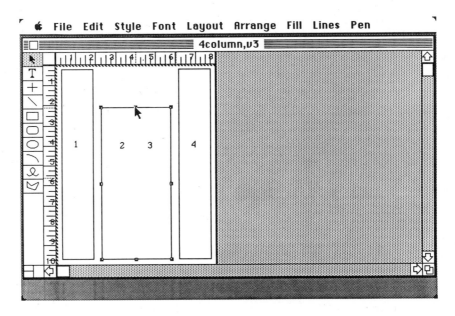

Using MacDraw to experiment with page designs.

The quality of these MacPaint graphics is not as good as that of the graphics you create with MacDraw, MacDraft, or a similar object-oriented drawing program. MacPaint creates a bit-mapped image at a fixed resolution that does not change when you print it on a high-resolution printer. As soon as you superimpose one image on top of another with MacPaint, the bottom image vanishes. In an object-oriented drawing program such as MacDraw, however, each object you draw is a separate, individual object that is re-created at the resolution of whatever device it is working with. When it is presenting information on the screen, MacDraw uses the screen's resolution to represent objects.

In a MacPaint document, jagged edges that appear in a circle drawn on the screen also show up in the final document. The smoothing option of the LaserWriter removes some of the "jaggies" and stepladder effects. A MacDraw or MacDraft circle, however, although it appears similar on the screen, appears at a greater resolution on the printer, because MacDraw can match the resolution of the output device. Therefore, a LaserWriter prints a circle at 300 dots per inch, and it looks very smooth. MacDraw evens the appearance of objects by translating them into PostScript commands. MacDraw graphics print at an even higher resolution on a typesetting device such as the Linotype Company Series 100 Linotronic 100 and Linotronic 300, which feature resolutions of 1270 and 2540 pixels per inch, respectively.

Clip Art

A plentiful supply of clip art disks is available for the Macintosh. These disks are usually composed of MacPaint documents—a slight drawback, since MacPaint uses a 72-pixel-per-inch bit map (the resolution of the Mac's video display), and these images sometimes look poor on the LaserWriter, especially when you enlarge them. Eventually, a second generation of clip art disks that contain images and designs in MacDraw files will emerge. MacDraw creates PostScript output you can size, position, and re-create at the resolution of the output device to take advantage of the higher resolutions of the LaserWriter and other PostScript output devices such as the Linotype typesetting machines.

Fonts

Font disks for the Macintosh contain stylized typefaces. These disks fall into two categories: Macintosh screen fonts (those shown on the video display) and PostScript fonts used by PostScript printers and typesetting machines. Designed to look good on the video display, screen fonts print on either the ImageWriter or LaserWriter, but since these fonts are not optimized for PostScript, the edges of characters look jagged. Screen fonts are often included on clip art disks. Although you can sometimes use these fonts as graphic elements for design effect, they are not really acceptable as typefaces.

PostScript font disks are collections of typefaces from Adobe, Apple, and others that produce beautiful results on the LaserWriter, Linotype Series 100 typesetters, and other high-resolution PostScript printers. PostScript font disks also contain screen fonts so you can view the typefaces on the Mac's display.

COMMUNICATIONS

The first of the secondary application-software types useful for desktop publishing, communications software, works with a modem to connect your computer to a telephone line. It allows you to send and receive files between a personal computer and another personal computer, a minicomputer, a mainframe computer, or an on-line information service. Your computer becomes a tremendous research tool as you tap into hundreds of millions of pieces of information stored in on-line systems.

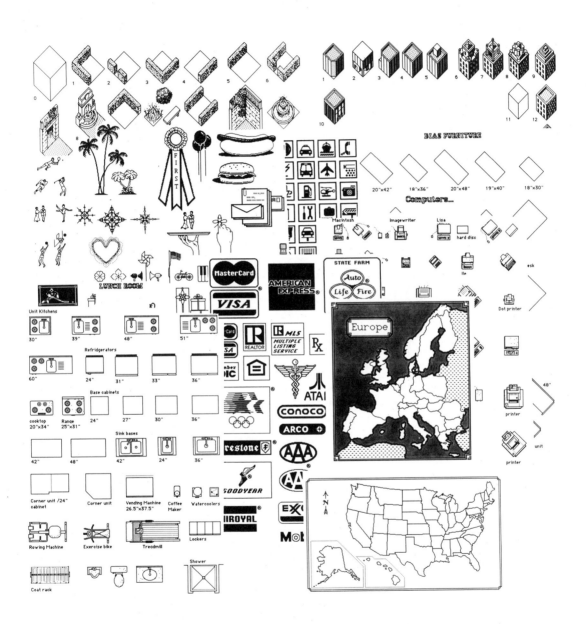

Clip art from ClickArt.
Courtesy of ClickArt, Miles Computing, and Image Bank Software.

Communications Software

MacTerminal is a general purpose communications program with which you communicate with other personal computers, certain DEC and other minicomputers, and some mainframe computers. It lacks some of the advanced automatic log-in capabilities of programs such as InTouch and MicroPhone, two other excellent general purpose telecommunications programs.

Some specialized communications programs may prove beneficial for your desktop publishing applications. For example, SmartCom II from Hayes Microcomputer Products sets up two interconnected Macintoshes to draw interactively on the same document by using a set of drawing tools similar to those of MacPaint. This ability can be effective for sketching out diagrams or ideas with someone at a remote location.

Dow Jones Software's Straight Talk is especially well suited for retrieving information from the more than 40 databases contained in the Dow Jones News/Retrieval service, as well as information from other information services.

Similarly, Mead Data Central has a special Macintosh communications package that puts you in touch with its Nexis and Lexis databases. Nexis offers information from more than 14 newspapers, including the *Washington Post, Financial Times*, and *Japan Economic Journal*; 40 magazines, primarily Time-Life and McGraw-Hill publications; 12 wire services, including AP, UPI, and Reuters; 50 newsletters; the New York Times Information Bank; *Encyclopedia Britannica*; the National Automated Accounting Research System; the Lexpat patent database; and others. Nexis also contains several full-text databases of government information, including the Federal Register, Code of Federal Regulations, Federal Reserve Bulletin, and weekly compilation of presidential documents. The service adds an estimated 20,000 articles each week.

Lexis is an on-line database of legal information that gives you instant access to the full text of federal cases and the case law of all 50 states. It comprises two citation services called Auto-Cite and Shepard's Citation and four law libraries: Federal, State, United Kingdom, and French. The Federal Law Library contains ten component libraries: general information; tax law; securities; trade law and regulations; patent, trademark, and copyright; communications; labor; bankruptcy; energy; and public contracts.

Straight Talk

Straight Talk automatically logs you in to MCI Mail, Dow Jones News/Retrieval service, and most other on-line services. When you use it in conjunction with Dow Jones News/Retrieval, Straight Talk provides access to business and economic news, security quotes, financial and investment services, and general news and information. Another advantage of Straight Talk is that it works with Dow Jones's Spreadsheet Link program to collect data from the News/Retrieval service and automatically enter it into an Excel spreadsheet. This feature can be especially helpful if you are using your desktop publishing system to publish financial, investment, or securities information.

LIST PRICE • $95

SYSTEM REQUIREMENTS • Macintosh, modem (Apple Modem, Hayes Smartmodem, Novation 103/212 Smart-CAT, Novation Smart-CAT +, or POPCOM X100), Apple ImageWriter or LaserWriter optional

Dow Jones Software
P.O. Box 300
Princeton, NJ 08540
(609) 452-2000

DATA TRANSFER

As desktop publishing becomes more widespread in the business community, the transfer of electronic data from person to person, office to office, department to department will become increasingly important. Products that facilitate data transfer among Macintoshes, IBM PCs, and other computers will be crucial for two main reasons: Many businesses already have banks of PCs in place, and Macs will see increasing use as business computers—often in formerly PC-bound offices. You can transfer files to and from a Macintosh for formatting and layout in several ways, from simply transmitting them with a modem to using special file transfer products such as those we highlight here. (Product descriptions are found on pages 110 through 114.)

MacLink

Dataviz's MacLink communication program links IBM PC series computers and the Macintosh via a direct cable connection or modems. It enables you to transfer files and translates between Displaywrite/DCA on the PC series computers and several word processing programs on the Macintosh, including MacWrite and Microsoft Word. The two-way translators retain paragraphs, margins, and typestyles—as well as converting text to its new format—which means that users can move files easily from one machine and word processing program to another. Some versions of MacLink can convert PC text files into usable word processing files on the Macintosh. MacLink also transfers Lotus 1-2-3 files to Jazz or Excel on the Macintosh.

LIST PRICE • $125; eight-foot interface cable, $30

SYSTEM REQUIREMENTS • Macintosh and IBM PC series computer, interface cable or modems

Dataviz, Inc.
16 Winfield Street
Norwalk, CT 06855
(203) 866-4944

DATABASE PROGRAMS

Database programs are also important tools for desktop publishing. You can incorporate databases into documents and publications such as business forms, financial reports, directories, vendor lists, catalogs, customer lists, price lists, parts lists, mailing lists, sales reports, financial reports, abstracts, and indexes.

Although many database programs for the Macintosh can accomplish these tasks, it's important to find a program that allows you to include graphics and text in reports and one that gives you flexibility in report generation. Programs such as MegaForm from MegaHaus do a good job of formatting information in business forms but are not particularly powerful database programs. A database program such as Omnis 3 is powerful, but it lacks many sophisticated report formatting capabilities. For small-scale applications, Forethought's

MacCharlie Plus

MacCharlie Plus from Dayna Communications is a more powerful version of Mac-Charlie, a software and hardware product that lets Macintosh 512K and Macintosh Plus users use IBM PC series software and connect to mainframe computers and Apple or IBM networks. The basic MacCharlie Plus coprocessing system includes a single disk drive, 256K RAM, ten function keys, Apple's Switcher program, and MS-DOS 3.1 and GW-BASIC software. Upgrades can include a second disk drive, memory upgrades to 640K RAM, an internal or external hard disk drive, and an expansion chassis for the addition of up to six IBM PC-compatible cards or a hard disk drive. Macintosh and IBM application programs can run simultaneously on this system, and Apple's Switcher program provides quick access to all of them.

LIST PRICE • $1295

SYSTEM REQUIREMENTS • Macintosh 512K or Macintosh Plus

Dayna Communications, Inc.
50 South Main Street
Salt Lake City, UT 84144
(800) 531-0600
(801) 531-0600

FileMaker and Singular Software's Interlace database programs mix text and graphics in reports. Both are good choices for desktop publishing applications. FileMaker is a single-file database program, whereas Interlace is a relational database program with which you link information from multiple files. Interlace is more sophisticated; FileMaker is easier to use.

For applications that require more advanced database management, you can team up two database programs to publish materials. One program works as the database "engine" that manages the information, and the other works as a report formatter that gives you flexibility in designing the database's output. The combination we recommend is the Omnis 3 (described on page 115) program as your database engine and the FileMaker program as the report handler.

InterBridge

InterBridge from Hayes Microcomputer Products, Inc., connects several AppleTalk Personal Networks to allow more efficient use of Macintosh 512K and Macintosh Plus computers, fileservers, modems, LaserWriter printers, and other output devices. The product enables direct connection of networks in close proximity, such as departments within an organization. It also allows remote connection of distant networks, such as branch offices of a business, with modems. InterBridge works with the Hayes Smartmodem line of modems, including the Smartmodem 2400.

LIST PRICE • $799
SYSTEM REQUIREMENTS • Macintosh 512K and/or Macintosh Plus computers, AppleTalk Personal Networks

Hayes Microcomputer Products, Inc.
P.O. Box 105203
Atlanta, GA 30348
(404) 449-8791

After you've manipulated information with Omnis 3, you can transfer the final data for publication to FileMaker. FileMaker is an excellent report formatter for desktop publishing applications on the Macintosh because you can cut and paste graphics from Mac-Paint, MacDraw, MacDraft, and similar programs into FileMaker layouts for use as logos, diagrams, complex forms, digitized images, and so forth. In addition to giving you flexibility in intermixing text, graphics, and data fields in a report format, FileMaker sets you up to create a variety of layout formats for use with the same data. A single database can result in numerous different reports and forms.

Using the Omnis 3/FileMaker combination, you can also read files created by database programs on Apple II computers, systems based on the CP/M operating system, and many minicomputers and mainframes. Publishing information derived from databases, focused and targeted, presents one of the greatest opportunities in desktop publishing.

TOPS Local Area Network

The TOPS local area network from Centram Systems West can connect two or more completely different computer operating systems, so that a Macintosh can share files with an IBM PC or an Apple II can link to a VAX. Any computer on a TOPS network can function as a fileserver, which means that files can move from one workstation to another without delay. This product solves the problem of machine incompatibility by translating requests from individual machines into universal requests that the TOPS software recognizes.

For example, a Macintosh user can view the directory of the hard disk of an IBM PC AT. The directory appears in the Macintosh format, as icons on a desktop. You can access and work with files stored on remote drives, exactly as if they were internal to your own machine, regardless of the type of operating system.

TOPS software and hardware are compatible with the AppleTalk networking system, and versions that work with other networking systems such as Ethernet and the IBM token ring network are under development. For the Macintosh, the only necessary hardware is a cable; for the IBM PC series and compatible computers, you need an add-on card; and UNIX and ProDOS machines will also require a card. TOPS can link up to 254 devices, with a recommended maximum of 32 users per network, and has provision for linking more than 65,000 networks together.

LIST PRICES • Macintosh node, $149; IBM PC network adapter, software, and manuals, $349; LaserLink utility software (provides channel from the IBM PC to the Apple LaserWriter), $325

SYSTEM REQUIREMENTS • Macintosh, other computer systems optional

Centram Systems West
2372 Ellsworth Avenue
Berkeley, CA 94704
(415) 644-8244

SPREADSHEETS

Because of the Macintosh's graphics, most popular spreadsheets for it have features that create charts and graphs representing information derived from the spreadsheet. We recommend the Excel spreadsheet program from Microsoft for desktop publishing. A

EtherMac

EtherMac is an AppleTalk extension of 3Com's EtherSeries line of network products. With the EtherMac, up to 31 Macintosh computers can share one of 3Com's 3Server hard disk drives on an AppleTalk network (see "Ethernet" and "AppleTalk" in chapter 6). The 3Server is the standard fileserver for all of 3Com's networks, so you can also use it to store files from Ethernet networks on an IBM PC, meaning that Macintosh users can share files with IBM PC users. An Apple LaserWriter in such a setup can print jobs from Macintoshes as well as from PCs.

The 3Server, which comes with 512K of RAM, expandable to 896K, can store information from both an AppleTalk and an Ethernet network at the same time. It is basically an IBM PC-compatible product. The EtherMac network software must be loaded onto the 3Server from an IBM PC, and the Mac can access the software only with the help of Apple's MacTerminal communications program and a serial cable. You also need a 3Server Port Expansion board to connect the AppleTalk network to the hard disk. The EtherMac system is most appropriate for offices with an existing Ethernet network of IBM PC computers. EtherMac lets you connect to such a network by linking a Macintosh-only AppleTalk network to it, after which you can use the EtherShare file transfer software to move data between the two types of computers. In fact, you can hook up several AppleTalk networks to an Ethernet network.

An adjunct product, DiskPlus, is a 3Com 3Server Expansion Disk and an accessory kit (cable and software) to attach the Expansion Disk to the SCSI port on the Macintosh Plus. It can act as a network server for smaller groups than the EtherMac system can accommodate—six Macintosh users at most. You can link as many as seven of the 70-megabyte hard disks, for 490 megabytes of storage. For a single user, the 30-millisecond access time of the disk drive means very fast access to data (an IBM PC XT, in contrast, has track-to-track access times of 70 milliseconds, with far less data per track).

LIST PRICES • 3Server hard disk drive with cabling: 36 megabytes, $7995; 70 megabytes, $8995; 3Server Port Expansion board, $695; 3Server Expansion Disk, $4995; DiskPlus accessory kit, $150

SYSTEM REQUIREMENTS • Macintosh and/or IBM PC series computers; DiskPlus requires Macintosh Plus

3Com Corporation
1365 Shorebird Way
P.O. Box 7390
Mountain View, CA 94039
(415) 961-9602

Omnis 3 Database Software

Omnis 3 is a powerful multiuser relational and hierarchical database program for the Macintosh computer with which you can design custom pull-down menus and work with up to 12 open files simultaneously. It offers 120 fields (areas for entering information such as name, address, and phone number, within a database record) per open file, with 12 screens/pages per entry format. It can also search for up to 50 criteria and sort nine level of subtotals at a time. Its file capacity is 64 megabytes.

An advantage of Omnis 3 is that it has utility programs that make it compatible with other database programs such as dBASE II and dBASE III on IBM PC series computers, as well as Lotus Jazz and Microsoft Excel. You can read information into Omnis 3 from IBM PC series computers, transmitting the files from the IBM PC to the Macintosh with a modem or connecting the computers directly at the same location in an AppleTalk network with file-sharing software such as TOPS. The utility software also provides access to mainframe systems.

LIST PRICE • $375

SYSTEM REQUIREMENTS • Macintosh

Blyth Software
2655 Campus Drive
Suite 150
San Mateo, CA 94403
(415) 571-0222

powerful program, Excel links information together from multiple spreadsheets and offers an assortment of chart and graph formats. You have a choice of five different area charts, seven different types of bar charts, eight different types of column charts, seven different types of line charts, six different types of pie charts, five different types of scatter charts, and four different combination charts. You can scale each of these chart types to any size within Excel and then cut and paste them into a word processing program if you want to drop them into a column of text, into a graphics program for further enhancement or embellishment, or into a page layout program.

Other programs for the Macintosh such as Microsoft Works and Jazz feature spreadsheets with graphics, but Excel not only provides the most powerful spreadsheet and a good variety of chart and graph types, but it also reads and writes Lotus 1-2-3 files, a feature missing in other programs (with Jazz, you can read, but not write to, Lotus 1-2-3 files). This capability is especially desirable if you are using a Macintosh as a desktop publishing workstation for information that originated with an IBM PC series computer, since Lotus 1-2-3 is the predominant IBM PC series number processing tool. You can send 1-2-3 files to the Macintosh by modem, or you can transmit them over an office network such as AppleTalk, using the TOPS network. Macintoshes and IBM PC series computers can share the same data via TOPS.

THE MACINTOSH IN DESKTOP PUBLISHING'S REALM

The three primary software tools of desktop publishing—page layout software, word processing software, and graphics software—along with the three secondary software tools—communications, database, and spreadsheet programs—provide a well-rounded software library for numerous desktop publishing applications. Your system is not limited to desktop publishing, however. The same computer system can manage your expenses, financial information, accounting, names and addresses of contacts, general office automation, word processing tasks, and so forth. With more than 1000 programs available for the Macintosh, it forms a foundation tool for both business and personal needs.

Even though the original version of the Macintosh had limitations that, ironically, made it a weak product for desktop publishing, this little machine catalyzed the phenomenon of desktop publishing. The Mac helped rescue computer-aided publishing from the hegemony of minicomputer and mainframe systems and, perhaps most important, it helped make publishing and page formatting a manageable task, rather than an arcane exercise in quasi-programming. Now that the Macintosh has grown along with desktop publishing, it takes its place with other tools of this new technology that puts a tremendous amount of computing and publishing power at your hands.

Chapter 6

The IBM PC Series and Compatible Computers

The IBM PC series is the leading family of personal computers for business. Although the PCs are not as well suited to desktop publishing as is the Macintosh, many excellent desktop publishing tools are available for this series of computers.

In this book, *the IBM PC series* refers to the IBM PC, XT, Portable, AT, and IBM-compatible personal computers. (The RT PC, which we examine in chapter 7, can be retrofitted to run PC series software, but we are treating it as a UNIX workstation.) We use *the IBM PC series* as a general term to describe this group of computers. The IBM-compatible computers have varying levels of compatibility, as do the computers in the IBM PC line itself. Certain desktop publishing programs require an IBM PC AT; others may require a PC XT, for example, or a certain minimum amount of memory, a special type of monitor, or a display adapter card.

Since computers in the IBM PC series come in so many configurations, it is important to determine the system requirements of any software or hardware accessories you plan to use with your IBM PC series computer. The general rule is first to determine what software you will use and then determine what hardware you need to use that software to its full potential.

Because of the many different configurations of IBM PC series computers, keep in mind that although software may work with a particular configuration, its performance improves, sometimes substantially, when you use a different setup. For example, Microsoft Windows can run on an IBM PC system, but it works much better on a beefed-up system, such as one that has an Enhanced Graphics Adapter display card, also known as an EGA card. This card presents a much clearer on-screen display of typefaces and multiple fonts than you can get with a regular IBM PC graphics adapter card or equivalent.

Similarly, many programs, including Windows, perform much better when you use them on the IBM PC AT, since this computer contains a more powerful processor. If you are assembling a desktop publishing system based on IBM PC series computers, be sure to test the software you plan to use on the exact configuration with which you intend to use it. If you are buying your system from a retail dealer, the dealer should allow you to test software before you agree to proceed with the purchase.

Although the Macintosh computer has the most to offer in the field of personal computer desktop publishing at this time, the IBM PC series is in a strong second place. Many businesses, for example, already have settled on PCs for general office tasks, and, in such cases, an IBM PC series computer may be the only one available for you to use as a desktop publishing tool.

Early good, general purpose, easy to use typesetting and page layout programs for IBM PC series computers are DO-IT from Studio Software and ClickArt Personal Publisher from T/Maker. If you are knowledgeable about computer programming, you can use the TEX typesetting language with an IBM PC series computer to produce excellent results. Also, a version of the Macintosh PageMaker program from Aldus Corporation is under preparation as of this writing for the IBM PC AT. This program promises to be a powerful software tool for desktop publishing with IBM PC series computers.

If you are a novice computer user, you should hire a reputable computer consultant who is knowledgeable about desktop publishing to assist you in selecting the proper software and hardware for your application. You don't need a lot of technical knowledge to run your IBM PC series computer, however. Although it requires a little more time and effort, you can produce output with an IBM PC series computer that is as good as output you can create with a Macintosh.

TECHNICAL DETAILS

The main representatives of the IBM PC series are the IBM PC, the IBM PC XT, and the IBM PC AT. The other computers in the IBM PC series, including the compatibles, are usually comparable to one of these three systems. Since more technical knowledge is necessary to assemble and operate a desktop publishing system with an IBM PC series computer than with a Macintosh, we are providing a general technical description of the PC series computers and a discussion of how these technical details affect use of these computers for desktop publishing.

With two floppy disk drives that store 360K of data each, the IBM PC is the standard model. This computer puts a maximum of 640K RAM on the system board. The IBM PC XT is virtually identical to the basic IBM PC, except that the XT contains one floppy disk drive and one ten-megabyte hard disk drive. The IBM PC AT, however, is a more advanced computer based on a more powerful processor, with higher-capacity disk drives and internal memory. All three of these models have three main components, however: a system unit, a monitor, and a keyboard.

The system unit is the rectangular metal box that is the heart of the computer. It contains the disk drives, the power supply, and the system board (also called the motherboard). The system board contains the central processing unit (CPU), memory chips (RAM), and expansion slots for addition of hardware options. Several plug-in boards are necessary to complete the system, since these boards operate the disk drives; to connect the video display; and to connect printers and other devices such as an AppleTalk board or other communications board for hooking up a modem or communicating with other computers in a local area network.

The CPU, the brain of the computer system, performs arithmetic, logical, and data manipulation operations. The CPU runs programs and controls the computer's operating system. It processes information by using a system of zeros and ones known as binary digits, or bits. Each bit represents a tiny "switch" that is either on or off. If the switch is on, that bit receives an assigned value of 1; if the switch is off, the bit gets a value of 0. A group of 8 bits is called a byte.

The IBM PC and XT use the Intel 8088 microprocessor as their CPU. The 8088 is a 16-bit microprocessor with an 8-bit bus. It is called a 16-bit microprocessor because it manipulates information in groups of 16 bits. The term *8-bit bus* refers to the 8088's moving 8 bits of information (i.e., 1 byte) at a time when it communicates with external devices. A 16-bit CPU such as the 8088 can address 1024 kilobytes of internal memory (RAM), but because of the operating system design IBM uses, the computer can use only 640K of memory at a time. IBM's system sets aside the remainder of the memory for the video display adapter, the hard disk controller, and other internal instructions the computer uses.

The IBM PC AT and its compatibles, however, use the newer Intel 80286 CPU chip. The 80286 is a true 16-bit microprocessor with a full 16-bit data bus. The advanced design of this chip means it can directly address 16 megabytes of RAM, the same amount of RAM the 32-bit 68000 CPU of the Macintosh Plus computer can address. The IBM PC AT is a higher-performance computer than the regular IBM PC or PC XT.

Memory Considerations

Discussions of memory in personal computers can often be confusing, since the term memory describes a variety of different data storage areas within a computer. The two main types of memory are remote storage memory, such as disk drives and tape cartridges, and internal memory, such as RAM and ROM. RAM (random access memory) is a temporary storage area directly accessible by the CPU. It is known as random access memory because the CPU can skip from one memory location to another, thereby accessing any portion of it virtually instantaneously. Since RAM is solid state, or electronic, memory that is stored on densely packed circuits within a microprocessor chip, it is known as volatile memory—its contents vanish when the system's power is turned off. RAM is the active work space a computer program uses. Some programs need more RAM than others, so you need to find out the minimum your software requires for proper operation.

Originally the IBM PC came with only 16K of RAM installed on its board, but IBM soon increased the standard amount of RAM to 64K. As memory chips with more storage capability became less expensive, the computers generally came with 256K of RAM. Many dealers now install a full 640K of RAM as a standard amount on IBM PC XT and compatible systems. RAM for the AT is usually calculated in half-megabyte (512K) increments, with 512K and one-megabyte configurations predominating.

ROM, or read only memory, is the other type of internal memory. It is called read only memory because it contains instructions the computer reads. ROM cannot serve as a temporary storage area and differs from RAM in that its contents are permanent and don't disappear forever when you turn the computer off. The IBM PC and XT contain 40K of ROM, and the AT contains 64K.

Expanding a PC System

Unlike the Macintosh, which is a complete system, ready to run right out of the box, the IBM PC series is a component system. The system unit and keyboard are the base on which components are added. The first component you will need to decide on is the video display monitor. Monochrome and color are the two main types of monitors. Other decisions concern the type of printer you will attach to your computer, since different types of printers require different interface cards that you have to insert into expansion slots inside the system unit of your computer. You usually need to know exactly what accessory hardware, such as printers, modems, or networks, you'll be using, before you can determine the components you need to assemble.

Some expansion slots within your computer will already be filled with circuit boards that control the disk drives or add extra memory and the like. Since the number of slots inside the computer is limited, many manufacturers conserve space by combining two or more functions on a single board called a multifunction board.

Computers in the IBM PC series have different numbers of expansion slots. The IBM PC has five full-length expansion slots. The PC XT and the IBM Portable PC have eight slots each that are physically and electronically identical to those of the PC but are slightly closer together than the PC's slots. This close proximity is important only if you are using multifunction boards that are too thick to fit next to each other. Make sure your combination of add-on boards fits inside your computer if you have an XT or a Portable. In the XT, only six of the eight slots are full-length slots similar to those of the PC. The other two slots are shorter because the inside of the XT system unit is more crowded. In the case of the Portable, one of the expansion slots is unusable for expansion boards. Of the remaining seven slots, three accommodate full-length boards, and four accommodate only short boards. Because of these limitations, the Portable has not been an extremely popular model; the IBM PC-compatible Compaq computer has had much better sales.

When you buy an IBM PC, two of its expansion slots are usually already filled, one with a display adapter and the other with a floppy disk drive controller. In the XT, four slots are usually filled: one with a video display adapter, one with a floppy disk drive controller, one with a hard disk controller, and the other with a communications interface, to which you can connect a printer or a modem.

The AT has eight full-length expansion slots, six of which have an additional 36-pin connector that is required for communication between the CPU and boards that use a full 16-bit data bus. Most of the memory expansion boards available for the IBM PC cannot work with the AT because the 16-bit data bus requires more connectors than the number IBM PC memory boards provide. The majority of the other types of expansion boards that work with the IBM PC and XT, however, do work with the AT as well, even though they don't fill the slots with the additional 36-pin connector.

MASS STORAGE DEVICES

Most IBM PCs and compatibles are equipped with two floppy disk drives that each store 360K worth of data, or about 360,000 characters (a character is equivalent to one letter of the alphabet, one numeral, a punctuation mark, a mathematical symbol, or a space). The IBM PC XT and a growing number of compatibles have one 360K floppy disk drive and an internal hard disk drive capable of storing ten megabytes of data, or ten million characters.

A 360K floppy disk is a thin, circular sheet of mylar encased in a protective jacket. When you place the disk into the disk drive, the drive spins the mylar inside the jacket, and a magnetic head, similar to those that read and record music on tapes, moves back and forth across the disk surface as it rotates and reads or writes information from or onto the disk surface. Each of the floppy diskettes costs only several dollars and stores approximately 240 double-spaced typewritten pages' worth of information.

A hard disk drive works in a similar manner, with a rotating disk and magnetic heads that read information from and write it to the disk. Instead of a thin, mylar, flexible surface, however, a hard disk drive houses a hard platter coated with a metal oxide. Because you cannot remove the platter, hard disk drives are also called fixed disk drives.

The AT comes equipped with one floppy disk drive and either a 20- or 40-megabyte hard disk drive. The PC and XT system unit has two bays in the front designed to fit full-height disk drives, either a full-height $5\frac{1}{4}$-inch floppy disk drive or a full-height $5\frac{1}{4}$-inch hard disk drive. You can buy non-IBM half-height components and place two $5\frac{1}{4}$-inch half-height drives into one bay and a hard disk, or even two half-height hard disk drives, into the other bay. Such a setup requires a lot of electrical power, however, and may overload your system, so be sure to match the power requirements of disk drives if you're adding these to your system.

Compartments in the AT for three disk drives can accommodate two half-height floppy disk drives and a hard disk drive or a single half-height floppy disk drive and two 20-megabyte hard disk drives. The AT floppy disk drive can read a standard IBM PC format with 360K storage or can use its own high-capacity format, which stores 1.2 megabytes on a single diskette. The 360K floppy disk drives store information on both sides of the diskette, using 40 tracks on each side. Each track has nine sectors containing 512 bytes each. The higher-density PC AT drives achieve their greater storage capacity by writing information on both sides of the disks with 80 tracks per side and 15 sectors per track. When you buy blank diskettes for IBM PC series computers, you will need soft-sectored, double-density, double-sided, 48-tpi (tracks per inch) diskettes for use with the 360K double-sided drives. For the AT's high-capacity drives, you will need soft-sectored, double-density, double-sided, 96-tpi diskettes.

Not only do hard disk drives provide greater amounts of storage, but they also work at a higher speed than do floppy disk drives—two important considerations if you plan to publish a lot of pages and maintain large databases. In fact, most hard disk drives are about 10 to 20 times faster than floppy disk drives, which rotate at a mere 300 rpm. Hard disk drives rotate at about 3600 rpm. This high-speed rotation allows the read/write head to find any information stored on a hard disk platter in about 90 milliseconds. Hard disk subsystems from different manufacturers are available for the IBM PC series. These storage devices comprise two main categories: hard disk drives that fit inside the system unit and those that are self-contained in an external unit. The external drives are bulkier and take up extra desk space, but they're usually better protected against accidental bumps and overheating, which can occur inside the computer.

Another option you may want is a cassette tape backup device for your hard disk drive. A tape backup keeps an archival copy of information stored on your hard disk drive. This archival copy can be a real lifesaver if your system breaks down. To avoid data disaster, make an archival copy of the contents of your hard disk drive at least once a week. If you copy the files from your hard disk drive onto floppy diskettes, you'll need about 30 diskettes to store 10 megabytes' worth, and the diskettes alone can cost more than $100. A tape backup system can store 10 or 20 megabytes on a single data tape that is not much larger than a standard audiocassette tape.

Although hard disk drives are available with storage capacities in excess of 100 megabytes, a new high-capacity medium called the CD-ROM stores 500 megabytes or more on a removable diskette. CD-ROM diskettes are similar to the compact discs that audio systems use. CD-ROMs are read only, however; that is, information cannot be written on them. Using CD-ROMs is a convenient way to store a lot of information such as an encyclopedia or large database.

MONITORS

Unlike the Macintosh and Macintosh Plus, which have a built-in standard display, the IBM PC series can use monitors that offer different-size screens, colors, and qualities of text and graphics display. Selecting a good monitor and accompanying display adapter is one of the most important aspects of putting together a desktop publishing system with an IBM PC series computer.

A video monitor is similar to a television, except that the only channel you receive is the computer. Video monitors are known by a variety of names such as *monitor*, *display*, *computer screen*, or *CRT* (cathode ray tube, the type of tube you find in a television). Although these words are often used interchangeably, *display* is the general term that describes all types of monitors, video displays, liquid crystal displays, plasma displays, and so on. The term *monitor* refers to the television-like display that contains a cathode ray tube.

A monochrome monitor displays only one color; a color monitor displays many colors. Monochrome displays are green, white, or amber. As we mentioned earlier, monochrome monitors are generally sufficient for most desktop publishing applications. The most common type of IBM monitor is the IBM 5151 Monochrome Display, also known as the IBM Personal Computer Display. This monitor has an $11\frac{1}{2}$-inch diagonal screen and a green phosphor video monitor. Monochrome monitors are best for displaying text for word processing and spreadsheets. If you plan to purchase an Enhanced Graphics Adapter, however, a color monitor may make sense, since the Enhanced Graphics Adapter creates very-good-resolution images on a color monitor and uses color to provide a more attractive monochrome display.

The most prevalent IBM color monitor is the IBM Color Display, a medium-grade RGB display (*RGB* stands for *red-green-blue*, one type of color monitor; the other type is called *composite*). If you're getting a color monitor for desktop publishing applications, it is wise to pair it with the Enhanced Graphics Adapter. IBM manufactures two RGB monitors for the Enhanced Graphics Adapter and its companion card, the IBM Professional Graphics Controller. The IBM Enhanced Color Display is designed for use with the Enhanced Graphics Adapter, and the IBM Professional Graphics Display provides the best resolution when you use it with the IBM PC Professional Graphics Controller two-board package.

Special monitors are available that display 1024×1024 pixels, and even-higher-priced, higher-resolution monitors can display 2048×2048 and even 4000×4000-pixel resolution. (Most software does not yet take advantage of these high-resolution monitors, however, and their cost is prohibitive. Although these higher-resolution displays hold great promise for the future, the most sensible choice for a display is currently one such as the IBM Enhanced Color Display with the IBM Enhanced Graphics Adapter.

The monitor is the means by which the computer displays information. The quality of the display in an IBM PC series computer depends not just on the type of monitor you choose but, more important, on the type of display adapter board. In order to use a monitor, an IBM PC series computer requires a display adapter board to capture signals from the motherboard and control the display of the video screen.

DISPLAY ADAPTER BOARDS

IBM offers three main display adapter boards for the PC series. The marketing of various boards from third-party developers is based on some type of comparison to these three IBM display adapter board standards. The two most common display adapter boards IBM sells are the Monochrome Display and Printer Adapter, and the Color/Graphics Adapter. The third board IBM produces, which is less common than the other two and more expensive, is the IBM Enhanced Graphics Adapter.

All three of these adapters work with the PC, XT, AT, and many of the compatible computers. Owners of older IBM PCs should note, however, that their computer may require a new ROM BIOS module (BIOS Update Kit #1501005) in order to use the Enhanced Graphics Adapter Board, since the older ROM does not work with this board. All three of these boards can generate 25 lines of text with 80 characters per line. The similarities end there, however.

An important consideration in a discussion of display adapter boards is the board's on-screen resolution. *Resolution* refers to the degree of discernible detail in an image. The standard measurement system for resolution of video displays and other output devices such as printers is a unit called a pixel. *Pixel*, which stands for *picture element*, refers to the smallest display space a computer can independently assign an intensity, brightness, or color. Text, graphics, and other images on a video screen are made up of many tiny dots, each of which is a pixel. The number of pixels the board can display and the board's ability to position the pixels determines the resolution of on-screen text and graphics. As a general rule, the greater the resolution of the board, the greater the number of pixels that can appear on the screen at the same time. In other words, the higher the number of pixels a board produces, the sharper the on-screen images.

A point to keep in mind is that the resolution of a display adapter board is totally different from the resolution of a monitor. The resolution of the display adapter board is the more critical, because no matter how many pixels a monitor is capable of displaying, it cannot display any more pixels than the adapter board can generate. Even if the display board can produce a high-resolution image, the resolution of the image may be limited by the capability of the monitor, which is why you should match the monitor to the display adapter board.

The resolution of the IBM Monochrome Display and Printer Adapter board is 720 × 350 pixels, for a total of 252,000 pixels on the screen at one time. The IBM Color/Graphics Adapter board has a maximum resolution of 640 × 200 pixels, for a maximum of 128,000 pixels on the screen at once. Note that the IBM Color/Graphics Adapter has only about half the resolution of the IBM Monochrome Display and Printer Adapter.

The IBM Enhanced Graphics Adapter, on the other hand, can display 640 × 350 pixels, for a total of 227,500. The Enhanced Graphics Adapter is also available in tandem with another graphics controller board in a package IBM calls the IBM PC Professional Graphics Controller. The two boards take up two adjacent slots inside your computer. The Professional Graphics Controller has two modes: a Color Graphics mode that emulates most PC software and an Expanded Graphics mode that can generate 640 × 480 pixels, for a total of 307,200 pixels on the screen at a given time. Currently, not much software works with the IBM PC Professional Graphics Controller, however, and the IBM Enhanced Graphics Adapter still remains the best choice for a desktop publishing system based on an IBM PC series computer.

The IBM Monochrome Display and Printer Adapter is the most common display board. This board works with a monochrome monitor and produces clear and crisp text on the screen but cannot display graphics. The Monochrome Display and Printer Adapter creates characters that comprise a matrix 9 dots wide by 14 dots high, for a total of 126 dots, or pixels, per character. This resolution is quite a bit sharper than the text of the Color/Graphics Adapter, which generates characters in a matrix 8 pixels wide by 8 pixels high, for a total of only 64 pixels per character. Since the Monochrome Display and Printer Adapter board devotes almost twice as many pixels to each character, the displayed characters are clearer and crisper on the screen. If your main use for the computer is simply as a text entry, word processing, or spreadsheet workstation, the Monochrome Display board and a monochrome monitor may be all you need. If you want to display various sizes of fonts on screen, however, and have true boldfacing, italicizing, and other details for a WYSIWYG system, the Monochrome Display and Printer Adapter with a monochrome monitor will not be suitable because it cannot display graphics. When you're using different fonts or sizes and styles of type, you have to create the characters with computer graphics, rather than with a built-in text generator on the Monochrome Display and Printer Adapter board.

The IBM Color/Graphics Adapter is the most widely used graphics board with the IBM PC series. The low text resolution of this board makes it a poor choice for use in a desktop publishing system, however. If you need graphics in your application, you're much better off spending the extra money for an IBM Enhanced Graphics Adapter board. By combining the features of the Monochrome Display and Printer Adapter and the Color/Graphics Adapter, this board also works with many different monitors.

When you're using a program such as Aldus's PageMaker for the IBM PC AT, an Enhanced Graphics Adapter will be part of the system requirements. Programs such as Microsoft Windows let you use the IBM Color/Graphics Adapter, but the programs also work with the IBM Enhanced Graphics Adapter. The clarity of the screen image that the Enhanced Graphics Adapter produces is strikingly different when you run Windows on a regular Color/Graphics Adapter and an Enhanced Graphics Adapter. Ask your dealer for a demonstration of Windows with both of these adapters, and you'll see that the Enhanced Graphics Adapter is much better and easier on the eyes.

The Enhanced Graphics Adapter is available in many memory configurations. You can expand the standard board with the Graphics Memory Expansion Card and additionally expand it with the Graphics Memory Module Kit. If you can afford it, get the extra memory, since it provides smoother scrolling of graphics across the screen. Another advantage of having the IBM Enhanced Graphics Adapter is that you can load RAM-resident character sets with characters up to 8 pixels wide and 32 pixels high.

The IBM Enhanced Graphics Adapter provides a bit-mapped graphics display, as does the Apple Macintosh. With bit-mapped graphics, every pixel the screen displays has a corresponding bit or series of bits in the computer's internal memory that directly corresponds to it. The direct correspondence of bits to pixels allows the computer to manipulate bits in memory to change the image on the screen directly.

Non-IBM Display Boards

Before you buy a non-IBM display board, make sure the software you intend to use works with that board. The capabilities of some non-IBM boards exceed those of the IBM display boards, and you may find that your software will yield better graphics resolution if you use a non-IBM board. The software should dictate the type of display adapter board you use, however. If the software requires a particular type of board, use that board. If better performance and graphics quality are likely with another board, then consider using it. It's a good idea, though, to test any non-IBM display board and determine that you like its performance before you buy it.

One of the most popular non-IBM display boards is the Hercules Graphics Card. This board, or card, is compatible with the IBM Monochrome Display and Printer Adapter and paints a 720 × 348-pixel bit-mapped graphics display. Some boards deliver a resolution as high as 1024 × 1024 pixels, but you should ascertain that the software you buy can utilize such high resolution. It is pointless to pay a lot of money for a pixel-packed board if your software does not work with that board any better than it would with one that costs less.

Another consideration when you select a display adapter is whether or not you need color. Most desktop publishing output devices such as laser printers and typesetters are not capable of reproducing color output. Therefore, color is usually not a factor when you're putting together a desktop publishing system. Graphics capability is important, however, especially if you are using WYSIWYG programs such as DO-IT; PageMaker; or Microsoft Windows, which uses a graphics-oriented operating system similar to the Macintosh's.

PRINTERS FOR PCS

One of the toughest decisions you'll face in assembling a desktop publishing system that uses an IBM PC series computer is choosing the proper printer or printers. Scores of printers, in all different shapes, sizes, and prices, that produce widely diverse qualities of print, are on the market. The print quality sometimes has little to do with the price of the printer—you cannot simply assume that because a printer is more expensive, it will produce higher-quality output. Sometimes greater expense is related to faster output, perhaps of lower quality than that of a less expensive printer. (For more information on printers, see chapter 9.)

An extremely popular printer for an IBM PC series computer is the IBM Graphics Printer, a dot matrix printer manufactured for IBM by Epson; an equivalent Epson-label printer is also available. The IBM Graphics Printer has a 9-wire printhead that creates characters in a 9-dot-high by 9-dot-wide matrix. The printer features a variety of print styles, ranging from 5 to $16\frac{1}{2}$ characters per inch (*cpi*), with a 10-cpi print style being the most common. The graphics resolution is 120 dpi horizontally by 216 dpi vertically.

PAGE PRINTERS FOR PCS

Page printers constitute one of the main components of a desktop publishing system. The most popular page printer for the IBM PC is the HP LaserJet. Other printers that work with the PC are the Apple LaserWriter, which is gaining rapid popularity with IBM PC users, and the Corona Laser Printer, which is used primarily with the PCTEX system.

Several ways are available to connect the IBM PC to the Apple LaserWriter. You can use the PC MacBridge AppleTalk network board or use another AppleTalk board. The LaserWriter also has an RS-232 interface for connection to IBM PC series and other computers. You use your computer's RS-232 serial interface and a standard communications program to communicate with the LaserWriter, much as you would with another computer via a modem or data terminal. Communication with the LaserWriter occurs at a variety of transmission speeds, with 1200 bits per second (bps) and 9600 bps being most common; the LaserWriter Plus can go even faster, with 19,200 bps being the most frequent speed.

The general guidelines for communication with the LaserWriter are to set your communications program to 8 data bits, 1 stop bit, no parity, and use the *XON/XOFF* communications protocol. You can have the LaserWriter report its current status by sending it a *Control-T*, and you can stop any current job with a *Control-D*. To start a programming session, send the LaserWriter a *Control-D* followed by a *Control-T* to make sure the printer is free for your use; then send it the *Execute* command so it will ready itself for your PostScript instructions.

Other laser printers for the IBM PC include those manufactured by Genicom, AST, and Xerox.

When you select a page printer for your IBM PC series computer, match the printer's capabilities to the ability of the software and also to your needs for the system. If you want advanced graphics and a rich assortment of typefaces, typestyles, and type sizes—and are using software, such as DO-IT or PageMaker, that works with graphics and text to create elaborate page layouts—then the Apple LaserWriter or another PostScript-compatible printer may be best suited to your needs. If you will use only a few typefaces, styles, and sizes and do not require graphics, the HP LaserJet or another of the lower-cost page printers may be acceptable. Keep in mind, however, that with most of these lower-cost printers, you need to insert additional font cartridges to change fonts or download fonts from the host computer. Also, the graphics capabilities of these

Using the LaserWriter Plus with an IBM PC Series Computer

You can connect the LaserWriter Plus to any serial data source that uses the RS-232 communications standard. The LaserWriter Plus uses the 25-pin connector for RS-232, but it actually employs only six of the pins. The pins' signal assignments are:

Pin Number	Signal Assignment
2	transmit data
3	receive data
4	request to send (optional)
6	data set ready (optional)
7	signal ground
20	data terminal ready (optional)

The LaserWriter Plus needs to use only pins 2, 3, and 7. You have to connect pins 4, 6, and 20 only if the host computer requires them for DTR data flow control. The availability of DTR flow control in the LaserWriter Plus makes little difference to Macintosh users but helps the printer work better with other computers such as those in the IBM PC series.

To use an IBM PC with the LaserWriter Plus's 25-pin RS-232 serial connector and DTR data flow control, issue the following commands on the IBM PC:

```
MODE COM1:9600,n,8,1,p
MODE LPT1:=COM1:
```

Then connect the computer to the printer with a cable that uses all six of the pins mentioned above and set the LaserWriter's communications switch to the 9600 position. Send the printer the following commands from the IBM PC to use DTR with PostScript:

```
serverdict begin 0 exitserver
statusdict begin
25 9600 4 setsccbatch
end
```

and issue the following commands if you want to use the printer in Diablo 630 emulation:

```
serverdict begin 0 exitserver
statusdict begin
25 9600 4 setsccinteractive
end
```

systems are usually limited, so find out if the host computer can take over the burden of creating graphics—i.e., whether your software can create the graphics to send to the printer on its own. You should check with the software's producer to find out what type of page printer is recommended.

PLOTTERS AND IBM PCS

A plotter is a special-purpose printer whose main use is creating charts, graphs, line drawings, and schematics. Most plotters employ a print mechanism consisting of a mechanical arm that moves one or more pens. The pen or pens can draw smooth curved lines and circles that look cleaner than curves and circles done on a dot matrix printer or a low-resolution page printer. Many statistical and scientific programs work with pen plotters but cannot utilize high-resolution output devices such as PostScript-compatible page printers and typesetting machines. If you need to incorporate pen plotter output into your publication, you'll have to mechanically paste the plotter graphics into spaces you leave for them in your document.

Two popular plotters for IBM PC series computers are the HP 7470A plotter from Hewlett-Packard, which works with $8\frac{1}{2} \times 11$ inch sheets of paper; the PC Plotter 595 and 695 from Houston Instruments (the 595 works with $8\frac{1}{2} \times 11$ inch paper, and the 695 can work with graphics of up to 11×17 inches); and the IBM XY/749 plotter, which features a built-in microprocessor for generating circles, arcs, axes, and so forth.

Although no manufacturers have announced any PostScript-compatible plotters at the time of this writing, it is possible that such a device will debut sometime in the near future. A PostScript-compatible plotter would have broader applications in desktop publishing than do standard plotters.

PRINT BUFFERS AND PCS

A print buffer is a section of memory that a computer can use to temporarily store information being sent to a printer. The memory for a print buffer can be in an external device, or it can be part of a memory card or multifunction card. Printers operate much more slowly than computers do, which means the computer can be held up during the printing of a document, unable to take care of any other tasks until the printer completes the document. With a print buffer, a PC system can send the contents of the document at electronic speeds to a certain area of memory. The computer is then free to work on other tasks. The print buffer gradually feeds data to the printer as it can print it.

A buffer is especially useful when you're employing a slow-printing pen plotter, letter-quality printer, or dot matrix printer. A buffer can be a tremendous asset and dramatically improve the performance of your system if you are using a dot matrix printer or page printer as a page proof device and are controlling the printer directly with software, rather than communicating with an "intelligent" printer through a page description language such as PostScript.

Print buffers of a megabyte or more can be useful with laser printers, such as the HP LaserJet, that do not have internal computers. If a personal computer system has to create the bit map that produces the final document and send that bit map to the printer for the creation of each page, the computer must transmit a tremendous amount of information to the printer. For example, on an $8\frac{1}{2} \times 11$ inch piece of paper, you have a 7×10 inch live text or graphics area that you are printing at 300 dpi; that is 70 square inches times 300 dots vertically times 300 dots horizontally, for a total of 6,300,000 dots. Each dot in a bit-mapped graphics system corresponds to a bit of memory. Therefore, storing a full-page image takes nearly 800K of RAM. If you had to wait for the computer to send this information bit by bit to the printer, it would tie up a lot of time on your system. If you have a print buffer large enough to hold the entire document or at least an entire page of the document at a time, you will be able to free up your computer for other uses while the document is printing.

When you're calculating how much RAM your print buffer needs, you have to figure out the size of each section of data going to the printer. In our previous example, if the software sends one page at a time to the printer and a page contains 6,300,000 dots, you will need a buffer that has at least 800K. A general guideline for determining whether you need a print buffer for your desktop publishing application with the IBM PC is to consider what type of printer you'll be using with the system and if you will be using that printer as a page proofing device. For example, if the printer is going to print only raw text and your final output is produced on a typesetting machine, you may not need a print buffer.

Similarly, if your software uses PostScript, the entire bit map for a document does not need to be sent to the printer; instead, the printer receives only a PostScript description, which is considerably smaller, for that document. For example, the same 6,300,000-bit 7 × 10 inch page requires only 5K or less of information if you send it as a PostScript document. PostScript relies on the intelligence of the printer to recreate the page according to the description the PostScript document contains. Therefore, if you are using an intelligent printer such as an Apple LaserWriter, the Dataproducts PostScript printer, or the QMS PostScript printer, your computer will not have to transmit the entire bit map, and you will not really require a print buffer unless you are printing documents of more than five or ten pages. Then the length of the PostScript documents themselves may dictate use of a buffer. (For more on PostScript, see chapter 8).

MODEMS, NETWORKS, AND COMMUNICATIONS

Since modems allow your computer to communicate with other personal computers and with mainframe computers and information services, a modem is an important part of a complete desktop publishing system. With the IBM PC, you can choose between two types of modems. The first variety is the external modem, which is a self-contained device that connects to an RS-232 serial interface port on your computer. The PC XT often comes with an RS-232 interface board. If you do not have a board that provides an RS-232 serial port for a modem, you will need to get either an RS-232 serial interface board or a multifunction board that offers this port.

An external modem also requires a cable to connect the modem to the RS-232 board on the back of the computer. Different boards and different modems often require cables with different wiring, which can become especially confusing and difficult, and it is a good idea to buy your modem and cable from a dealer who guarantees that they work with the serial board or multifunction board you are using. The cable between the modem and the serial board can be one of the largest sources of problems in connecting a modem to an IBM PC series computer.

The other type of modem you can use is an internal modem, or modem board. These boards do not have an external unit and require no special cabling. You simply plug the board into an expansion slot inside the system unit and plug the phone line directly into the back of the board through the back of the computer.

An advantage of external modems is that you can use them with a variety of different computers. For example, a Hayes 1200-bit-per-second (bps) Smartmodem external modem works with both the IBM PC and the Apple Macintosh. Also, many external modems such as the Hayes Smartmodem feature LED indicator lights on the front of the modem that give you information about the status of your call. Internal modems have the advantage of being easier to hook up and not taking up any desk space, but they do occupy a slot inside the computer.

Many communication software programs are designed for use with the Hayes Smartmodem, which is available both as the Hayes Smartmodem 1200, the 1200-bps external modem we recommend for IBM PC series computers, and the Hayes Smartmodem 1200B, the internal modem that is functionally equivalent to the Smartmodem 1200. Most software is meant for use with these popular modems, so if you purchase other than a Hayes modem, you should find one that uses the same instruction set. Some modems—the Apple Modem and the Novation Smart-CAT, for example—are compatible with the Hayes commands.

MICRO TO MAINFRAME LINKS

Using a modem to transfer documents and other data, it is possible to link personal computers to mainframe computers. This method often presents certain difficulties, however. One of the most common problems is that mainframes and other large computer systems are often designed for connection to a specific terminal model. If your communications software can emulate that type of terminal, you may be able, using only a modem, to connect your PC series computer to a host mainframe. Modem speeds can become a limiting factor, though, if a large amount of information must be transferred. Another difficulty in linking PCs to mainframe computers with only a modem is that many mainframes use the *EBCDIC* (Extended Binary Coded Decimal Interchange Code) system for representing data, and many personal computers use the ASCII (American Standard Code for Information Interchange) system. ASCII uses 7 bits for representing data, defining 128 different characters. EBCDIC, on the other hand, uses a full 8 bits for each character and has a character set of 256 characters. Because EBCDIC has characters that are not available in ASCII, and ASCII even has characters that are unavailable in EBCDIC, obtaining an exact translation between the two data encoding systems is not always possible.

Luckily, you can find devices and software that work together to promote much more efficient communication between personal computers and mainframes. Such communication can be important for desktop publishing in corporate and business settings, since you may be publishing information stored in your company's mainframe. Although electronic publishing software is available for mainframes, it is much more complicated and expensive than personal computer software, since mainframe hardware and software are both costly. Retrieving information from a mainframe with a personal computer and typesetting and publishing it with a desktop publishing system is more efficient and less expensive than using a mainframe electronic publishing system.

Large organizations with IBM mainframes and minicomputers often use IBM PC series computers as their personal computers, so corporate desktop publishers need to know how to hook up their PCs to bigger systems. Since this task is frequently complex, it is wise to consult someone in the data processing department of your organization or to get an outside consultant to determine exactly what hardware configuration and software you need to enable your IBM PC series computers to communicate effectively with the corporate mainframe or minicomputer.

The most prevalent devices for connecting IBM PC series computers to mainframes and minicomputers are protocol converters. They translate information from one computer system into another computer system's format. Protocol converters usually come in the form of plug-in boards that fit into an expansion slot inside the system unit, although they are also available as standalone external devices you can hook up to an RS-232 serial communications port.

IBM mainframes use a variety of specifications for communicating with remote terminals. Four of the most common are the IBM 3270, the IBM 3780, and the IBM 2780 terminal protocols; and the IBM 3770 Remote Job Entry (RJE) protocol.

Mainframes and minicomputers manufactured by Digital Equipment Corporation use the DEC VT-52 and VT-100 class of terminals. You need to find out what type of remote terminals can work with your corporate mainframe or minicomputer systems. With this information in hand, you can determine what hardware and software your personal computer system needs in order to emulate the appropriate terminal and communicate effectively with your central corporate computer.

DATA TRANSFER

Before the introduction of the IBM PC, IBM offered an office automation system based on the IBM Displaywriter series of dedicated word processors. IBM continues to sell the Displaywriter for office automation, along with several other systems such as the IBM 6670 Information Distributor, the IBM 5520 Administrative System, and the IBM Office System 6.

So its customers can use IBM PC series computers with IBM office automation equipment, IBM has developed several products to facilitate information interchange. The simplest is the Displaywriter/Personal Computer Attachment Convenience Kit, which hooks IBM PC series computers up to IBM Displaywriter word processing systems. Another, more expensive, product is the IBM Personal Computer DisplayComm Binary Synchronous Communications Program, which permits document exchange with the IBM Displaywriter, the 6670 Information Distributor, the Office System 6, and IBM mainframes equipped with special software. This program is designed for use with IBM's DisplayWrite series of personal computer word processing software.

A standard format for documents known as DCA (Document Content Architecture) is emerging from IBM. DCA, a protocol that governs document formatting, deals with factors such as typeface, typestyle, and paragraph format. Several companies, including Apple, have thrown their support behind this standard, and software for IBM PC series computers and the Macintosh can work with documents in this format.

When selecting software for an IBM PC series computer, you may want to find programs that work with DCA documents. Another product available from IBM is the IBM 5520/Personal Computer Attachment Program, which exchanges information between IBM PC series computers and the IBM 5520 Administrative System.

PC TO MACINTOSH LINKS

Recent advances in hardware and software technology now let you get the best of both worlds by combining IBM PC and Macintosh systems. You can create documents on an IBM PC system with an ordinary word processing program and send them to a Macintosh for formatting, laser printing, and/or typesetting. One Macintosh can collect documents from several interconnected IBM PC series computers and integrate the assembled documents into a single body of text you combine with graphics and other design elements to create a publication.

Many kinds of hardware, such as AppleTalk, Ethernet, and IBM's networks, move documents rapidly among various computers. With software such as TOPS from Centram Systems West, the Macintosh can share data easily and conveniently with IBM PC series computers. Since IBM PCs predominate in many large businesses, numerous Macintosh software applications work with files created on IBM PC series computers. An example is the Excel spreadsheet program on the Macintosh, which can read and write files in the Lotus 1-2-3 format.

A desktop publishing application in business publishing that employs a lot of charts, graphs, and representations of financial data created on spreadsheets can use a Macintosh connected to an IBM PC series computer, read the 1-2-3 files, and exploit Excel's advanced graphics to end up with publication-quality charts and graphs much more easily than is possible on the IBM PC with Lotus 1-2-3.

Similarly, Microsoft Word on the Macintosh can exchange files with Microsoft Word on the IBM PC. You can write a report, for example, on an IBM PC computer and send it over a network to a Macintosh for printing on an Apple LaserWriter connected to the Macintosh, or you can convert it into a PostScript document with page layout software on the Macintosh and print it on a typesetting device such as a Linotype typesetter.

Among the products that have emerged to put PCs and Macs/LaserWriters in touch with each other are PC MacBridge, MacLink, and MacCharlie Plus. As their names indicate, these products bridge the gap between the two computer systems or merge them into one functional system.

MacLink

Dataviz's MacLink communication program links IBM PC series computers and the Macintosh by a direct cable connection or modems. It enables you to transfer files and translates between DisplayWrite/DCA on the PC series computers and the MacWrite and Microsoft Word word processing programs on the Macintosh. The two-way translators retain paragraphs, margins, and typestyles—as well as convert text to its new format—which means that users can move files easily from one machine and word processing program to another. Some versions of MacLink convert PC text files into usable word processing files on the Macintosh. MacLink also transfers Lotus 1-2-3 files to Jazz or Excel on the Macintosh.

LIST PRICE • $125; eight-foot interface cable, $30

SYSTEM REQUIREMENTS • Macintosh and IBM PC series computer, interface cable or modems

Dataviz, Inc.
16 Winfield Street
Norwalk, CT 06855
(203) 866-4944

PC MacBridge

Tangent Technologies Ltd. is pegging the "real impact" of its PC MacBridge product on the acceptance of AppleTalk as what Tangent calls a viable local area network. PC MacBridge is a hardware/software combination that puts PC users in connection with the Apple LaserWriter. The hardware part is a short slot card that functions in IBM PCs and ATs and some compatible computers. The compatibles in which it won't work are those with speeded up clocks. To the card, you connect the AppleTalk connector and cable, both available from Apple. The software part of this product, called the Apple Bus Link Access Protocol, puts your PC on the network. Other elements of the software drive the LaserWriter and send mail and files to Macintoshes on the network. To use the LaserWriter, you must have PostScript files, and LaserScript files convert your PC files into PostScript. The files that LaserScript can convert to PostScript are WordStar 3.3, MultiMate 3.3, ASCII, Diablo 630, Lotus 1-2-3, and Microsoft Word. This product is clearly aimed at office network applications; among the business-related features it adds to the Macintosh Office is electronic mail, the ability to send messages to associates via your computer.

LIST PRICE • $650

SYSTEM REQUIREMENTS • IBM PC or AT, some compatibles; AppleTalk connector and cable

Tangent Technologies
5720 Peachtree Parkway
Suite 100
Norcross, GA 30092
(404) 662-0366

MacCharlie Plus

MacCharlie Plus from Dayna Communications is a more powerful version of Mac-Charlie, a software and hardware product that lets Macintosh 512K and Macintosh Plus users use IBM PC series software and connect to mainframe computers and Apple or IBM networks. The basic MacCharlie Plus coprocessing workstation includes a single disk drive, 256K RAM, ten function keys, Apple's Switcher program, and MS-DOS 3.1 and GW-BASIC software. Upgrades can include a second disk drive, memory upgrades to 640K RAM, an internal or external hard disk drive, and an expansion chassis for the addition of up to six IBM PC-compatible cards or a hard disk drive. Macintosh and IBM application programs can run simultaneously on this system, and Apple's Switcher program provides quick access to all of them.

LIST PRICE • $1295

SYSTEM REQUIREMENTS •   Macintosh 512K or Macintosh Plus

Dayna Communications, Inc.
50 South Main Street
Salt Lake City, UT 84144
(800) 531-0600
(801) 531-0600

Additionally, several Macintosh database programs, such as Omnis 3, Factfinder, and others, can read database files created on IBM PC series computers and integrate them into typeset-quality reports. Interconnecting IBM PC series computers and Macintoshes not only makes for a flexible desktop publishing system, but it also means businesses can expand their existing systems, while preserving much of their initial investment.

LOCAL AREA NETWORKS

Local area network (LAN) is a broad term that refers to any two or more computers connected by some type of cable. A local area network not only facilitates communication among computers, but it also allows computers connected to it to share common resources such as hard disks, printers, and even modems. Each device connected to a network is called a node. Numerous networks are available for IBM PC series computers, ranging from low-speed networks that use RS-232 serial communications to high-speed varieties such as Ethernet. Since page printers, typesetting machines, and other tools of desktop publishing can be expensive for individual tasks, a network, which allows a group of computers to share hardware resources, can save your organization money. Networks also cut costs by exchanging information among different computer models.

One specific way a network can save you money is by dividing hard disk resources among several users. Two methods of designing hard disks to work with networks have evolved. In the first approach, the hard disk is a "diskserver," and in the second, it is a "fileserver." Which strategy you use is mainly a software consideration.

A diskserver splits a hard disk into separate sections, each dedicated to a single computer. For example, with a 20-megabyte hard disk and four computers connected to a network, the hard disk is partitioned into four 5-megabyte volumes. Each computer connected to the network gets an individual 5-megabyte volume for its own use. Each computer can use only one volume, however, and cannot access files in any other computer's volume.

A fileserver, on the other hand, allows all the computers hooked to the network to share a common storage device, with common access to files that that device contains. For instance, a 20-megabyte hard disk acting as a fileserver provides a common 20 megabytes of storage, and files stored on it can all be accessed by any of the computers attached to the network. Likewise, any of the network's computers can save files in the common 20-megabyte area. Fileserving, therefore, is more useful to desktop publishing—since it allows computers to share files—than is diskserving, which is merely a convenient way of splitting up space on a hard disk for separate use by individual computers. If you are getting a hard disk to connect to your network for use in desktop publishing, make sure this hard disk is a true fileserver that provides common access to files. Such common access becomes critical when several people have to work on the same report or article.

As we point out elsewhere in this book, the Macintosh is the computer best suited to desktop publishing because of its low price and the availability and quality of the hardware and software that work with it. With a network, you can connect IBM PC series computers to one or more Macintoshes. You're then in the enviable position of writing documents on the PCs, and then using the Macintosh system to format and print the documents.

The combination of PCs and Macintoshes is the most effective way to use IBM PCs for desktop publishing—especially for businesses, where many PCs are likely to be in place. To match the capabilities of the Macintosh for desktop publishing, you need an IBM PC AT with an Enhanced Graphics Adapter Card, additional RAM, and page layout software such as DO-IT or PageMaker. It is much less expensive to get PageMaker for a Macintosh than it is to get a similarly equipped IBM PC AT. Even if you go to the expense of equipping an AT, it is still not as flexible a desktop publishing tool as the Macintosh, because the Macintosh has more supplementary software such as clip art and adjunct hardware such as inexpensive video digitizers and scanners. Many of these companion products that are useful for desktop publishing applications are not as readily available for IBM PC series computers.

Although many networks exist for IBM PC series computers, the most useful ones for desktop publishing applications are AppleTalk, Ethernet, Omninet, and IBM's token ring network. The token ring network allows interconnection of personal computers, minicomputers, mainframe computers, and numerous peripherals, and all of these networks can connect IBM PCs and Macintoshes. If you do not plan to use a Macintosh or other non-IBM computer immediately, you can incorporate them later. IBM provides various methods for hooking IBM PC Networks up to the token ring scheme, and Apple is developing several strategies for connecting Apple products to the network. Because of its flexibility, the IBM token ring network appears to be the leading contender for the position of predominant IBM networking system.

AppleTalk

AppleTalk is one of the least expensive networks available for the IBM PC. Although slow by network standards, it is much faster than the highest-speed modems. AppleTalk boards for the IBM PC series are available from Tangent Technologies, which offers the PC MacBridge, and Centram Systems, maker of an IBM PC AppleTalk board in combination with its excellent TOPS network software. Other manufacturers, including Apple, are considering producing AppleTalk boards for IBM PC series computers. It is not necessary to have a Macintosh connected to the network when you are using AppleTalk. If you decide on AppleTalk as a network to connect other AppleTalk-compatible devices such as the Apple LaserWriter, the Dataproducts laser printer, or a Linotype PostScript-compatible typesetting machine, you should also purchase the TOPS networking software from Centram Systems West.

TOPS

With TOPS software, any disk drive, whether it's a hard- or floppy-disk drive, connected to any computer hooked up to the AppleTalk network can share files with any IBM PC series computer or other computer such as a Macintosh connected to the system. This filesharing ability means you can access, for example, a disk drive in an AT from an IBM PC or Compaq. It also lets you use any PC series computer to access information in a Macintosh disk drive—either the Macintosh's floppy disk or a hard disk—or in another storage device connected to the system. Likewise, it gives a Macintosh access to information in a PC AT or other IBM PC series computer. File access and exchange are easy with TOPS.

Ethernet

Ethernet is a high-speed network originally developed by Xerox that transmits information at lightning-fast speeds, up to ten megabits per second. The predominant supplier of Ethernet adapter boards, cabling, and network software for IBM PC series computers is 3Com Corporation. 3Com's Ethernet system allows connection of as many as 1024 devices. Using 3Com's 3Server Ethernet fileserver, a group of IBM PCs can share files on a common hard disk. A version of the 3Server lets you partition the hard disk and create a separate volume for Macintosh users, with software that converts documents from the PC volume to the Macintosh volume (see "EtherMac" in chapter 5).

Omninet, from Corvus Systems, transmits information at about one megabit per second and provides for connection of up to 64 devices to the network. This network, which has been available for personal computers for many years, has the advantage of intermixing a variety of computers such as the IBM PC series, the Macintosh, and the Apple II series, in the same network. Although each operating system requires a separate partition and separate volume on the hard disk (i.e., a diskserver setup), you can transfer text files among volumes, and systems that share a common operating system have fileserver access to their volume on the hard disk.

The IBM PC Network developed for IBM by Sytek operates at

TOPS Local Area Network

The TOPS local area network from Centram Systems West connects two or more different computer operating systems. A Macintosh, for example, can share files with an IBM PC, or an Apple II can link to a VAX. Any computer on a TOPS network can function as a fileserver, which means that files move from one workstation to another without delay. This product solves the problem of machine incompatibility by translating requests from individual machines into universal requests that the TOPS software recognizes.

Say you have a Macintosh and you want to view the directory of the hard disk of an IBM PC AT. The directory appears in the Macintosh format, as icons on a desktop. You can access and work with files stored on remote drives, exactly as if they were internal to your own machine, regardless of the operating system.

TOPS software and hardware are compatible with the AppleTalk networking system, and versions that work with other networking systems such as Ethernet and the IBM token ring network are under development. For the Macintosh, the only necessary hardware is a cable; for the IBM PC series and compatible computers, you need an add-on card; and UNIX and ProDOS machines will also require a card. TOPS can link up to 254 devices, with a recommended maximum of 32 users per network, and allows linkage of more than 65,000 networks.

IBM PC series computers can connect into an AppleTalk network via Centram's AppleTalk-compatible network adapter card. The PC-only version of TOPS runs up to 800K bits per second, almost four times the 230K bits per second of AppleTalk. Laser-Link utility software provides a channel from the IBM PC to the Apple LaserWriter, using the TOPS network adapter. Anything you can print on an IBM graphics-capable printer, you can also generate on the LaserWriter.

LIST PRICE • Macintosh node, $149; IBM PC network adapter, software, and manuals, $349; LaserLink utility software (provides channel from the IBM PC to the Apple LaserWriter), $325

SYSTEM REQUIREMENTS • IBM PC series computers, other computer systems optional

Centram Systems West
2372 Ellsworth Avenue
Berkeley, CA 94704
(415) 644-8244

two megabits per second. IBM suggests that you use an IBM PC AT as your fileserver, although you don't have to. Sytek has recently announced its intention to use the IBM token ring network, however, and it is unclear what role the IBM PC Network will play in the future, since the token ring network allows more efficient communication.

Novell NetWare

An alternative to IBM's PC Network is the NetWare series of local area network products from Novell, Inc. Many people consider the NetWare products to be the best for interconnecting IBM series computers. The only drawback of NetWare is that it does not yet work with the Macintosh. Novell offers two versions of the NetWare software: Advanced NetWare, which provides an MS-DOS network operating system that accommodates multiple fileservers, bridges, and gateways; and its more advanced relative, SFT NetWare 286, which has all the main features of Advanced NetWare plus disk backup, media correction capabilities, and other options. Both of these software systems can use all three of Novell's network hardware systems: G-Net, ARCNET, and ProNET. G-Net is a baseband CSMA/CD network that operates at 1.43 megabits per second and allows up to 50 devices to be interconnected over a distance of up to 7000 feet; ARCNET is a token-passing network that operates at speeds up to 2.5 megabits per second; and ProNet is a high-speed token-passing network that operates at speeds up to 9.94 megabits per second.

DESKTOP PUBLISHING SOFTWARE FOR THE IBM PC SERIES

The Macintosh may have put personal desktop publishing on the map, but more PCs than Macintoshes are currently in use and more desktop publishing programs are available for the PC series than for the Macintosh. First we look at a series of page layout programs for the PCs.

DO-IT

Studio Software refers to its DO-IT software package as "an automated art board that can handle just about any pre-press function." What that means is that you can use this extensive software package to lay out pages for page printing or typesetting. In its method of iconic interaction, DO-IT retains concepts and terminology from mechanical layout methods—blue pencil, rulers, T-square, magnifying glass, and so forth. This approach to page layout follows the trend toward easy-to-use, symbolic operation—i.e., terminology that relates to the task at hand (layout) as opposed to command line computer tasks.

To use DO-IT, you take stories, articles, or whatever you have written with your IBM PC series computer or "exact compatible" and run them through the program to end up with formatted pages. DO-IT has lots of features and capabilities, but you need a hard disk to use the package effectively, since it comes from Studio Software distributed across at least 11 floppy disks.

DO-IT works with numerous word processing programs and the following output devices, among others: laser printers—LaserWriter, Hewlett-Packard LaserJet, Lasergrafix series, Imagen 800/3; typesetters—Alphatype CRS, Autologic APS-5 and Micro-5, Linotype Company Series 100 and 200; plotters—Hewlett-Packard 7470A, Houston Instrument/Bausch & Lomb DMP Series.

LIST PRICE • $1800

SYSTEM REQUIREMENTS • IBM PC XT or AT or exact compatible; 512K minimum, 640K recommended; hard disk; laser printer or typesetter

Studio Software
17862-C Fitch
Irvine, CA 92714
(800) 437-4496

MagnaType

The quick brown and furry fox jumped over the lazy and
listless dog. The quick brown and furry fox jumped over the
lazy and listless dog. The quick brown and furry fox
jumped over the lazy and listless dog. The quick brown
and furry fox jumped over the lazy and listless dog. The
quick brown and furry fox jumped over the lazy and
listless dog. The quick brown and furry fox jumped
over the lazy and listless dog. The quick brown and
furry fox jumped over the lazy and listless dog. The
quick brown and furry fox jumped over the lazy and
listless dog. The quick brown and furry fox jumped
over the lazy and listless dog. The quick brown
and furry fox jumped over the lazy and listless
dog. The quick brown and furry fox jumped
over the lazy and listless dog. The quick brown
and furry fox jumped over the lazy and listless dog. The quick brown and furry fox
jumped over the lazy and listless dog. The
quick brown and furry fox jumped over the
lazy and listless dog. The quick brown
and furry fox jumped over the lazy and
listless dog. The quick brown and furry
fox jumped over the lazy and listless
dog. The quick brown and furry fox
jumped over the lazy and listless
dog. The quick brown and furry fox
jumped
over the lazy
and listless
dog. The quick
brown and furry
fox jumped over
the lazy and list-
less dog. The
quick brown
and furry fox
jumped over
the lazy and
listless dog.
The quick
brown
and
furry fox jumped
over the lazy and listless dog.
The quick brown and furry fox jumped over the
lazy and listless dog. The quick brown and furry fox jumped
over the lazy and listless dog. The quick brown and furry

"Wine Glass" shape created with MagnaType.

MagnaType is a personal computer version of a $100,000 composition system that can generate PostScript coding and output documents to many typesetters, including Linotype's, as well as the Apple LaserWriter printer and any other PostScript-compatible device. It includes a word processing program and five methods of hyphenation. (DOS files from various other word processing programs are compatible with the system.) You use short mnemonic codes to control the configuration of your text. The system can store an unlimited number of fonts, with any 16 stored in memory at a time.

The program's multitasking ability lets you take care of several functions at once — sending material to a typesetter while simultaneously creating another document, for example. With a companion product called MagNet, MagnaType works in a network with as many as eight other computers.

Another auxiliary product, MagnaPage, has these pagination features: vertical justification, widow and orphan control, and single- and multiple-line running heads and feet, among others. The paging commands work with outside programs such as database managers, which means you can prepare data such as parts catalogs or directories for typesetting.

LIST PRICE • $1000

SYSTEM REQUIREMENTS • IBM PC XT, AT, or other PC-DOS-compatible computer; 512K RAM; hard disk drive

Magna Computer Systems, Inc.
14724 Ventura Blvd.
Sherman Oaks, CA 91403
(818) 986-9233

SuperPage

A newsletter produced with SuperPage.

SuperPage from Bestinfo is interactive, menu-driven, WYSIWYG software that facilitates typesetting, pagination, composition, and graphics. You use the PC's cursor keys to create page layouts that you can use on the screen and then store for reuse. You can specify up to 40 columns, with boxes for sidebars or art and spaces for headlines, dropped caps, and the like. After you've established your page layouts, you can "pour" text into them—it automatically wraps around the spaces you've designated. You are limited to eight fonts per page, and editing text after page layout is cumbersome.

SuperPage automatically wraps columns; aligns lines from column to column; balances short columns; vertically justifies; eliminates widows and orphans; and provides automatic headers, footers, ruled backgrounds, and page numbers. The product has a 20,000-word hyphenation dictionary. It can accept scanned original art or graphics and scale it to fit any space.

The software works with many typesetters and laser printers, as well as dot matrix printers. You can get your documents to a typesetter with a modem or use a conversion device to transfer them directly from a disk. SuperPage can also work within a network.

Bestinfo also offers a scaled-down version of SuperPage to provide an intermediate level of sophistication and performance between casual desktop publishing systems and complete typesetting composition systems. It lets you typeset text from word processing programs and features column justification, kerning, line hyphenation, bulleting, and paragraph indentation. You can select from eight preset font styles of 127 characters each.

One hundred page styles are possible in page layout. The program lets you channel scanned graphics and PC Paintbrush files onto pages for positioning, scaling, and cropping. To merge text with page designs, you can wrap text around windows designated for graphics.

LIST PRICE • SuperPage, $7000; lower-end version, $500-$700, depending on options

SYSTEM REQUIREMENTS • IBM PC XT, AT or compatible computer, PC-DOS, 512K RAM, IBM monochrome monitor, and large-option or Hercules Graphics Card; LaserWriter or other laser printer; mouse or digitizing tablet optional

Bestinfo
33 Chester Pike
Ridley Park, PA 19078
(215) 521-0757

PagePlanner

PagePlanner is among the best known and most successful composition software packages for the IBM PC series. It unites text entry, hyphenation/justification, and page makeup in one package. The program relies heavily on menus for presenting its options, which include extensive editing facilities, storage of partially completed pages, proportional column display, and reverse type. You manipulate text with the cursor keys and function keys.

ShapeSet is an enhancement to PagePlanner for preparing advertisements. You use the cursor to draw an outline of a symmetrical or asymmetrical area into which text fits automatically.

PagePlanner is not a WYSIWYG product. It was intended to automate pasteup, and page layout is its strength. It is best at showing solid blocks that represent text, formatted in columns, with space allocated for illustrations. Although it doesn't show actual text or illustrations, it gives you a reasonable idea of what a page will look like and then lets text flow automatically into the area designated for it.

The system has software options that enable it to work with a range of phototypesetters including the Compugraphic 8300, 8400, and 8600; the Linotype Linotronic 100 and Linotron 202; and the Lasercomp.

LIST PRICE • $3995 (includes page layout and ShapeSet programs, exception dictionary, bridge to a word processing program, and output drivers for a printer and typesetter)

SYSTEM REQUIREMENTS • IBM PC series computer with IBM Graphics Card or Hercules Graphics Card, or other MS-DOS- or CP/M-based computer; 512K RAM; hard disk drive recommended

PagePlanner Systems, Inc.
463 Barell Avenue
Carlstadt, NJ 07072
(201) 933-4700

Other software helps turn your IBM PC series computer into a desktop publishing system. The rest of this chapter is a sampler of such software.

ClickArt Personal Publisher

ClickArt Personal Publisher from T/Maker is a low-cost on-screen page layout system for the IBM PC and compatible computers that simultaneously mixes text and "clip art" graphics on the screen. It performs on-screen and printed proportional spacing and kerning. This WYSIWYG system lets you perform simple text and graphics entry and formatting and gives you libraries of canned images. ClickArt works with Epson, Okidata, and compatible printers, Apple's LaserWriter, and Hewlett-Packard's LaserJet. A unique feature of this product is that it is compatible with fonts and MacPaint documents from the Macintosh.

The basic ClickArt product costs $185. Laser fonts and drivers for the LaserWriter or LaserJet cost an additional $150. Each of these ClickArt image packages costs $49.95:

- Personal Graphics: more than 150 contemporary images of famous people, animals, cars, and symbols, including Rodin's *The Thinker*, Michelangelo's *David*, Einstein, various arrows, and borders
- Publications: more than 500 images for enhancing business communications, including two- and three-column layout headers, borders, illustrated alphabets, maps, cartoons, and phrases
- Letters: large alphabets, for fliers, overheads, and posters
- Holiday Images: including Christmas, Hanukkah, Thanksgiving, Easter, Valentine's Day, and special events

LIST PRICE • See text

SYSTEM REQUIREMENTS • IBM PC, XT, AT, or compatible computer; 384K RAM, IBM color card or Hercules Graphics Card; two disk drives

T/Maker Company
2115 Landings Drive
Mountain View, CA 94043
(415) 962-0195

Harvard Presentation Graphics

Harvard Presentation Graphics from Software Publishing Corporation combines text, graphs, and charts to help businesspeople prepare presentation graphics. It generates high-quality output on many kinds of peripherals, from dot matrix printers to laser printers. You can also put what you produce on 35mm slides, using an outside slide service bureau. The product has 13 custom-designed fonts, 16 colors, and extensive formatting and layout options, including three-dimensional graphs and unlimited text sizes. Its Chart Editor feature lets you enhance charts with symbols and text.

Among the files it reads directly are Lotus 1-2-3 spreadsheet data and graphs, PFS:Graph files, and ASCII text or data files. It also transfers files to PFS:Write for inclusion in word processing documents. You can run it on the 3Com network, and it works with the Enhanced Graphics Adapter card and various printers, plotters, and film recorders.

LIST PRICE • $395

SYSTEM REQUIREMENTS • IBM PC series computer or compatible; 256K RAM

Software Publishing Corporation
1901 Landings Drive
Mountain View, CA 94043
(415) 962-8910

Personal Bibliographic Software Products

Personal Bibliographic Software offers several bibliographic products for the IBM PC series and Macintosh. Among them are Professional Bibliographic System, a text formatting and database system that enables users to compile and manage an extensive database of bibliographic citations. It can hold up to 1000 citations on a floppy disk and as many as 30,000 on a hard disk, in any bibliographic format. A companion program called Biblio-Link reformats downloaded records from the OCLC, RLIN, Dialog, and BRS on-line systems for data management. The Index Plus utility disk lets users create indexes, based on the records in their databases. It also provides for mass deletion of duplicate records and the merging of databases.

LIST PRICE • Professional Bibliographic System, $295; Biblio-Link BRS, $195; Index Plus, $95

SYSTEM REQUIREMENTS • IBM PC, PC XT, or PC AT; Macintosh; or OCLC M300 Workstation

Personal Bibliographic Software, Inc.
P.O. Box 4250
Ann Arbor, MI 48106
(313) 996-1580

Concept 100 Publishing System

The Concept 100 System.

The Concept 100 system from Concept Technologies, Inc., consists of a graphics controller and software that turn an IBM PC, XT, or AT, as well as several compatible computers, into a publishing system. You can use it interactively to create and edit high-resolution text and graphics, and to lay out pages. The package uses various de facto or proposed industry standards, which means it can work with various printers, plotters, and displays. One of these printers is the ConceptWriter, sold by Concept Technologies to complement the software and form a full-fledged publishing system. The 300-dpi laser printer produces eight pages per minute on plain paper or transparencies. This printer is essentially a daisywheel emulator, although it can produce bit-mapped images. The system also works with Lasergrafix printers by QMS, of which Concept Technologies is a subsidiary.

LIST PRICES • Concept 100, $2195; ConceptWriter, $5995

SYSTEM REQUIREMENTS • IBM PC, AT, XT, or compatibles

Concept Technologies, Inc.
P.O. Box 5277
Portland, OR 97208
(503) 222-7080

The DataCenter

The DataCenter.

Corporate Data Sciences sells The Data-Center, a system that works with the IBM PC XT or AT. The DataCenter includes the GD/P (Graphics Display/Processor) high-resolution monitor, VTEXT text format-ting software, and CDS 2300 laser printer. Optional graphics drawing software and a three-dimensional spreadsheet are available.

The GD/P has a 17-inch-diagonal, high-resolution, full-page, portrait-style (oriented like a printed page) screen. The screen resolution of 1024×1024 pixels is useful for computer-aided design and computer-aided engineering. The screen has its own graphics microprocessor for almost instantaneous refresh.

VTEXT uses the GD/P hardware to display documents on the screen as they will appear printed. The VDRAW option helps you generate detailed images on a main-frame or PC; edit them on the GD/P with a mouse, keyboard, or both; display them on the screen; integrate them within VTEXT text; and print them on the laser printer. The software can rotate three-dimensional objects on the screen.

VESS is an optional spreadsheet with data display in three directions, data transfer among reports, and display of an entire report or balance sheet on the screen.

LIST PRICES • $13,895 for the complete DataCenter; $7600 without laser printer; PC mouse, $150; VDRAW, $750; VESS, $590

SYSTEM REQUIREMENTS • IBM PC XT or AT, 512K RAM, 10-megabyte hard disk drive, 8087 (XT) or 80287 (AT) coprocessor, serial port (for VDRAW), parallel port (for printer)

Corporate Data Sciences, Inc.
2560 Mission College Blvd., #102
Santa Clara, CA 95054
(213) 674-3117

Multi-Lingual Scribe

Multi-Lingual Scribe from Gamma Productions, distributed by Software Resource, is a word processing program for Hebrew, Greek, Arabic, and Russian that displays foreign language characters on the screen with vowel points and accents. It also displays most European languages, with their peculiar diacritical marks (umlauted a [ä], for example). Languages that read right to left are displayed that way. Each language is memory resident, and you select it by pressing a key; no disk swapping is necessary. Usual word processing features such as block move, search and replace, headers and footers, print preview, unlimited document size, subscripts, and superscripts are included. The package has keyboard layout charts and press-on keyboard labels for the four languages. Output devices include several Epson and Epson-compatible dot matrix printers, IBM graphics printer, Okidata, C-Itoh Prowriter, NEC 8023A dot matrix printer, and the Corona LP300 Laser Printer.

LIST PRICE • $349.95; demo, $15 plus $3 shipping ($15 applicable to purchase price)

SYSTEM REQUIREMENTS • IBM PC, XT, AT, or 100 percent graphics-compatible computer; DOS 2.0 or higher; 320K RAM; IBM or Hercules Color Graphics Card or 100 percent compatible card; black-and-white composite or color monitor; one disk drive; any of these printers: Epson RX, MX, FX, LX, 1500 or compatible; IBM Graphics Printer; Okidata printer (with IBM emulation); C-Itoh Prowriter; NEC 8023A dot matrix printer; Corona LP300 laser printer

Gamma Productions, Inc.
710 Wilshire Blvd., Suite 609
Santa Monica, CA 90401
(213) 394-8622

Distributors:
Software Resource
East Coast: (800) 223-1143 or (201) 390-0999
West Coast: (800) 851-9010 or (800) 851-9009 (California)

Chapter 7

Workstations

Although the term *workstation* dates from 1931 and originally meant "an area with equipment for a single worker," since about 1980, the term has taken on a new meaning. It now refers almost exclusively to a type of computer technology: "a usually intelligent terminal connected to a data processing or word processing network."

Computer workstations were conceived for technical applications such as computer-aided design and mechanical engineering. Many workstations have large screens (up to 19 inches diagonally) and high-resolution displays—ideal for designing integrated circuits and the like. Such technical applications still constitute the primary use for workstations, but, with the development of page description software, workstations are seeing use as desktop publishing tools. With the introduction in early 1986 of the IBM RT PC workstation, workstation technology took a turn away from an almost total concentration on the technical arena toward a wider audience (we cover the RT PC later in this chapter).

The user interface of many workstations is similar to that of the Macintosh computer from Apple. These machines have mouse pointing devices and pull-down and pop-up menus. Because of these built-in facilities, workstations have inherent potential as desktop publishing tools. You can think of these workstations as big, fancy (and expensive) Macintoshes. Since they have larger and higher-resolution screens, workstations are good for WYSIWYG text manipulation—particularly since a full-size representation of an $8\frac{1}{2} \times 11$ inch page can appear on the screen. (We've already pointed out that under certain conditions, a Macintosh can function as a workstation. Like many computer terms, *workstation* is imprecise, and the distinctions between workstations and personal computers are becoming blurred. For convenience, the devices referred to in this section are the so-called technical workstations.)

Various page description and editing packages exist for workstations. Since workstations are designed with network applications in mind, they provide employees of a publishing operation the opportunity to pass documents back and forth electronically. At this stage of their development, workstations hold the most promise for business publishing, partially because of their cost. Workstations are expensive, costing anywhere from about $7000 to nearly $100,000, depending on the capabilities and configuration of the machine. Workstations at the low end of the price spectrum are so-called diskless nodes that must be connected to other workstations and computers in a network. Standalone workstations have their own data storage (disks or tapes); you must pay proportionally more for the computing autonomy standalone workstations offer, although workstation manufacturers are expanding the capabilities of their machines while lowering prices.

Although numerous companies manufacture computer systems called workstations, the market is dominated by a few manufacturers, and we are concerned here with those whose systems are suitable for desktop publishing applications.

A Sun Microsystems standalone workstation.

Among these manufacturers are Apollo, Sun Microsystems, Silicon Graphics, Cadmus, and IBM, all of whose products are similar. Most workstations are based on the operating system UNIX. Designed for networking, they have a Macintosh-like user interface. Like the Macintosh, they use the Motorola 68xxx family of microprocessors. They are heavily oriented toward technical applications. As workstation manufacturers have moved into the desktop publishing market, however, they have developed and offered packages that transcend or mask the complexities of UNIX and its cumbersome editors and typesetting commands (see *troff* in chapter 8).

IBM RT PERSONAL COMPUTER

The IBM RT Personal Computer, or IBM RT PC, is the most powerful personal computer system IBM is offering at the time of this writing. The IBM RT PC is a supermicro workstation that uses RISC (reduced instruction set computer) hardware and software architecture to improve the performance of the computer. IBM's RISC software architecture is based on a scaled-down version of IBM's 370 mainframe computer instruction set. RISC uses a limited set of instructions to perform complex tasks, thus reducing the software overhead necessary to perform tasks and completing the tasks more quickly than standard personal computer technology can accomplish them.

The RT PC comes in several different models that carry a base price of $12,000 to $23,000—several times higher than the cost of an IBM PC AT. Unlike the PC AT and other IBM PC series computers that employ the PC-DOS, or MS-DOS, operating system, the RT PC uses UNIX. Software for the RT PC is expensive compared to IBM PC series software. The RT PC's version of UNIX is called AIX, which stands for Advanced Interactive Executive. In technical terms, AIX is a "multiuser, multitasking, demand-paged, virtual-memory operating system optimized for 32-bit RISC architecture." AIX, initially priced at $3400, was codeveloped, with IBM, by Interactive Systems Corporation of Santa Monica, California, and includes the basic features of AT&T's UNIX System V, as well as added features drawn from the Berkeley Version 4.2 UNIX and Interactive's own IN/ix.

An unusual feature of the RT PC's AIX version of UNIX is that it not only accepts UNIX-style commands, but it also accepts PC-DOS-style commands, which the software converts into UNIX equivalents. If you actually want to run PC-DOS or MS-DOS programs, however, you have to purchase special coprocessor equipment that includes a $995 AT coprocessor board with an 80286 CPU and the $1000 VRM (Virtual Resource Manager), which controls how PC-DOS and AIX applications share system resources such as disk drives, memory, and video. The RT PC has a peripheral bus similar to that of the IBM PC and PC AT and works with the IBM PC's standard monochrome adapter card and the IBM Enhanced Graphics Adapter; it does not work with the standard IBM Color Display Adapter or the Professional Graphics Adapter. Instead, IBM offers three new display adapters for the RT PC: The IBM Advanced Monochrome Display, with 720×512 pixel resolution in a single color; the IBM Advanced Color Graphics Display, with 720×512 pixel resolution in 16 colors; and the IBM Extended Monochrome Display, with a 1024×768 pixel display that could be excellent for WYSIWYG desktop publishing applications.

One drawback of this system is that it does not use the Intel family of CPUs that are in other IBM PC series computers, so the software for this machine has to be created from scratch, and this situation probably means limited availability of products for at least the first year after the RT's introduction in early 1986. Initial software efforts have looked promising, however. Interleaf, a leading supplier of electronic publishing software for workstations, is converting its software to run on the RT PC. At the time of this writing, Interleaf was selling a system based on a Sun Microsystems workstation for around $60,000 for an entry level system including hardware and software. According to Interleaf, a similar system based on the IBM RT PC will soon cost less than $30,000 for an entry level system.

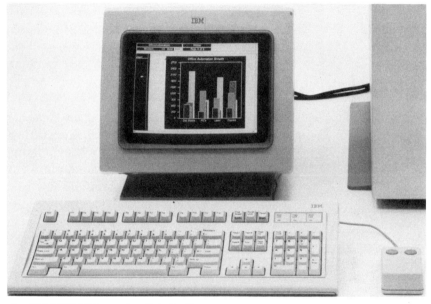

An IBM RT PC running Interleaf.

The Interleaf software per se is already available for the RT PC. The version of Interleaf IBM sells is Workstation Publishing Software with a document content architecture (DCA) filter, an interchange format among word processors. All IBM branches and selected authorized IBM Personal Computer dealers sell the WPS software at $1995 per copy.

Shortly after this book is published, Interleaf plans to sell its Technical Publishing Software directly. Typesetter and scanner interfaces are planned; prices will be higher than the price for the WPS version of the software from IBM.

Other software packages announced for the RT PC are Applix IA, a text processor (also known as Alis) from Applix, Inc., and Samna+, a text processor with spreadsheet from Samna Corporation. Because there is no clear standard for windowing on the RT PC, Interleaf,

Applix, and Samna are all using their own independent windowing schemes.

The RT PC will probably be a good solution for people who need more power and capabilities than a Macintosh or Macintosh Plus can give them but don't want to pay the higher price for a Sun or Apollo workstation. A possible contender in this middle ground for electronic publishing systems is the so-called "open Mac," or "Macintosh II," rumored to be under development at Apple. This machine, reportedly scheduled for release in early 1987, will be a low-cost supermicro workstation with a 68020 processor and a 17-inch full-page display option that will compete with the IBM RT PC, Sun, Apollo, and other workstations.

WORKSTATIONS AS PUBLISHING SYSTEMS

Cambridge, Massachusetts-based Interleaf makes the most popular electronic publishing systems for workstations. If you buy a complete Interleaf hardware/software system, you get a Sun, Apollo, or Digital Equipment Corporation workstation running Interleaf software. In addition to the workstation and software, the complete system features a choice of two 300-dpi laser printers (made by Imagen) and an image scanner. The lower-end printer is rated at eight pages per minute and has 300-dpi resolution. It uses the Impress page layout and description language from Imagen. The higher-end printer is considerably faster, pumping out pages at 26 per minute under optimum conditions. This printer is based on Interleaf's own RIPrint page description language.

With the scanner, you can incorporate photographs and other artwork into your documents (the scanner is about the size of a standard office copier). For higher resolution of printed images, the Interleaf system can send output to typesetters with image processing capabilities. Some of these typesetters include Monotype Lasercomp, Compugraphic 8600G, Autologic APS-Micro 5G, Linotype Linotronic 300, and all models from International, Inc.

Interleaf offers two kinds of software for its systems: Workstation Publishing Software and Technical Publishing Software. Using Interleaf is somewhat similar to working with a page layout project on a Macintosh, but Interleaf can do much more and is accordingly more difficult to learn and use.

Sun Microsystems is using Interleaf to produce various marketing documents, as well as shipping forms and price lists. According to the *Journal of Commerce*, other companies that have adopted

---

CadMac

Cadmus, of Lowell, Massachusetts, leaves no doubt that using its workstations is akin to working with a Macintosh. One line of Cadmus workstations is called CadMac. The Cadmus ad slogan boasts: "The simplicity of the Macintosh with the performance of a mainframe." In other words, working with CadMac workstations is similar to working with Macintoshes, and you get the advantage of a larger screen: 17 inches diagonally.

Since the CadMac system is "source compatible" with the Macintosh, you can run Macintosh applications on the CadMac's larger screen. In addition to having a bigger screen, the CadMac offers more disk storage space. You can use this larger disk space as a fileserver for a network of Macintoshes, connected by the AppleTalk network. The CadMac also works with the LaserWriter and PostScript. It has the same graphics tools, Core and GKS, that come with most workstations.

LIST PRICE • $25,000 with 2 megabytes of RAM, an 80-megabyte disk, and a 30-megabyte tape system—this machine is based on the MC68020 microprocessor; a CadMac system based on the slower MC68010 chip lists for $21,000

SYSTEM REQUIREMENTS • PostScript-compatible page printer

Cadmus Computer Systems
500 Suffolk Street
Lowell, MA 01854
(617) 453-2899
(800) 221-3384

Interleaf for in-house desktop publishing include

- American Can, which uses Interleaf to quickly produce briefing books for the board of directors
- Wyeth Laboratories, which uses the Interleaf system to create custom forms for each new product that goes through R&D
- Investment banking house Lazard Freres, which employs its Interleaf system to produce customized corporate finance proposals, replete with charts and graphs

A page made up with Interleaf.

- Hewlett-Packard, which uses Interleaf to produce user documentation for software and hardware products
- Apollo, which the October 16, 1985, issue of *MIS Week* noted was using Interleaf publishing software companywide for most in-house technical publishing

List Prices: A fully equipped Interleaf system, complete with fast laser printer and scanner, costs in excess of $100,000; licensing fees are applicable for buyers who get the software for other workstation systems

System Requirements: Apollo, DEC, IBM, or Sun workstation; laser printer; scanner (optional)

Interleaf, Inc.
1100 Massachusetts Avenue
Cambridge, MA 02138
(800) 241-7700

Chapter 8

Page Description Languages

Page description languages allow computers to define what printed pages will look like. These languages are fundamental to desktop publishing because they let you describe pages precisely and reproduce them on many different kinds of output devices such as page printers and typesetting machines. Page description languages such as PostScript, TEX, InterPress, and *troff* also provide standard ways to represent pages. Thus, products from different manufacturers can use the same page descriptions—you can create and edit a document on a system from one manufacturer, print it on a laser printer made by another company, and typeset it on a typesetting machine from yet another firm.

By adopting standard conventions for describing pages, companies do not force you to buy all the components of your system from a single manufacturer.

Although quite a few page description and graphics languages can be used for describing pages, three languages have emerged as the leading standards: PostScript, developed by Adobe Systems; TEX, developed by Stanford University professor Donald Knuth; and InterPress, from Xerox. Of the three, PostScript seems to be taking a clear leadership position and offers numerous compatible products. The next-strongest contender is TEX, since it is excellent for formatting long and/or complex documents. InterPress, which shares a common heritage with PostScript, has not gained as much momentum as a standard, which is probably due to Xerox's uncertain promotion of InterPress as a standard; originally Xerox used InterPress only for Xerox products, and when the company finally saw the wisdom of promoting InterPress as a standard language, PostScript had already entrenched itself in the market. At the time of this writing, IBM has not announced any endorsement of a particular page description language. Whatever language IBM adopts, however, is likely to gain a great deal of momentum as a standard, if it is not one already.

POSTSCRIPT

PostScript is a computer graphics language (also called a page description or formatting language) that describes pages of text and graphics and reproduces the descriptions on a printer, typesetting machine, or other output device. PostScript was developed by Adobe Systems of Palo Alto, California, as an OEM product for Apple's LaserWriter, with the hope of PostScript's catching on as a standard graphics language for page description.

Companies other than Apple have adopted PostScript, since the language works with many systems including the Macintosh, IBM PC series, some DEC systems, and UNIX- and TEX-based systems, and it provides a common meeting ground for various hardware and software manufacturers.

PostScript's roots go back to the Evans & Sutherland Computer Corporation, ca. 1976, where John Warnock, a founder of Adobe, was working with John Gaffney. Warnock and Gaffney created a graphics language called the Design System to build complex three-dimensional databases for use in computer-aided design (CAD).

In 1978, Warnock joined the near legendary Xerox Palo Alto Research Center (PARC), site of the development of many original Macintosh concepts. At PARC, Warnock and his colleague Martin Newell revived the language as JaM (for John and Martin); Newell used JaM for experimental VLSI microchip design, while Warnock turned his attention to investigating potential applications for the language in printing and graphics arts. Warnock's and others' work on JaM led to both Xerox's Interpress printing protocol and PostScript.

In 1982, Warnock and Chuck Geschke founded Adobe Systems. Their goal was to create PostScript, a third incarnation of the Design System and JaM, to describe two-dimensional pages and control raster image printers—printers that produce images composed of tiny dots.

The success of PostScript has been phenomenal, due mainly to Apple's success with the LaserWriter and an agreement Apple forged with Adobe and Linotype Company to create PostScript versions of the Linotype typesetting machines and the ITC typeface library, which includes the entire Mergenthaler, Linotype, Stempel, and Haas typeface libraries. PostScript has emerged as a standard among page description languages; many hardware and software companies now make PostScript-compatible products—from page layout and graphics software for the Macintosh and IBM PC to page printers and typesetting machines.

PostScript describes pages by using mathematical formulas that represent shapes rather than by specifying individual pixels in a bit-mapped graphic image (the small dots that comprise an image are known as picture elements, or pixels). It translates images into the tiny dots that make up text, graphics, and halftones on printed pages. PostScript encodes typefaces into outlines that a laser printer reconstructs at the proper size and then fills in to solidify the outline. This approach has several advantages: computer memory is conserved, and many different types of output devices can re-create

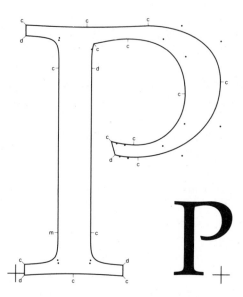

A PostScript outline of the letter P, and the letter filled in.
Illustrations courtesy of Adobe Systems.

the standard PostScript format at a wide range of resolutions.

PostScript's unique system of typeface definition creates characters in a wide variety of typestyles and sizes. This approach can cut typesetting costs considerably, since typefaces are traditionally sold by the font (a set of characters of a single typeface, typestyle, and size). In other words, most typesetting machines require separate purchases for 9-point Times Roman, 12-point Times Roman, 12-point Times Roman italic, and so forth. On the other hand, a single purchase gets you the Times Roman typeface for a PostScript system in all the major typestyles—plain text, italic, bold, underline, outline, shadow, small caps, superscript, and subscript—and in virtually any type size (the Apple LaserWriter, for example, can produce any size from 3 points up). You don't pay separately for each variation.

As an example of how little memory PostScript requires to create a typeface collection, a complete alphabet of 210 characters takes up only 15K to 20K bytes, including all point sizes and typestyles. Since the compact PostScript page description requires only a tiny percentage of the memory required to store a bit-mapped image, it conserves computer RAM and disk storage and accelerates data communication.

PostScript has two main components, the page description vocabulary used by the personal computer and the interpreter that converts page descriptions into a form a particular printer can use. The PostScript page description vocabulary allows you to specify sizes and positions for text and graphics on a page; the interpreter translates the page description into tiny dots that form the printed image. The interpreter software usually runs on a special type of printer controller known as a *raster image processor*, or *RIP*, inside a host computer or, more commonly, inside the printer. The RIP has to work hard to print at high resolutions, and many RIPs are powerful computers in their own right. For example, the RIP in the Apple LaserWriter has several megabytes of memory and a faster microprocessor than the Macintosh, which means that it packs more computing whallop than either the Macintosh or the IBM PC AT.

By using this very powerful graphics language, you can integrate and manipulate text, digitized images, and other graphics on a page. PostScript creates halftones by generating dot or line screens that correspond to a particular printer, and it can even fashion color separations and make provisions for printing in full color when color page printers and other output devices become more widely available. PostScript's features include:

- the ability to construct arbitrary shapes from lines, arcs, and cubic curves
- painting commands with which you can outline a shape with lines of any thickness, fill it with any pattern or color, and merge graphics from digitized images or other sources
- the ability to use images of any resolution that are either digitized from samples such as photographs or generated synthetically by another computer

PostScript is a "device independent" language, which means it creates output files that are not tied to any particular output device. Device driver programs translate the device-independent output files into specific formats that control particular types of printers or other output devices. The same PostScript program can work with many different output devices, from dot matrix printers to laser printers and typesetting machines, at resolutions of less than 100 pixels (or dots) per inch to resolutions of more than 2000 per inch.

PostScript and Printers

The PostScript language is useful not only for describing pages and creating output; you can also exploit it as a programming language

PostScript can manipulate text and graphics by using mathematical formulas.

to control the special RIP computers that intelligent printers use to create the image on a page. PostScript page descriptions are usually generated automatically by application programs such as word processors, charting and drawing programs, page layout software, and other graphics programs. Although application developers do the majority of PostScript programming, you may want to write a PostScript program to take advantage of PostScript capabilities, such as translation, scaling, rotation, reflection, and skewing of images, that are not available in a particular application program.

Adobe has also developed a software package called TransScript that allows UNIX systems and systems that use other computer languages to use PostScript-based printers. It works with AT&T System V and Berkeley 4.2BSD versions of UNIX, as well as *troff*, *ditroff* (Documenters' Workbench), Plot files, Diablo 630 print files, Tektronix 4014 files, user-created PostScript print files, and other languages such as Scribe and TeX.

Adobe Systems, Inc.
1870 Embarcadero Road
Palo Alto, CA 94303
(415) 852-0271

TEX

TEX is a computer language for typesetting and page layout created by Stanford University computer science professor Donald Knuth during the 1970s. Knuth is the author of the well-respected multiple-volume computer text entitled *The Art of Computer Programming.* He is regarded as one of the world's top authorities on a special type of mathematical formulas known as algorithms, which are sets of rules for solving problems. Knuth had been frustrated by the available methods of typesetting mathematical formulas and developed TEX (sounds like *tech*) because he wanted a more sophisticated way to specify formulas that used unusual symbols and were therefore difficult to typeset and lay out accurately. Although TEX grew out of a desire to create good-looking mathematical formulas, it also contains advanced methods for handling ordinary text.

TEX gives its users a great deal of control over the placement of characters, symbols, and words on a page. It does not use the word justification and simple hyphenation that you'll find in many word processing and page layout programs; instead TEX inspects every character in a document and determines the optimum placement of each element on a page according to page layout criteria that you specify with TEX commands. TEX performs many complex calculations, such as determining exactly where each letter should be placed in relation to the other letters in a word, determining the proper hyphenation and placement of each word, and specifying layout and placement of paragraphs, titles, and other elements on each page. Unlike most other page layout systems, which examine only one line of type at a time when determining where to break lines or hyphenate, TEX inspects the entire paragraph, and often the end of a paragraph influences the way the first lines break. This system results in even spacing between characters and words and few hyphenated words.

TEX uses two primary concepts to describe pages and their contents: "boxes" and "glue." In the TEX system, a character of type is a box, a space is a box, a line of text is a long thin box composed of the character and space boxes, rules are even thinner boxes, graphic elements are boxes, and so on. The final page is a box that is a collection of all the various component boxes. The boxes are held together with a conceptual glue. The glue has three main characteristics, the space component, which represents the ideal space between boxes; the stretch component, which specifies the amount of extra space that is tolerable between boxes; and the shrink component, which represents the amount of space that can be removed if necessary. Another feature of TEX is that all of its commands use standard typewriter characters, so virtually any word processing system or text editor can serve as an input device.

Like PostScript, TEX creates a device-independent output file (also known in TEX jargon as a *DVI* file) that functions with a variety of device drivers to create output on many different types of output devices. Numerous device drivers are available for TEX to translate device-independent output files into the format required by different output devices. At the time of this writing, TEX offers more device drivers than PostScript does (especially for typesetting machines), but PostScript is rapidly overtaking TEX as a standard page description language, and probably more PostScript than TEX device drivers will be developed from now on.

FTLTEX for the Macintosh

FTL systems, Inc., has made the TEX typesetting package available on the Macintosh. FTLTEX converts TEX files into PostScript files, merging the capabilities of TEX with PostScript's graphics abilities to create a layout and typesetting system. The product works with the standard TEX fonts, as well as all of the Apple LaserWriter fonts in unlimited point sizes. You can also use it with several commercially available digitizer packages and merge digitized pictures with your typeset text. A preview window lets you see processed text before it prints.

LIST PRICE • $750

SYSTEM REQUIREMENTS • Macintosh Plus, PostScript-compatible printer, hard disk drive recommended

FTL systems Inc.
234 Eglinton Avenue East, Suite 205
Toronto, Ontario, Canada M4P 1K5
(416) 487-2142

PCTEX

This product is a full-fledged version of TEX82 from Donald Knuth, the originator of TEX. The basic package includes INITEX, a program that installs TEX; the complete TEX formatting language; LATEX, a comprehensive macro package that improves on TEX's forbidding interface; and the AMSTEX and VANILLA macro packages. With the PCDOT device driver, you can operate numerous dot matrix printers, including printers from Epson, Toshiba, and IBM. Each driver includes more than 230 fonts. More important for desktop publishing are the PCLaser device drivers for the Laser-Writer; QMS Lasergrafix 800 and 1200 printers; Imagen 8, 12, and 24/300 printers; the HP LaserJet; Corona LP-300 Laser Printer; and others. MF Medley includes 44 fonts from the Metafoundry, including Copperplate and Schoolbook.

LIST PRICES • PCTEX, $279; PCDOT, $100; PCLaser, $300; MF Medley, $100

SYSTEM REQUIREMENTS • IBM PC XT, AT, or compatible computer; DOS 2.0 or higher; 512K RAM; 10-megabyte hard disk. PCLaser requires a $909 JLASER card from Tall Tree Systems.

Personal TEX
20 Sunnyside, Suite H
Mill Valley, CA 94941
(415) 388-8853

MicroTEX

Like PCTEX, Addison-Wesley's MicroTEX is a full-blown version of Knuth's creation. Also like PCTEX, this product has drivers for dot matrix and laser printers, including the LaserWriter. To complement this product, Addison-Wesley publishes Knuth's *The TEXbook* and *TEX: The Program.* Another associated Addison-Wesley title is *LATEX: A Document Preparation System* by Leslie Lamport.

LIST PRICE • $495; additional printer drivers increase the cost

SYSTEM REQUIREMENTS • IBM PC, XT, AT, or compatible computer; 512K RAM; 10-megabyte hard disk drive

Addison-Wesley Publishing Company
Educational and Professional Technologies Division
Reading, MA 01867
(617) 944-6795

Products from Textset

Preview displays formatted documents on an IBM PC, XT, AT, or compatible computer that has either an IBM Enhanced Graphics Adapter card, a Hercules Graphics Card, or a Tecmar Graphics Master card. Although these cards are all monochrome, Textset plans to offer Preview with color cards.

Textset also writes device drivers to run various output devices, including the Laser-Writer, QMS Lasergrafix printers, and Autologic APS-5 typesetting machine, on the IBM PC, AT, XT, and compatible computers, as well as on higher-performance computers from DEC, Sun Microsystems, and Apollo. Textset also supplies custom drivers and provides typesetting services from TEX DVI files. Another service of the company is production and macro assistance for TEX manuscripts that must be reorganized to meet publishers' specifications.

Textset, Inc.
Box 7993
Ann Arbor, MI 48107
(313) 996-3566

INTERPRESS

Interpress is Xerox's standard format for rendering documents in final form, already prepared with page layout software, into print. It interprets page layout commands for text, graphics, multiple fonts, and pictures for laser printers, phototypesetters, plotters, and other output devices.

Xerox provides software that takes page layout specifications from a workstation and expresses them as an Interpress "master," which represents a series of instructions to the output device. This scheme divides the preparation of documents into two tasks: text creation and printing. The standard is independent of a workstation's or output device's specific characteristics, including resolution and the availability of certain fonts.

Designed to take advantage of the high-resolution text and graphics of laser printers, Interpress describes and manipulates the pages to be printed. It has numerous commands for describing text, graphics, and pictures, as well as commands for creating various shapes, rotating them, and scaling them. Interpress masters are intended for creation and interpretation by programs, rather than by people. The software within a printer interprets a master to print a document.

Interpress shares common roots with PostScript. Both languages derived from JaM, developed at Xerox PARC by John Warnock and Martin Newell. Xerox intended the Interpress standard for the use of other laser printer manufacturers, but it didn't publish the standard or license it out, for fear that Japanese printer makers would adopt it, undersell other manufacturers, and steal the laser printer market. Therefore, most of the key players in the laser printer market opted for the PostScript standard and have put their primary development efforts into PostScript-based products. Now Xerox is licensing the Interpress standard to various manufacturers, such as Burroughs Corporation and Digital Equipment Corporation, but PostScript has a clear lead. Strengthening PostScript's position as the primary standard, Interpress-to-PostScript convertors are expected to join the TeX-to-PostScript convertors that are already available.

TROFF

This UNIX typesetting language seems to elicit one of two reactions: people who have had close encounters with it seem either to love it or to hate it. *troff* is a complex set of commands that result in typeset output.

Its supporters point out that it is a "powerful" language with which you make sophisticated tables, charts, and other typeset output. Its detractors note that it requires a phenomenal number of commands to produce even the smallest deviations in standard text. Since each element of text must be preceded by a minimum of one command and most commands occupy a line each, a *troff* document that contains 500 lines of actual text can have well over 500 command lines.

A simple symbol, the registered trademark sign—an uppercase R enclosed by a circle (®)—requires the following string of commands

```
\u\o'\s-3R\s+3\(ci'\d
```

after the word that is to be denoted with this symbol. If you make one mistake in typing this lengthy command string, you will get disastrous, often amusing, results, such as the rest of the document's appearing in superscript. Since *troff* is not a WYSIWYG system, you have to wait until you have typeset or printed your document to see the results.

Some UNIX-based systems, such as Sun workstations, have a feature called Preview. Preview displays a document in a WYSIWYG fashion, so you can see what you are going to get before you waste too much paper.

Some *troff* commands are mnemonic. For example:

.B means *boldface*
.I means *italic*
.PS means *point size*
.VS means *vertical space*, or leading
.LP means *left paragraph*, or no indent

Complicated tables can be the bane of a *troff*er's existence.

In spite of its complexity, *troff* has a lot of adherents, but to use it effectively, you have to become almost completely proficient in it, which means learning all the commands or having a very large "cheat sheet" at hand. Furthermore, *troff* works in conjunction with a UNIX programming editor called *vi*, which in itself is difficult to use and is poorly suited for writing and editing prose.

In any case, the interface that *troff* presents does not constitute what we believe is an easy-to-use and efficient system. Compared to the Macintosh interface—based on readily understandable pictographs and words—*troff* is cumbersome.

SofType

SofType, from SofTest, is a formatting command language for use on a variety of computers and operating systems, including UNIX- and Xenix-based machines. SofType is always used in conjunction with an existing word processing program: LEX and Uniplex on UNIX and Xenix systems; and LEX, MultiMate, WordStar, and IBM DisplayWrite on MS-DOS and other machines. It adds about 15 English-like commands to those already present in the word processing program. When you use it with PC Paintbrush, SofType combines graphics and text and can incorporate images scanned with the MicroTek MS-300 Scanner.

SofType works with the Hewlett-Packard LaserJet and LaserJet Plus, Xerox 4045 and 2700 laser printers, and the following phototypesetters: Compugraphic 8400 and 8600; Varityper Comp/Edit 5810, 5900, and 6400; Autologic APS-5; and Linotype Linotron 202.

SofType costs $1000 for single-user computers and $1500 for multiuser computers. One font, either Helvetica or Times Roman, comes with SofType, in normal, bold, italic, and bold italic, in point sizes from 6 to 40. A complete extra font family is $400. SofTest also sells the PC Paintbrush Graphics Package with a mouse for $150 and the MicroTek MS-300 scanner (with integration software) for $2750.

LIST PRICE • see text

SYSTEM REQUIREMENTS • IBM PC XT/AT and compatible computers; a word processing program such as MultiMate, WordStar 2000, Samna Word III, WordPerfect, DisplayWrite 3, LEX, or Uniplex

SofTest, Inc.
555 Goffle Road
Ridgewood, NJ 07450
(201) 447-3901

Chapter 9

Output Devices

Once you've formatted a document or publication, you're ready to get it into camera-ready condition for printing. The quality of the camera-ready output depends on your requirements, such as the nature of the subject matter and the publication itself. The two main kinds of output devices are printers and typesetting machines. The latter devices produce the finest-quality output. Although printers come in three varieties—dot matrix, letter-quality, and laser—laser printers give desktop publishing its greatest potential.

PRINTERS

Most laser printers create typefaces at a resolution of about 300 dots per inch. Typesetting machines usually print at three main resolutions: about 700, 1200, and 2400 dots per inch. In contrast, the ImageWriter II dot matrix printer's resolution is about 72 dots per inch, yet other dot matrix printers have much higher resolutions—up to 960 dpi. The variety of different output devices and their respective printing resolutions has spurred discussion about what differentiates "typeset output" from "typeset quality" and "near typeset quality," and so forth.

As a publishing paradigm, we suggest that any printer that can produce proportionally spaced characters in a variety of typefaces (e.g., Times Roman and Helvetica), typestyles (e.g., italic and boldface), and sizes (e.g., 9 point and 12 point) can produce "typeset output" of "typeset quality." Even though many output devices print typeset-quality output, the type of device you choose influences whether the quality of the typesetting is suitable for your needs. Some of the low-cost dot matrix printers (such as the ImageWriter II) can even create typeset text in color, but the quality of the output is suitable only for personal publishing applications and some business publishing applications. Three-hundred-dpi laser printers produce good enough typeset text that an untrained eye usually can't perceive the difference between it and typography from a typesetting machine. Next come typesetting machines, with their 700-to-2400-dpi resolution. *Typeset quality* and *near typeset quality* are two terms with ambiguous and ill-defined meanings. You will be the best judge in determining what is typeset quality within the context of your needs.

DOT MATRIX PRINTERS

Dot matrix printers are inexpensive and use either small pins, a spray of ink, or thermal transfer to create a matrix of dots that form individual characters, hence the name *dot matrix printer.* Some of these printers print only a fixed number of different characters and may provide only one or two fonts for printing. Other dot matrix printers can be programmed to individually control each dot in each matrix. Using the computational ability of the computer, many dot matrix printers can produce graphics and low grade typeset-quality printing. Using dot matrix printers can be an inexpensive way to see what final typeset-quality output will look like. Although the dot matrix print may not be suitable for final reproduction, it is adequate for judging relative positioning of text and graphics on the page; space in the margins; length of columns; location of word breaks at the end of columns, pages, and lines; and other qualities.

The final output device can be either a page printer, such as a laser printer, or a typesetting machine. By using a dot matrix printer to produce page proofs, you may be able to have individual workstations or computer setups whose users create documents and proof them on dot matrix pages. You can then send the diskette for processing by a computer hooked up to a page printer, telecommunicate the data, or send it via a network to a page printer or typesetting machine.

If you can program your dot matrix printer to print graphics, the resolution of the graphics will determine how good the output will look. Just as the video monitors we discussed earlier have resolutions that determine the quality of what you see on the screen, dot matrix printers and page printers, as well as typesetting machines, are all based on a technology of creating characters by arranging tiny dots. Page printers and typesetting machines can position the dots much more accurately and squeeze many more dots much closer together, therefore fooling the eye into perceiving these characters as being solid and fully formed. Dot matrix printers place the dots less accurately, and the resolution of characters is not as good as a page printer's or laser printer's, but the technology has certain similarities. You can get a general idea of the relative output quality from the resolution rating, which—as with monitors—is measured as the number of dots vertically by the number of dots horizontally. For example, the Apple ImageWriter II dot matrix printer prints about 72×72 dots per inch. Sometimes the terms dots per inch and lines per inch are used to describe resolution, with dots per inch generally referring to horizontal resolution (i.e., the number of dots per linear inch) and lines per inch referring to vertical resolution.

The Apple ImageWriter II Printer

The low-cost ImageWriter II dot matrix printer produces output suitable for general correspondence, accounting, and drafts of documents that you can later have printed by a service bureau that has either a LaserWriter or another PostScript-based page printer such as a Linotype typesetter. Since the ImageWriter prints any of the fonts the Macintosh displays on the screen, you can use the ImageWriter II as a page proofing device. It features an optional $225 sheet feeder and has an optional AppleTalk board so that, like the LaserWriter, it works with more than one Macintosh at a time when it's connected to an AppleTalk network.

LIST PRICE • $599

SYSTEM REQUIREMENTS • Any RS-232-compatible computer (Macintosh, Apple II, IBM PC, TRS-80, etc.)

Apple Computer, Inc.
20525 Mariani Avenue
Cupertino, CA 95014
(408) 996-1010

Many terms come into play in discussions of the output quality of dot matrix printers. You may hear salespeople or even manufacturers use the terms *draft-quality printing, correspondence-quality printing*, or even *letter-quality printing* when they make claims about particular models or brands of dot matrix printers. These terms are nebulous. To decide what kind of resolution you need, look at actual samples of printer output.

On the following page are samples of daisywheel and draft-quality dot matrix output. This page was printed on a laser printer. Compare it with the rest of the book, which was printed on a phototypesetter.

Another point to keep in mind when selecting a dot matrix printer for a desktop publishing application is that different printer manufacturers use different internal software commands to control graphics. Find out if the software you plan to use requires a particular type of printer.

Making Money with the Techniques of
Desktop Publishing

You can use the techniques
described in this book to make
money.

* If you give lectures, you can
  make extra money by selling your
  books, pamphlets, and brochures
  at presentations. You can avoid
  the expense of paying for these
  doucments to be professionally
  prepared by doing them yourself;
  you can also make them more
  attractive, and thus more likely
  to sell, by giving them the
  professional look available with
  the techniques of desktop
  publishing.

* If you write for mathematical or
  scientific publications, you can
  make your articles more likely
  to be accepted by including your
  own formatted chemical and
  mathematical forumlas, and so
  on.

Making Money with
the Techniques of
Desktop Publishing

You can use the techniques described
in this book to make money.

* If you give lectures, you
  can make extra money by
  selling your books,
  pamphlets, and brochures at
  presentations. You can
  avoid the expense of paying
  for these documents to be
  professionally prepared by
  doing them yourself; you can
  also make them more
  attractive, and thus more
  likely to sell, by giving
  them the professional look
  available with the
  techniques of desktop
  publishing.

* If you write for
  mathematical or scientific
  publications, you can make
  your articles more likely to
  be accepted by including

When you purchase a dot matrix printer for use in a desktop publishing system, get a tractor feed instead of a friction feed printer. Some printers offer both options built in. A tractor feed mechanism uses fanfolded, continuous sheets of computer paper with a line of small holes along the sides. This paper is perforated so you can tear it into $8\frac{1}{2} \times 11$ inch sheets. A friction feed mechanism presses a piece of paper between two rubber wheels or between a rubber wheel and a platen and uses friction to advance the paper. Tractor feed is usually more desirable because the tractor mechanism grabs the holes in the side of the paper and controls the movement of the paper precisely. Friction feed sometimes lets the paper slip, especially if the rubber wheel has become hard with age or if the paper has a particularly smooth surface. Because of slippage, the printing can become distorted or compressed.

An ink jet printer is a special type of dot matrix printer that sprays superheated dots of ink onto the paper with a high-precision ink jet. Because ink jet technology squirts ink at a page rather than hammering pins onto paper, ink jet printers are much quieter than other types of dot matrix printers. If you are particularly sensitive to noise, ink jet printers may appeal to you. Perhaps the most popular ink jet printer is the small, lightweight ThinkJet from Hewlett-Packard. It prints in its Draft mode at 150 characters per second (cps). If you settle on a ThinkJet printer as a page proofing device, you should use the special bond paper that Hewlett-Packard supplies, or its equivalent, even though it is expensive. It has a special gloss finish that prevents the ink from bleeding as much as it does into regular paper, so you'll get crisper, clearer graphics. Some types of paper don't work well at all with the ThinkJet, so before you buy a big supply of paper for your ThinkJet, try to test paper samples.

LETTER-QUALITY PRINTERS

Some printers print text only in a fixed font. An example is a letter-quality printer, so called because it produces typewriter-like output that you can use for correspondence (*daisywheel printer*, *correspondence-quality printer*, *fully formed character printer*, and *impact printer* are other terms for these printers).

Daisywheel printers dominate the letter-quality realm, and they work much like typewriters. Leading producers of daisywheel printers are Qume, Diablo, and NEC. These printers have a flat, circular print wheel with thin tabs that extend from the center like the petals of a daisy, hence their name. Each tab has a character at its end. A small metal hammer in the printhead mechanism strikes the wheel as it spins around like a propeller. Daisywheel printers are generally more expensive than dot matrix printers because the timing mechanism and mechanics of the printhead are sophisticated and costly to produce.

Although letter-quality printers see the most use in offices, they do have applications in desktop publishing. Some of them can print proportionally spaced characters. Under software control, they justify the type to turn out columns of text, which can be pasted up by hand and reproduced for newsletters, periodicals, and even some books. To change typefaces, typestyles, or type sizes, however, you have to change the printer's print wheel by hand, a time-consuming process that restricts the number of typefaces you can use in your documents. If you're publishing a newsletter and using a letter-quality printer, you might want to consider having the front page and perhaps the subsequent pages designed with a typeset logo and a stylized page layout into which you can just drop the columns of text.

Another drawback of daisywheel printers is that they are noisy and relatively slow. It can take more than a minute to print a page on a daisywheel printer. Also, if you have more than one of these printers going in the same office, you often have to fit each with a sound enclosure because the noise can be deafening.

Daisywheel printers grind out characters at about 10–50 per second (cps), whereas dot matrix printers print at 50–200 cps and more. Laser printer speeds, in contrast, are measured in pages per minute (eight single-spaced pages per minute—the top speed of the Apple LaserWriter—equals approximately 440 characters per second). A major drawback of daisywheel printers is that they have only limited graphics capabilities, which means that you cannot use them to produce charts, graphs, or any other type of graphics.

LASER PRINTERS

Laser printers are the most prevalent type of page printers used in desktop publishing. They work much like advanced photocopying machines. In essence, a laser printer creates an imaginary image from the bit-map data contained in a computer's memory, and the imaginary image is reproduced in the same manner as an original image is photocopied.

How a Photocopy Machine/Laser Printer Works

With a photocopy machine, you place an original document on the glass, and a strong light in the machine reflects off the original image. The reflected image hits a light-sensitive drum, which then comes in contact with the toner and ink. Ink adheres to the drum only where the reflected image creates dark areas that become electrostatically charged. The ink then transfers to a piece of paper. A laser printer works in much the same way, except that a laser beam, rather than reflected light, creates the image on the photosensitive drum. After the laser beam "etches" the image onto the drum, the rest of the process is virtually identical to what occurs in a standard photocopy machine.

Laser printers vary considerably in price, performance, and capabilities. The latter two factors largely determine price. Although some laser printers can spit out pages much faster than others, the primary determinant of price is the printer's "duty cycle," or the number of pages the printer can produce per month. For large-volume publishing endeavors, a laser printer with a light duty cycle is a potential risk. Laser printer duty cycles typically run from 3000 to 40,000 pages per month.

Laser Printers Categorized

Laser printers for desktop publishing fall into two main groups, those that are simple print engines and those that contain an internal computer. The printers in the first category, which includes the HP LaserJet and Corona Laser Printer, are usually less expensive than the second type, which include both a computer and a print engine. The second type of printer is typified by the Apple LaserWriter and QMS printers. The most useful printers for desktop publishing are those with internal computers that use the PostScript graphics language; PostScript is rapidly becoming the standard language for page description in desktop publishing systems (for more on PostScript, see chapter 8). In the remainder of this section, we'll examine PostScript-based laser printers and those that do not use PostScript.

The "print engine" we refer to above is the mechanism that puts images onto paper. Several companies produce these so-called engines, and the majority of light-duty laser printers such as the LaserWriter build their products around the engines manufactured by three engine makers.

Canon Engine. Canon is the big name in laser printer engines. The Canon LPB-CX is behind the LaserWriter, the LaserJet, some of the QMS printers, and a laser printer Canon itself makes.

Ricoh Engine. Of the other two engine makers, Ricoh is giving Canon its stiffest competition. Digital Equipment Corporation and Burroughs have chosen the Ricoh 4080 for their laser printers.

Hitachi Engine. Canon's other competitor is Hitachi, which makes the SL-100 engine. The Qume LaserTEN is based on this engine, as is Genicom's laser printer.

Other engine makers are Fuji, Xerox, NEC, Sharp, Konishiroku, Kyocera, and Casio.

APPLE LASERWRITER

In January, 1985, Apple Computer stunned the typesetting industry and kicked off desktop publishing with the introduction of the LaserWriter printer. The LaserWriter represented a significant price/performance breakthrough in printing.

Before Apple developed this machine, the primary use of laser printers was with minicomputers and mainframes. These printers cost between $15,000 and $100,000 and more. Huge, floor-standing devices, they used laser technology to achieve speed rather than high-quality printing. Scientists, however, were already determining ways to use lasers to create high-quality printing and graphics.

History of the LaserWriter

The LaserWriter's history began at Stanford University in the late 1970s when people there were pursuing ways to make practical use of the TEX typographic software that Stanford Professor Donald Knuth, a math and computer algorithms genius, had developed. Several people involved with TEX were trying to obtain low-cost page proofs without having to go to the considerable expense of running film proofs from a phototypesetter. The idea of using a modified desktop photocopy machine as the marking engine for a laser printer emerged.

At about that time, Canon announced a low-cost laser marking engine. The TEX aficionados and other computer typography supporters immediately pressed Stanford to obtain one of these new Canon print engines to let them determine if they could create a laser printer that would work with TEX. By 1980, the people at Stanford had a working prototype of this "grandfather" of desktop laser printers.

The Stanford students who were closest to the laser printer project formed their own company, Imagen, to develop and market their own versions of the printer. During their first months of operation, the Imagen founders built a printer, similar to Apple's LaserWriter, that contained the same Canon print engine the LaserWriter would eventually use. Although their printer also employed a powerful on-board microcomputer based on the 68000 chip, it was not as powerful as Apple's system. The Imagen printers sold for about $15,000 to $25,000 each.

Apple improved on the Imagen design by increasing the speed of the internal processor, increasing the amount of ROM and RAM inside the printer, and adding a built-in page description language called PostScript.

The LaserWriter was a breakthrough product not only because it was more powerful, more intelligent, and less expensive than other laser printers, but also because it came with software, PostScript, that allowed Macintosh application programs to produce typeset output—not only on the LaserWriter, but also on the higher-resolution Linotype Company Series 100 typesetting machines.

The LaserWriter Today

Since Apple introduced the original LaserWriter, the company has developed the LaserWriter Plus, which has almost three times as many typefaces and typestyles, as well as other enhancements. Both printers feature the Canon LBP-CX laser marking engine, a 12-MHz 68000 microprocessor, and a large amount of RAM and ROM. The LaserWriter is rated at eight pages per minute maximum. The printer's powerful internal computer creates a greater variety of text and graphics at a higher resolution than any other printer in its price range. Using any computer capable of RS-232 serial communications—such as a Macintosh, IBM PC series computer, Apple II, or CP/M system—you can program the LaserWriter's computer.

The original LaserWriter came with four typefaces: Times Roman, Helvetica, Courier, and Symbol. The LaserWriter Plus contains these four and an additional seven: Avant Garde Gothic, ITC Bookman, Helvetica Narrow, New Century Schoolbook, Palatino, ITC Zapf Chancery, and ITC Zapf Dingbats.

The LaserWriter Plus has twice the internal ROM, which means about double the amount of built-in instructions. The increase in ROM allows for the additional typefaces, as well as an improved version of the PostScript language. The new version is 30 to 40 percent faster in internal processing. The increase in performance comes only in procedures that are already stored in memory. Procedures that must be interpreted from a file or string do not accelerate as noticeably. The LaserWriter Plus prints pages faster than its predecessor by allowing PostScript programs to operate while the printer is building a page image. This symbiosis shaves about six seconds off the time required to print a page. Apple has improved the efficiency of the LaserWriter's AppleTalk communications by using more of the printer's RAM as a buffer. The printer generates large characters more quickly and retains typeface definitions longer. The result is faster switching among various typefaces, typestyles, and sizes.

The LaserWriter Plus's serial communication is better in two ways: The maximum transmission speed has increased from 9600 bps to 57,600 bps, and the *DTR* (Data Terminal Ready) hardware data transmission protocol is now an alternative to the *XON/XOFF* software data transmission protocol to speed data communications.

LASERWRITER TYPEFACES AT 12-POINT SIZE

This typeface is Times Roman, which is available on the LaserWriter and LaserWriter Plus.

This typeface is Helvetica, which is available on the LaserWriter and LaserWriter Plus.

This typeface is Courier, which is available on the LaserWriter and LaserWriter Plus. The next example shows the symbols in the Symbol typeface, on the LaserWriter and LaserWriter Plus.

θωερτψυιοπ[]∴ασδφγηφκλ;϶ζξχϖβνμ,./ ΑΣΔΦΓΗϑΚΛ;϶ΖΞΧςΒΝΜ,./ ℑ♠≤‵⁰/ƒ∞≈ …∠↑∊•↔♦ ×←⊥⌡≠®™∩ ♣∂⊗♥ ∅ℜ⊃—|⊕ ℘≡≅∝″≥√∧∨⇔⇐⇑⇒⇓Ωϒ〈®∇±∈ ©™ Σ⎛⎝⎧↓✝©∏∪|⎩⎰⎱⎨⎛ 〈⟨→⎡⎛ ·⌡〉⎞|⎠x

This typeface is Avant Garde Gothic, which is available only on the LaserWriter Plus.

This typeface is ITC Bookman, which is available only on the LaserWriter Plus.

This typeface is Helvetica Narrow, which is available only on the LaserWriter Plus.

This typeface is New Century Schoolbook, which is available only on the LaserWriter Plus.

This typeface is Palatino, which is available only on the LaserWriter Plus.

This typeface is ITC Zapf Chancery, which is available only on the LaserWriter Plus. The following example shows the elements of the Zapf Dingbats typeface, which comes only with the LaserWriter Plus.

✿✂✁✃✄✆✇✈✉✌ ✝□▶❀□▼❘◆❁□□✳✴❄◉▲✣✤✳✴✳✴✴●✚❁▌❘✳❖✿◼◯❂❈❦☞✴✴✳✴✴✴ ☆★☆✳✴✳✴✳♣✦✧✰✪✫✬✭✮✯✰②❤❣❢⑤♥❧❥⑥⑦⑦②⑥②♠♣ ⑨①✳⓪⓪⑨⑨→⑧❲⑩①⑤✦→⑦↬③⑩⑨⑧⑥❩④⑤❞⑩⑦⑧↔↦➤↗↣→➔→↦➡➾➩→ ➢⑧⑥⑤➢➤↪➥❘➤⇨④③⑩→⑨❩↬⇦⇨⇨⇨⇨⇩⇨⑧③❫➳⟵⇕➵➸➳⟶➳①

The Apple LaserWriter Plus.

How to Use the Apple IIe with the Apple LaserWriter

You can use an Apple IIe computer with a Super Serial Card and a word processing program such as Apple Writer 2.0, with its internal supervisory language, WPL, to produce text and graphics on the LaserWriter. In fact, with certain utility programs, the Apple II can use more of PostScript's abilities than the Macintosh can. The Apple Writer/Apple II combination bypasses AppleTalk and allows you to go directly to the LaserWriter's RS-232C connector. It lets you use the LaserWriter's Diablo emulation mode or create your own custom routines in PostScript to control the final page. Using Apple Writer on an Apple IIe is more economical than many of the other methods of producing page graphics with a LaserWriter. The commercial utility programs for this combination include automatic form letter generators, envelope addressing, tutorials, isometric drawing routines, bumper stickers, demos, menus, business cards, and page layout formatters.

Corona LP300

The Corona Desktop Printshop.

The Corona LP300 laser printer (also known as the Desktop Printshop) comes from Corona Data Systems, maker of IBM PC-compatible standalone and multiuser computer systems. Based on the Canon LBP-CX engine, it offers 300-dpi resolution and prints graphics and text at up to eight pages per minute. The LP300 accepts letter-, legal-, and larger-size paper, fed from a paper tray holding about 100 sheets. The printer, which weighs 55 pounds and fits easily on a desktop, comes standard with 16 fonts, plus many more optionally available at about $30 each. The fonts are downloadable; that is, they can reside in memory, rather than requiring a font cartridge.

As supplied, the LP300 prints true subscripts and superscripts. The controller for the printer is installed within the computer, so it can use the memory of the computer to store graphics. With a one-megabyte RAMdisk installed, the LP300 prints a full-page bit map of graphics at 300-dpi resolution. Many word processing, spreadsheet, and database programs, as well as other personal computer applications, are compatible with the LP300, which emulates Epson printers, and it interfaces with the IBM PC and compatible computers. Toner is kept in a developer cartridge that needs replacement after approximately 3000 pages. The printer comes with an interface card that fits into a standard expansion slot, and the package also includes a software printer driver.

LIST PRICE • $2995

SYSTEM REQUIREMENTS • IBM PC or compatible, MS-DOS, 256K RAM (512K for best use of graphics)

Corona Data Systems, Inc.
275 East Hillcrest Drive
Thousand Oaks, CA 91360
(800) 621-6746
In CA (805) 495-5800

QMS Printers

QMS Lasergrafix family.

QMS Smartwriter.

One of the major manufacturers of laser printers is Quality Micro Systems (QMS) of Mobile, Alabama. The QMS line of printers is extensive, ranging from the $2000 KISS to the $30,000 Lasergrafix 2400.

Smartwriter

The Smartwriter is QMS's low-end laser printer. Based on Motorola's MC68000 microprocessor, the Smartwriter gives 300-dpi resolution. Its speed is rated at up to eight pages per minute; as with any laser printer, the number of pages per minute it produces is related to the complexity of the task: The more complex the printing operation—that is, the more characters on the page and the greater percentage of the page devoted to graphics—the fewer pages per minute.

The Smartwriter can print on both sides of letter- and legal-size pages. Its paper tray holds 17- and 21-pound stock, but for duplex printing (printing on both sides of the paper), you must hand-feed sheets of up to 34-pound paper. Manual operation is also required for envelopes, postcards, and transparencies. The toner and photoreceptor drum are both housed in a user-replaceable cartridge. The recommended duty cycle is up to 3000 pages per month. The Smartwriter's firmware includes simulations of Qume, Diablo, and Epson typefaces. The firmware also contains ANSI X3.64 graphics and seven fonts.

With 128K of RAM, the Smartwriter is programmable. You can intermix text and graphics on a page, reverse images, and draw lines and boxes. A plot/pixel mode lets you bit-map logos, signatures, and other images. An additional 78K of RAM is available for forms overlay and downloading of fonts. Optional font cartridges, each with up to 40 additional fonts in a variety of typefaces and point sizes, are available for the Smartwriter. The Smartwriter has a list price of $3850.

A stripped-down version of the SmartWriter is called the KISS (Keep It Smart and Silent). Based on the MC68000 processor, the KISS emulates Epson, Diablo, and Qume printers. This 6-page-per-minute, 300-dpi laser printer costs only $2000.

Lasergrafix 800

Listing at $7995, the Lasergrafix 800 is closer in price to Apple's LaserWriter. This printer has many of the same features as its less expensive cousin the Smartwriter. For example, it is also rated at eight pages per minute (depending on the application), and its print resolution is 300 dpi. Like the Smartwriter, it has a recommended duty cycle of 3000 pages per month.

QMS PS 800

This is the PostScript-based version of the Lasergrafix 800, and it is the first in a planned line of QMS PostScript printers. By the time this book comes out, QMS plans to offer a 24-page-per-minute PostScript printer.

Lasergrafix 1200

The next rung on the QMS ladder is the Lasergrafix 1200. As with other QMS printers, the model number indicates the number of pages per minute the printer can produce—12, in this case. The main differences between this printer and the Smartwriter and 800 are its size and duty cycle. Weighing in at nearly 300 pounds, this printer needs a floor for placement. At a list price of nearly $20,000, the 1200 begins to approach the cost of a true typesetting system, and its resolution is still only 300 dpi.

Lasergrafix 2400

QMS's top-of-the-line laser printer is the Lasergrafix 2400. Under optimum conditions, this printer can churn out pages at the rate of 24 per minute. Other than differing in print speed and price (nearly $30,000), it is similar to the 1200. At 325 pounds, it weighs 260 pounds more than the Smartwriter. In spite of the price differential between the high and low end of QMS printers, the 2400 delivers the same 300 dpi as the Smartwriter does.

LIST PRICES • KISS, $2000; Smartwriter, $3850; Lasergrafix 800, $7995; QMS-PS, $7995; Lasergrafix 1200, $19,995; Lasergrafix 2400, $29,995

Quality Micro Systems, Inc.
P.O. Box 81250
Mobile, AL 36689
(205) 633-4300

Imagen Printers

Imagen printers.

Imagen offers four lines of laser printers: ImageStations, the Imagen 8/300 Printstation, the Imagen 12/300, and the Imagen 24/300 Printstation.

ImageStations

The ImageStation group comprises three printers: The Executive, The Designer, and The Innovator. All of these printers employ laser electrophotography using dry toner. A disposable cartridge (the company recommends replacement every 300 sheets) contains 60 percent of the moving parts. Print speed is rated at eight pages per minute, and print resolution is 300 dpi. The ImageStations accommodate three sizes of paper and permit hand feeding of envelopes and paper smaller than $8\frac{1}{2} \times 11$ inches. These printers also accommodate legal-size paper and size A4 (8.3 inches × 11.7 inches).

ImageStations' dimensions are relatively compact; the combined weight of the engine and image processor is 72 pounds. The image processor is based on a 68000 microprocessor system. RAM capacities of the Executive, Designer, and Innovator respectively are 256K, 512K, and 1.5 megabytes. These machines feature an array of software, starting with Imagen's own Impress page layout and description language for typesetting and graphics. The ImageStations can emulate Diablo 630 ECS and Qume Sprint 11 letter-quality typefaces. Dot matrix emulation of Epson FX-80 and IBM 5152 printers is also available. The ImageStations have a Tektronix 4014 graphics terminal emulator and a line printer emulator. The printers provide a variety of communications protocols.

Several standard and optional fonts are available on the ImageStations. The standard ones are various subsets of Courier and dot matrix fonts. Among the optional choices are Times Roman, Helvetica, and the Pi set, a graphic arts font that ranges in size from 6 to 24 points in regular, bold, and italic; 36 point is available in regular only.

8/300 Printstation, 12/300, 24/300

Imagen's 8/300 Printstation is similar in capabilities to the ImageStations. Higher-level products from Imagen are the 12/300 and 24/300 printers. The 12 and 24 in the model designations refer to the number of pages each machine prints per minute. The resolution of all Imagen printers is the same: 300 dpi. Whereas the ImageStations and 8/300 Printstation are relatively light, the 12/300 and 24/300 weigh 152 and 365 pounds, respectively.

LIST PRICES • ImageStation series, priced according to memory; 8/300, $8950; 12/300, $15,800; 24/300 Printstation, $29,950

Imagen Corporation
2650 San Tomas Expressway
P.O. Box 58101
Santa Clara, CA 95052
(408) 986-9400

Hewlett-Packard LaserJet and LaserJet PLUS

Hewlett-Packard's LaserJet printer is one of many laser printers that use the Canon LBP-CX print engine. Perhaps the best description of this printer is "daisywheel emulator," but one that prints 10 to 40 times as fast as a daisywheel printer and can mix graphics and text.

You can get up to nine fonts for the LaserJet, in 10- or 12-pitch or proportional spacing. Two fonts are built into the printer, and the others come in plug-in cartridges that cost $225 each for three fonts, meaning you can mix up to five fonts in any one document. You can print in both "portrait" (the way a page is usually printed) and "landscape" (rotated 90 degrees) orientations.

You don't have to change the toner in this printer. Approximately every 3000 pages, you replace the electrophotographic cartridge, the housing for the toner. The printer handles letter-size paper and also has optional legal- and larger-size paper trays. You can use the printer for envelopes as well as transparencies for overhead slides.

The LaserJet prints characters at 300 dpi. It can also produce graphics to fill a fourth of the page at 300 dpi, half the page at 150 dpi, or the whole page at 75 dpi. Through its RS-232 interface, it connects to most computers with a serial port, and its HPIB (Hewlett-Packard Interface Bus, IEEE-488) interface is for connection to Hewlett-Packard computers.

A limitation of the HP LaserJet is that it cannot use the PostScript page description language. Although the LaserJet and LaserJet PLUS can produce typeset materials at a resolution of 300 dots per inch, which is the same resolution as that of Apple's LaserWriter, their fonts are available in a much more limited range of sizes and styles than what is available with the Macintosh and a LaserWriter. For this reason, the HP LaserJet is not an adequately versatile printer to take full advantage of the capabilities of the Macintosh.

The LaserJet PLUS has more memory, which lets you download fonts and graphics at a higher resolution. It can fill half the page at 300 dpi or the whole page at 150 dpi. It also accepts all the cartridges of the original LaserJet.

Used with an IBM PC series computer with a JLASER board from Tall Tree Systems of Palo Alto, California, either printer can produce full-page bit-mapped graphics. This board also sends TeX output to both printers.

LIST PRICE • LaserJet, $2995; LaserJet PLUS, $3995

SYSTEM REQUIREMENTS • see text

For information on Hewlett-Packard products, contact your local Hewlett-Packard sales and support office or nearest regional office, as listed in the White Pages of the phone book.

Qume LaserTEN

The LaserTEN.

Qume Corporation has been known mainly for daisywheel printers. In November 1985, the company released a laser printer based on the Hitachi engine. At a speed of ten pages per minute, the 300-dpi LaserTEN printer is jointly manufactured by Hitachi and Qume's Taiwan facility. The compact LaserTEN emulates Qume's entire line of daisywheel printers, plus many daisywheel and dot matrix printers from other manufacturers. It offers fonts in sizes from 7 to 24 points and can print up to 19 fonts per page. The LaserTEN downloads fonts into its user memory of either 128 or 512K. It features replaceable modular toner, developer, and drum vs. the one cartridge in which all of these elements are stored in other printers and that all must be replaced when only one runs out or malfunctions.

The printer addresses individual dots in its Graphics mode and has a front-load 250-page input paper tray and face-down collated output, as opposed to the face-up output of most competitors in its price range. You can design forms and graphics on the host computer and then store them in the LaserTEN's memory; an overlay feature permits printing text and then overlaying the forms and graphics simultaneously on the page.

Two fonts are built in; the rest are supplied in font cartridges, as many as three of which can be used simultaneously. A manual feed slot permits printing on transparencies, envelopes, and odd-size paper. The LaserTEN's duty cycle is 5000 pages per month; the drum lasts up to 30,000 pages, and the toner cartridge is replaced once every 5000 pages.

LIST PRICE • 128K model, $2795; 512K model, $3395

SYSTEM REQUIREMENTS • IBM PC XT/AT or compatible, IBM PC network with DOS 3.1; ITT XTRA/XP

Qume Corporation
2350 Qume Drive
San Jose, CA 95131
(408) 942-4000

Talaris 810 Laser Printer

The Talaris 810 Laser Printer from Talaris Systems has three emulation modes (Epson FX-80, Diablo 630 ECS, and Qume Sprint) that provide compatibility with a wide range of software. It contains 12 standard built-in fonts. In addition, Talaris offers optional font cartridges with up to 16 fonts from Talaris's library of more than 800 computerized fonts. The T810 prints proportionally formatted text with the MASS-11 word processing package, and it lets you format files with the TEX formatting language and use the Talaris DVI processor to drive the T810. The ANSI 3.64 language and Epson FX-80 emulation give the printer its graphics capabilities. The print speed is eight pages per minute, and the resolution is 300 dpi. The 18-inch-wide by 12-inch-high by 16-inch-deep T810 weighs 75 pounds.

LIST PRICE • $3850

SYSTEM REQUIREMENTS • any computer with a Centronics parallel or an RS-232C serial interface

Talaris Systems, Inc.
P.O. Box 261580
San Diego, CA 92126
(619) 587-0787

Xerox 4045

Xerox, the company whose trademark has all but become synonymous with photo-copying, makes a huge array of large, floor-standing laser printers, one of which spews out pages at a rate of 120 per minute at 300 dpi. These devices are beyond the scope of desktop publishing, but Xerox does make a desktop laser printer, the 4045, that doubles as a copying machine. It prints full-page bit-mapped graphics at 150 dpi and 300 dpi "nominal" (text and 5 × 7 inch graphics) at about ten pages per minute. An unusual feature is an optional cassette tray that feeds as many as 50 envelopes through the printer. The 4045 can handle more paper at once than older laser printers can: 250 letter- or legal-size sheets on the input side (optional paper cassettes offer other sizes) and 100 sheets in the output tray. An optional sequencer collates up to 50 sheets of paper.

With extra memory, the 4045 can have up to 128 fonts on line at once, including those in font cartridges—it can store the contents of as many as four cartridges simultaneously. Its monthly volume is 2000-10,000 pages, compared with the 3500 of other inexpensive laser printers.

The base price of the printer is $4995; the copier option adds $400 to the price. With a $1395 interface sharing device (ISD), four computers can share the printer. To connect it to personal computers, you need a $250 RS-232 interface. Other options, such as extra memory and IBM 3278 dot matrix printer emulation, increase the price further. The 4045 works with many software packages.

LIST PRICE • Depends on configuration; see text

SYSTEM REQUIREMENTS • Personal computer interface

Xerox Corporation
101 El Segundo Blvd.
El Segundo, CA 90245

TYPESETTING MACHINES

Typesetting machines produce top-quality output by printing at very high resolutions on glossy photographic paper. They are far and away the most expensive components of an electronic publishing system; most machines cost more than $20,000. Although lower-cost page printers may suffice for many publishing jobs, most book and magazine publishers, and many businesses, require high-quality output for some, if not all, of their work.

Typesetting machines are raster image (producing images with many tiny dots) output devices that print directly on film at resolutions that are generally in the range of 1000 to 2500 dots per inch. A few systems exceed 5000 dots per inch in resolution, however. The typesetting machines that are most important to desktop publishers are the Series 100 Linotron 100 and Linotronic 300 from Linotype Company, a division of industrial conglomerate Allied-Signal. The advantage of these two typesetting machines is that they can be equipped with a PostScript RIP (raster image processor) that prints PostScript documents at the fine resolution that only a true phototypesetting machine can manage. PostScript compatibility is doubly important because lower-cost PostScript-based printers such as the LaserWriter can serve as page printers to produce inexpensive page proofs. The ability to produce low-cost page proofs means you can eliminate the expensive process of producing them on the phototypesetter, a process over which you have much less control. This savings alone can, over time, justify the purchase of a desktop publishing system.

If you want to be able to use a typesetting machine for final output and are using your page printer only as a proofing device, you should make sure that you get an integrated software and hardware setup that allows you to use both page printers and typesetting machines. With some software, you may be able to create typeset graphics only on a specific laser printer—the HP LaserJet, for example—with a specific font cartridge or, in some cases, even a custom font cartridge that comes with the software. This type of software may not be able to communicate with a typesetting device to produce higher-quality output.

Using a page printer that is compatible with the PostScript page description language, which is emerging as the standard for page printers and typesetting machines in desktop publishing applications, ensures your ability to communicate that same PostScript page description to a PostScript-compatible typesetting device to obtain higher-quality typeset output on the typesetting machine. Laser printers that are not PostScript-compatible may be excellent for a specific application, but they are not as flexible as the PostScript-compatible page printers.

Linotype Typesetting Machines

The Series 100 Linotronic 300.

The Series 100 Linotron 100 is the most economical PostScript-based typesetter. It uses a 68000 microprocessor and a helium neon laser to print at resolutions of up to 1270 dots per inch on paper or film up to 12 inches wide.

The Linotron 202, which is not PostScript-compatible, prints type in sizes from 1 point to 72 points in $\frac{1}{2}$-point increments and in 72–96 points in 1-point increments on paper or film up to 8 inches wide in the standard model, and up to 12 inches wide in the Linotron 202/W. The Linotron 202 printer prints at two resolutions: 975 scan lines per inch in the Standard mode and 1950 scan lines per inch in the High Resolution mode. This typesetting machine works with numerous software packages on many personal computers, including the IBM PC series, as long as they are compatible with Linotype's Cora typesetting code.

The Series 100 Linotronic 300, the highest-quality Linotype typesetting machine, is also the highest-quality PostScript output device available at the time of this writing. This typesetting machine prints type in sizes from 1 point to 186 points in $\frac{1}{10}$-point increments on paper or film up to 12 inches wide. It uses a 68000 microprocessor and a helium neon laser to create raster images at resolutions up to 2540 pixels per inch.

LIST PRICE • Linotron 100, $29,950; Linotron 202, $38,000-$59,000, depending on options; Linotronic 300, $57,900

Linotype Company
A Division of Allied-Signal
425 Oser Avenue
Hauppauge, NY 11788
(516) 434-2000

Alphatype

Alphatype CRS 9900.

Alphatype Corporation of Niles, Illinois, makes the Alphatype CRS 9900 and CRS 4900 phototypesetters and the accompanying Work Station II software/hardware package for the IBM PC series computers. The $60,000 CRS 9900 prints at resolutions up to 3858 dpi, at speeds of up to 10,000 characters per minute. Alphatype's CRS 4900 costs about $25,000 and produces up to 5300-dpi resolution at speeds of about 5000 characters per minute, or half the speed of the CRS 9900.

The Work Station II software/hardware package for the IBM PC lists for $1900 and includes a new keyboard with color-coded command keys and a special graphics adapter that displays composition codes and typesetting characters on the PC's monitor. The Work Station II software, which you can purchase separately for $960, turns an IBM PC series computer into an input and editing terminal that is compatible with Alphatype's composition system. Note that you must purchase the composition system, and it costs more than $50,000 with software and font libraries. In addition, a full-page video display called SoftVu is available for about $12,500; it features a $9\frac{1}{2}$-inch by $12\frac{1}{4}$-inch display area that shows pages as they will appear when printed.

LIST PRICE • see text

SYSTEM REQUIREMENTS • IBM PC series or compatible computer, 256K RAM, 10-megabyte or larger-capacity hard disk drive

Alphatype Corporation
7711 North Merrimac Avenue
Niles, IL 60648
(312) 965-8800

Autologic

Autologic's phototypesetters work with many personal computers, minicomputers, and mainframes through parallel and serial ports, paper tape, modems, and magnetic tape. These typesetters offer resolutions from 723 dpi to 3616 dpi. Fonts range in size from 4 to 160 points, in $\frac{1}{10}$-point steps. Many of the phototypesetters also include an optional laser printer, for 300-dpi proofing. The typesetters print on plain paper, resin coated (RC) photographic paper, film, and paper and metal plates. Many large newspapers and magazines use Autologic typesetters, often with a custom front end, a system of terminals that translate user input into the typesetting commands the phototypesetter requires.

Autologic's new APS-55 family of typesetters are called Page Image Processors. They integrate text and graphics in the same output, something that, until recently, phototypesetters could not do. The APS-55/200 is strictly a laser printer, using the Canon LBP-CX engine, and costs $18,500. The APS-55/300 is also a laser printer, with a resolution of up to 723 dpi and a price tag from $26,000 to $37,000 depending on the laser printer engine. The APS-55/400 prints on plain paper, RC paper, film, or plate, with resolutions up to 1000 dpi, and costs from $28,500 to $72,500. The APS-55/500 handles prescreened, digitized tone art and line art with a resolution up to 1000 dpi and starts at $42,500. The top-of-the-line APS-55/800 creates an image of a 16 × 22 inch 1000-dpi newspaper page in 70 seconds and is capable of up to 2000 dpi. A Graphics Accelerator provides special effects, including screened and reversed images, mirrored images, and character rotation. The 800 starts at $57,500.

The APS-Micro 5 machines print at 1000 lines per minute, up to 300 feet of film at a time. They print composed full-page layouts, at high resolutions, up to 3616 dpi in the $62,000 APS-Micro 5/45. Models 57 and 70 cost $63,000 and $64,000 respectively.

The APS-55 Bit Blaster is a page image processor coupled with a laser printer to produce proofs that are an exact duplicate of the typeset output. One model, costing $32,000, shares the typesetter's electronics by placing the page image processor in the typesetter; another model, costing $52,000, has its own electronics and can be used with and independently of any other APS-55 model. The Bit Blaster uses the Xerox Xp-12 engine.

LIST PRICE • see text

SYSTEM REQUIREMENTS • ICL (Input Command Language)

Autologic, Inc.
1050 Rancho Conejo Blvd.
Newbury Park, CA 91320
(805) 498-9611

Chapter 10

Input Devices

Input devices allow you to enter text and graphics into your computer. Keyboards, mice, graphics tablets, and even modems are all types of input devices. The discussion below involves special types of input devices known as scanners that allow your computer to see text and graphics and store the information for later use. We look at two basic types of scanners, optical character readers, which allow your computer to read text, and graphics digitizers, which let it capture and store graphic images. Note that although graphics digitizers can capture text as an image of characters, they cannot store the text as text files for use by other software such as word processing and database programs.

OCRS—OPTICAL CHARACTER READERS

Optical character readers, commonly called OCRs, provide a way to automatically transform typewritten and printed data into computer data files. OCRs can scan text and recognize characters such as letters, numbers, and punctuation marks, and convert them into a form that can be read by or transmitted to a computer. OCRs will be a tremendously valuable tool in the transition from the paper office to the electronic office, since much valuable information is stored on paper. OCRs let typewriters become low-cost data entry terminals, since OCRs can read the typewritten pages and convert them into computer files.

OCRs fall into two main categories, those that can read only a limited number of monospaced fonts and those that can read a wide variety of typefaces, typestyles, and type sizes, including proportionally spaced type. The first category of OCRs, those that can read only a limited number of fonts, are typified by desktop OCRs manufactured by Dest. Dest's OCRs sell in the $10,000-and-under range but have limited applications since they can read monospaced typewriter fonts but cannot read typefaces from books, magazines, newspapers, etc. The second category of OCRs, those that can read a wide variety of typefaces and styles, are typified by the Kurzweil Data Entry Machine. The Kurzweil OCR costs tens of thousands of dollars, but it can read virtually any typeface because you can program it to learn new typefaces. With a Kurzweil Data Entry Machine, you can read periodicals, telephone directories, books, and other data sources directly into a computer file at a speed of about a page per minute, depending on the print density. The ability to read information directly into a database can be a valuable tool for gathering information and data for publication. Although the Kurzweil OCRs are quite expensive now, look for their level of ability to be available at a lower cost over the next few years from Dest, Apple, IBM, and other companies.

Several companies now produce OCRs that double as graphics

digitizers. These dual-purpose devices recognize text and save it as a text file and also capture images for use as graphics or illustrations. Two devices that typify this type of hybrid scanner are the IOC Reader from Intelligent Optics Corporation of Hackensack, New Jersey, and the CompuScan PCS from CompuScan of Fairfield, New Jersey.

Formatting is not strictly a matter of using page-layout software to arrange text and graphics. You can also incorporate line and continuous-tone art into your documents by using input devices such as scanners and digitizers.

A digitizer transforms an image into digital information you can store in a computer's memory or in a mass storage device. You can then transfer that information to a bit-mapped screen, where you can edit it repeatedly, or to a high-resolution output device such as a laser printer.

DIGITIZERS, OR SCANNERS

You can use scanners to capture graphics and other artwork for use as illustrations, logos, etc., or you can scan other visual data for incorporation into a database. Scanners can create visual databases, an application well suited for storage on compact disks (CDs). Large libraries of scanned images for use in desktop publishing will almost certainly be sold on CDs within the next few years.

Video Digitizers

Video digitizers use the standard video signal produced by, typically, a video camera, but also by a VCR or even a television set that can emit a video signal. A video digitizer scans an image and turns each of its elements into a binary number. On a screen, each number translates into a different light intensity, known as *gray scale*. On a printer, the numbers translate into dot patterns called *pseudo halftones*. From a distance, these patterns look like continuous gray tones. Examples of video digitizers are Micro-Imager, MacVision, and MicronEye.

Micro-Imager

Micro-Imager, a video digitizer, takes input from a video camera, videocassette recorder, or videodisc. Color filters turn color images into black and white. The system comes with software for editing images and includes various patterning effects you can make. If unwanted features appear during scanning, you can clear them from any part of the image, and you can also print only the part of an image you have surrounded with a selection rectangle.

If you don't have a video camera (almost any camera will do, with the better-quality ones producing better pictures), you can get a Panasonic black-and-white camera for $175 and a black-and-white monitor for $150 from Servidyne.

LIST PRICE • $350

SYSTEM REQUIREMENTS • video camera, video monitor

Servidyne Systems, Inc.
1735 Defoor Place NW
Box 93846
Atlanta, GA 30377
(404) 352-2050

MacVision

The MacVision package consists of a box with processing electronics and a disk with software that copies digitized images into Macintosh documents. A cable runs from the box to the Mac's serial port, and another attaches to any video source, including a video camera. The box has controls for contrast and brightness. It takes about 20 seconds to scan a complete image to fill the entire screen, or 7 seconds to scan the image into a small window. You can copy the window into the Clipboard of the Macintosh desktop or from an application, and then you can paste it into the Scrapbook or the application. If you fill the entire screen, you must save it as a MacPaint document and call it up again for editing.

If you install the software on an application disk, you can then use MacVision while running the application and copy an image directly into the file with which you are working. Since the image is constantly updated until you stop the scan, you can adjust the focus on the camera and the contrast and brightness on the controller box until everything is just the way you want it.

By moving the camera during the scanning, you can distort or multiply the image for special effects. When you have captured an image to your satisfaction, you can print it immediately on an ImageWriter or LaserWriter, or save it on a disk.

LIST PRICE • $399

SYSTEM REQUIREMENTS • Macintosh, printer

Koala Technologies Corporation
3100 Patrick Henry Drive
Santa Clara, CA 95052
(408) 986-8866

Magic

Magic does not use the Macintosh's familiar pull-down menus; instead, all commands are on the screen, where you control everything, since Magic has no hardware controls. Magic displays 2.5 images per second, allowing easy on-screen fine-tuning of the images. Under software control, images can appear in black and white or in shades of gray. You have a choice of 38 patterns to use in the gray areas, and you can mix them any way you want.

To change the size of an image, you measure it with on-screen rulers and instantly invert or reverse it. If the image comes from a source other than a camera, you can also use a panning feature to digitize whatever part of the image you want (the Mac's screen does not accommodate an entire video image). Printers that reproduce Magic's images are the ImageWriter, the LaserWriter, and the LaserJet.

LIST PRICE • $399 ($150 for black-and-white video camera)

SYSTEM REQUIREMENTS • Macintosh, printer

New Image Technologies, Inc.
10300 Greenbelt Road, #104
Seabrook, MD 20706
(301) 464-3100

MicronEye

This complete digitizing package includes digitizer, software, IS32 OpticRam (the camera), lens, and tripod in a 2.5-pound package. You focus with the camera and set the exposure on the camera or through software.

MicronEye gives you three kinds of pictures: an instant single exposure, gray scale, or pseudogray scale; you can take several pictures and combine them into one shaded image. With the software, you can instantly change black to white and white to black. Only half the screen at a time, top or bottom, can be filled at a time. To fill the whole screen, you have to take two pictures and paste them together.

LIST PRICE • $395

SYSTEM REQUIREMENTS • Macintosh

Micron Technology, Inc.
Systems Group
1447 Tyrell Lane
Boise, ID 83706
(208) 386-3800

Optical Digitizers

An optical digitizer scans flat art with a tiny light beam and converts the amount of reflectance into digital information similar to that produced by a video digitizer. The number translation process for displaying the image on a bit-mapped screen and printing it on a printer are the same for optical digitizers as for video digitizers. ThunderScan and Scan 300 are optical digitizers.

ThunderScan

The ThunderScan optical digitizer scans flat images with a pinpoint beam of light. At each point the beam touches the scanned object, it produces a dot, which is assigned a gray value ranging from 1 to 32. The digitizer stores these dots and then reproduces them on the screen or on the printer in patterns whose densities are determined by the gray-scale values.

The scanning mechanism replaces the ribbon cartridge of an ImageWriter printer. While the printer moves a sheet of paper in minute increments along the platen, the scanner moves back and forth. To digitize a three-dimensional object, you first have to take a photograph of it. Scanning an entire $8\frac{1}{2} \times 11$ inch page can take as long as 20 minutes. You can reduce or enlarge the image during the scanning process and can specify ahead of time how much of the image is to be scanned.

Once you've captured the image, you can change its contrast, brightness, and gray-scale patterns. You can also edit all or part of the image, which you can save as a ThunderScan or MacPaint document.

LIST PRICE • $229

SYSTEM REQUIREMENTS • Macintosh, ImageWriter

ThunderWare, Inc.
21 Orinda Way
Orinda, CA 94563
(415) 254-6581

Scan 300

Scan 300 from Abaton Technology Corporation is an optical scanner that digitizes drawings, photographs, and graphics into either a Macintosh or an IBM PC. The 300-dpi resolution of this optical digitizer is the same as that of many laser printers, including the LaserWriter, HP LaserJet, and Corona LP-300.

Scaling, brightness, and contrast are adjustable. The Scan 300 works in conjunction with page makeup software—including PageMaker, ReadySetGo, and Macpublisher—that is available for personal computers.

It accepts line art and turns continuous-tone photographs into halftones. In the halftone mode, this digitizer produces pictures with up to 64 levels of gray, using 12 built-in halftone screens. It also has a "mixed mode" for scanning pages that combine line art and continuous-tone art.

With base dimensions of 15 by 17 inches and a weight of 18 pounds, the Scan 300 fits on top of a desk. It accepts $8\frac{1}{2} \times 11$-inch-wide by any length documents and can reduce input in both x and y directions from 95 percent to 25 percent in 5 percent decrements.

LIST PRICE • $2495

SYSTEM REQUIREMENTS • Macintosh or IBM PC and laser printer

Abaton Technology Corporation
1526 Coverfield Boulevard
Santa Monica, CA 90404
(818) 905-9399

MS-200 and MS-300 Image Scanners

These two scanners from Microtek Lab, Inc., scan text, drawings, graphics, pictures, or mixed images. The lower-priced MS-200 offers a resolution of 200 dpi, thus the model number 200. It has three modes: Test mode, including line art; Halftone mode, for photos and continuous-tone art; and Mixed mode. The scanner uses software—EyeStar for the IBM PC and VersaScan for the Macintosh—to control scaling, brightness, and contrast. You can get either software package with the scanner, depending on which computer you are using. The scanner is software-compatible with page makeup programs. The scanning speed is rated at 20 seconds for an $8\frac{1}{2} \times 11$ inch sheet. These scanners use a parallel interface (a serial interface is optional). Documents and art feed manually into the MS-200.

The more expensive MS-300 is similar to the MS-200, the main difference being that it gives you the option of 200- or 300-dpi resolution. It also weighs two pounds more than the MS-200—18 pounds as opposed to 16.

LIST PRICES • MS-200, $1700 with choice of EyeStar or VersaScan software; MS-300, $2300

SYSTEM REQUIREMENTS • Macintosh or IBM PC

Microtek Lab, Inc.
17221 South Western Avenue
Gardena, CA 90247
(213) 538-5369

Spectrafax Scanner

The Spectrafax scanner is the first color scanner for the Macintosh computer. It includes Macintosh color graphics editing software that the ImageWriter II uses to print Macintosh text and graphics in color. The product digitizes black-and-white or color photographs and art into a Macintosh 512K or Macintosh Plus with full Macintosh resolution. You can use the software that comes with the scanner, Colormate from SoftStyle, to touch up digitized color images; add color to MacPaint, MacWrite, and Microsoft Word text and graphics; and print the document on the ImageWriter II in up to eight colors. The package also includes PaintScan software, also from SoftStyle, with which you scan black-and-white images directly into MacPaint.

The scanner/Macintosh/Colormate combination lets you produce high-quality black-and-white illustrations and low-cost "separations" for color printing and limited-run color newsletters—all useful applications for desktop publishing. Other uses include color "comps" (to show an ad agency how an ad will look), color illustrations, and color overhead transparencies for presentations.

LIST PRICE • $3995

SYSTEM REQUIREMENTS • Macintosh 512K or Macintosh Plus, hard disk drive recommended

Spectrafax Corporation
2000 Palm Street South
Naples, FL 33962
(813) 775-2737

Afterword

THE POTENTIAL OF DESKTOP PUBLISHING

Desktop publishing is here now, and it promises to become the focus of more and more companies and individuals. With the Macintosh and LaserWriter, Apple, for example, is producing everything except all the necessary software to set up a complete desktop publishing system. Apple has confirmed its plans to promote this area of computer technology, and scores of other firms are actively selling and developing the tools desktop publishers want and need. Already, you have an array of products from which to choose, and more advanced tools are constantly appearing. As these tools become more technologically sophisticated and demand for them grows, look for prices to drop and for even more choices than you have today to emerge.

In spite of the growth of the industry and the technology, though, its applications are still in their infancy. Desktop publishing presents tremendous opportunities for enterprising people in nearly all areas of publishing—witness some of the success stories we have outlined throughout the pages of this book. It is because of these opportunities that we have written *Desktop Publishing*. We hope that all current and would-be desktop publishers have benefitted from and been inspired by this book.

Appendix A

Money-Making Ideas

_____
_____
_____
_____
_____
_____
_____
_____

If you don't already have a desktop publishing system for a specific purpose, you may be setting one up for something specific, such as publishing a newsletter. In such cases, you already have a good idea of how your hope to use your system to make money.

In this section of the book, we give you some money-making suggestions that may not yet have occurred to you. If you're thinking about buying desktop publishing tools, or if you already have some of the components—a Macintosh, for example—of a system, you may find the impetus in these pages to buy a desktop publishing system or to convert an infrequently used personal computer into a cash generator.

- **Newsletters.** Since we believe that desktop publishing will be a boon to newsletter publishers, we've devoted an entire chapter to the subject (see chapter 4).

- **The Great American Novel.** With a great deal of persistence, you might be able to print your own literature, distribute it, market it, and make money; and you'd be in good company. Mark Twain and Ernest Hemingway, for example, self-published early works before they hit the big time. More probably, small literary journals can set up an inexpensive desktop publishing system and, over time, save enough money in typesetting costs to pay off the system and turn a small profit.

- **Greetings.** A quick look around a gift or greeting card shop indicates that Americans have an insatiable appetite for greeting cards, of every variety: cute, cloying, funny, earnest, soft pornographic, derisory—you name it. With a desktop publishing system, a greeting card shop can make up personalized cards for customers on the spot. The shop either plugs a customer's information into a predesigned card format or makes up a request from scratch, charging proportionally more for the latter type. How about starting your own greeting card operation? You can market your operation through relatively cheap ads in regional and community publications. The computer, with appropriate software, can double as a bookkeeping system.

- **Attention, Shoppers.** A desktop publishing system is ideal for a low-print-quality shopper or advertiser with a fast turnaround. Shopper publishers can write their stories, make up their ads, and do their books on the system.

- **Service, Please.** A desktop publishing system can be the basis for many kinds of service bureaus, including:
  - Resume writing and printing
  - Thesis and dissertation printing
  - Flier printing
  - Overheads and transparencies printing
  - Personalized calendar printing

- **BMOC.** That's Big Mac On Campus. In spite of the efforts of Apple and other computer makers to get a computer into every dorm room, a recent study indicates that the majority of college student do not even use computers. Enterprising students (from the Business School, of course) can set up on-campus service bureaus, selling their fellow students everything from typeset resumes to beautiful papers. A good-looking paper might cause a prof to overlook spelling mistakes, factual errors, and other such irritants. With the price of tuition and associated expenses skyrocketing, a publishing system might not add hugely to college costs. Instead of a couple of chemistry textbooks, buy a laser printer.

- **Instant-Print Shops.** Anyone who's owned or worked in one of these establishments has seen horrifying examples of what customers bring in for "camera-ready" copy—fliers typed on a 1907 Underwood with several cracked letters and a ribbon that hasn't been changed since 1908, for example. Complementing this visual delight, often, are typos, missing words, grammatical nightmares, and incomprehensible prose. An instant-print shop set up to do desktop publishing can provide laser printing for cost-conscious customers and supply the output of typesetting machines such as the Allied Linotronic for customers with larger budgets. For a surcharge, it can clean the document up in the process. It can then print or duplicate the documents thus prepared. Like any other businessperson using desktop publishing, a print shop owner can use the same system to keep the books.

Desktop Service

An outfit in Palo Alto, California, demonstrates the potential of desktop publishing. Eight months after Vince Dorn started LaserWrite in mid-1985, the incorporated company had eight Macintoshes, two LaserWriters, and "an IBM clone." Three graphic designers, three technical writers, and a marketing consultant ran LaserWrite's operations. Dorn said the business approximately doubled revenues each month. LaserWrite was self-financed, Dorn noted, but the company was in the midst of discussions with venture capitalists, the goal of which was to start a chain of stores. Dorn expected to have 20-50 stores nationwide by the end of 1987. LaserWrite was also working on PostScript applications and was trying to involve Apple in a VAR (value added reseller) arrangement.

Currently, LaserWrite offers complete word processing, technical writing, training, and consulting services. Dorn says his firm can handle everything from concept to mailroom services, the latter via Federal Express ZAP Mail. LaserWrite even refills LaserWriter toner cartridges and produces custom cartridges with colored inks.

"Desktop publishing is more quality than quantity," according to Dorn. He says LaserWrite does offer copying services, but he refers to copying as a "quantity" task. He also indicates that many of his customers are switching from IBM PCs to Macintoshes for business publishing.

- **Copy Shops.** Copy shops can provide access to laser printers such as the Apple LaserWriter for a fee, allowing customers to prepare typeset documents for photocopying. Such a service can increase the shop's business and help it compete successfully with other copy shops, as well as instant-print shops.

- **Noncomputer Menus.** It's an immutable law of the universe that every menu, no matter how classy the restaurant, no matter how slick the menu, has at least one typo in it. Furthermore, some menus look like they came from the print shop that did the job for the guy with the Underwood with the bad ribbon. You can start a service that prints nothing but menus. You have to be a literate gastronome for this one, however.

- **Small-Town Desktop Publishing.** Virtually every municipal organization in a small town, from the Chamber of Commerce to the County Clerk, can use a desktop publishing system, which the town can chip in to buy in lieu of paying for a lawyer to lobby to have the next Summer Olympics held there. (See "Desktop Newspaper Publishing" in chapter 2 for examples of how small-town newspaper publishers are using the Macintosh to make graphics for their papers.)

- **Typesetting.** Use your desktop publishing system to set type. Print your own fliers to start advertising.

- **Pamphleteering.** If you live in a politically active area, all the polemicists in the neighborhood can keep you in business.

- **Lectures.** If you give lectures, you can make extra money by selling your books, pamphlets, and brochures at presentations. You can avoid the expense of paying for professional preparation of these documents by doing them yourself; you can also make them more attractive, and thus more likely to sell, by giving them the professional look available with the techniques of desktop publishing.

- **Scholarly Publications.** If you write for mathematical or scientific publications, you can increase your chances of having your articles accepted by including your own formatted chemical and mathematical formulas, and so on.

- **Layout and Design.** A layout and design shop can offer services to users of word processing software and telecommunicating microcomputers. Clients can send text via modem, and the layout and design specialists, using page layout software, can reduce the amount of time and effort that goes into the creation of good-looking documents.

Appendix B

Resource Guide

Adapter cards

Product: Enhanced Graphics Adapter Card
Company: IBM
Address: 1133 Westchester Avenue
White Plains, NY 10604
Phone: (914) 765-1900
List Price: $199–$524
System Requirements: IBM PC-series computer or compatible
Comments: Lets the PC approximate the graphics abilities of the Macintosh.

Advertising software

Product: Ad Scheduling
Company: Publisher Control Systems, Inc.
Address: 223 West 5th Street
Shawano, WI 54166
Phone: (715) 526-6547
List Price: Contact company for price
System Requirements: IBM PC series computer or compatible
Comments: Creates a run sheet for publication day. Develops analysis reports specific to sections of each publication.

Product: Advertising/Billing System
Company: WPL Associates, Inc.
Address: 1105-F Spring Street
Silver Spring, MD 20910
Phone: (301) 589-8588
List Price: Contact company for price
System Requirements: IBM PC series computer or compatible, CP/M-compatible computer
Comments: Manages accounting and production of advertising.

Product: The Advertising Manager
Company: Cross and Chartoff Associates
Address: 73 Tremont Street
Boston, MA 02108
Phone: (617) 742-1100
List Price: $2500
System Requirements: IBM PC series computer or compatible, 256K RAM
Comments: Manages billing of advertising space for periodical publishers.

Product: PTMS (Publisher's Total Management System)
Company: Flint Hills Software

Address: 725 Shelburn Place, P.O. Box 3791
Lawrence, KS 66046
Phone: (913) 841-4503
List Price: $250
System Requirements: IBM PC series computer or compatible, CP/M-compatible computer, 128K RAM
Comments: Tracks ads and production costs. Monitors advertising sales performance.

Bibliographic software

Product: Personal Bibliographic Software Products
Company: Personal Bibliographic Software, Inc.
Address: P.O. Box 4250
Ann Arbor, MI 48106
Phone: (313) 996-1580
List Price: Professional Bibliographic System, $295; BiblioLink BRS, $195; Index Plus, $95
System Requirements: IBM PC, XT, AT; Macintosh; or OCLC M300 Workstation

Budgeting software

Product: Magazine Budget Model
Company: Sheridan Software
Address: 1031 Sheridan Road
Evanston, IL 60202
Phone: (312) 869-1965
List Price: $495
System Requirements: IBM PC series computer or compatible, 64K RAM
Comments: Projects circulation, cash flow, and profit and loss of magazine for 72 months. Reports include subscriptions by source, circulation, and revenue summary. Analyzes 22 factors using what-if strategy.

Clip art software

Product: ClickArt Personal Publisher
Company: T/Maker Company
Address: 2115 Landings Drive
Mountain View, CA 94043
Phone: (415) 962-0195
List Price: $185; laser fonts and drives for LaserWriter or LaserJet, $150; image packages, $49.95 each
System Requirements: IBM PC, XT, AT, or compatible computer; 384K RAM; IBM color card or Hercules Graphics Card; two disk drives

Communications software

Product: Dow Jones Spreadsheet Link
Company: Dow Jones & Company, Inc.
Address: P.O. Box 300
  Princeton, NJ 08540
Phone: (800) 257-5114, (609) 452-1511
List Price: $99–$249
System Requirements: IBM PC, XT; Apple II, II Plus, IIe, or Macintosh
Comments: Gathers financial data from various Dow Jones News/Retrieval
  databases.

Product: MacLink
Company: Dataviz, Inc.
Address: 16 Winfield Street
  Norwalk, CT 06855
Phone: (203) 866-4944
List Price: $125; eight-foot interface cable, $30
System Requirements: Macintosh and IBM PC series computer, interface
  cable or modems

Product: MacTerminal
Company: Apple Computer, Inc.
Address: 20525 Mariani Avenue
  Cupertino, CA 95014
Phone: (408) 996-1010
List Price: $99
System Requirements: Macintosh

Product: MicroPhone
Company: Software Ventures Corporation
Address: 2907 Claremont Avenue, Suite 220
  Berkeley, CA 94705
Phone: (415) 644-3232
List Price: $74.95
System Requirements: Macintosh

Product: Pro-Search
Company: Menlo Corporation
Address: 4633 Old Ironsides Drive, Suite 400
  Santa Clara, CA 95054
Phone: (408) 986-0200
List Price: $495

System Requirements: IBM PC-series computer or compatible
Comments: Accesses Dialog 2, BRS, and on-line services. Lets you download search results, log on and log off automatically, and upload search strategies.

Product: Smartcom II
Company: Hayes Microcomputer Products
Address: P.O. Box 105203
Atlanta, GA 30348
Phone: (404) 449-8791
List Price: $149
System Requirements: Macintosh

Product: Straight Talk
Company: Dow Jones Software
Address: P.O. Box 300
Princeton, NJ 08540
Phone: (609) 452-2000
List Price: $95
System Requirements: Macintosh, modem; Apple ImageWriter or LaserWriter (optional)

Computer systems

Product: Apple IIe 128K System, Apple IIc
Company: Apple Computer, Inc.
Address: 20525 Mariani Avenue
Cupertino, CA 95014
Phone: (408) 996-1010
List Price: Apple IIe, $945; Apple IIc, $940

Product: Hewlett-Packard Vectra
Company: Hewlett-Packard Company
Address: Personal Office Computer Division
974 East Arques
Box 486
Sunnyvale, CA 94086
Phone: (800) FOR-HPPC
List Price: Contact company for price
Comments: IBM PC AT compatible, with improved performance at somewhat lower price

Product: IBM Personal Computer
Company: IBM
Address: 1133 Westchester Avenue
White Plains, NY 10604

Phone: (914) 765-1900
List Price: $1390–$2295

Product: IBM Personal Computer AT
Company: IBM
Address: 1133 Westchester Avenue
    White Plains, NY 10604
Phone: (914) 765-1900
List Price: $3995–$5795

Product: IBM Personal Computer XT
Company: IBM
Address: 1133 Westchester Avenue
    White Plains, NY 10604
Phone: (914) 765-1900
List Price: $2270–$3065

Product: IBM Portable PC
Company: IBM
Address: 1133 Westchester Avenue
    White Plains, NY 10604
Phone: (914) 765-1900
List Price: $2595

Product: Macintosh 512K, Macintosh Plus
Company: Apple Computer, Inc.
Address: 20525 Mariani Avenue
    Cupertino, CA 95014
Phone: (408) 996-1010
System Requirements: Macintosh 512K, $1999; Macintosh Plus, $2599

Data management software

Product: Microsoft Windows
Company: Microsoft Corporation
Address: 16011 NE 36th Way, Box 97017
    Redmond, WA 98073-9717
Phone: (800) 426-9400, (206) 882-8088
List Price: $99
System Requirements: IBM PC series computer or compatible, 192K

Data transfer hardware/software

Product: MacCharlie Plus
Company: Dayna Communications, Inc.
Address: 50 South Main Street
    Salt Lake City, UT 84144

Phone: (800) 531-0600, (801) 531-0600
List Price: $1295
System Requirements: Macintosh 512K or Macintosh Plus

Data transfer software

Product: IBM 5520/Personal Computer Attachment Program
Company: IBM
Address: 1133 Westchester Avenue
   White Plains, NY 10604
Phone: (914) 765-1900
System Requirements: Contact your local IBM Product Center for system
   requirements and price

Data transfer systems

Product: Displaywriter/Personal Computer Attachment Convenience Kit
Company: IBM
Address: 1133 Westchester Avenue
   White Plains, NY 10604
Phone: (914) 765-1900
System Requirements: Contact your local IBM Product Center for system
   requirements and price

Product: EtherMac and DiskPlus
Company: 3Com Corporation
Address: 1365 Shorebird Way, P.O. Box 7390
   Mountain View, CA 94039
Phone: (415) 961-9602
List Price: 3Server hard-disk drive with cabling: 36 megabytes, $7995; 70
   megabytes, $8995; 3Server Port Expansion board, $695; 3Server Expan-
   sion Disk, $4995; DiskPlus accessory kit, $150
System Requirements: Macintosh and/or IBM PC series computers;
   DiskPlus requires Macintosh Plus

Product: IBM Personal Computer DisplayComm Binary Synchronous
   Communications Program
Company: IBM
Address: 1133 Westchester Avenue
   White Plains, NY 10604
Phone: (914) 765-1900
System Requirements: Contact your local IBM Product Center for system
   requirements and price

Product: InterBridge
Company: Hayes Microcomputer Products

Address: P.O. Box 105203
    Atlanta, GA 30348
Phone: (404) 449-8791
List Price: $799
System Requirements: Macintosh 512K and/or Macintosh Plus computers,
    AppleTalk Personal Networks
Comments: Links AppleTalk networks.

Product: PC MacBridge
Company: Tangent Technologies
Address: 5720 Peachtree Parkway, Suite 100
    Norcross, GA 30092
Phone: (404) 662-0366
List Price: $650
System Requirements: IBM PC or AT, some compatibles; AppleTalk con-
    nector and cable

Product: TOPS Local Area Network
Company: Centram Systems West
Address: 2372 Ellsworth Avenue
    Berkeley, CA 94704
Phone: (415) 644-8244
List Price: Macintosh node, $149; IBM PC network adapter, software, and
    manuals, $349; LaserLink utility software, $325
System Requirements: Macintosh; other computer systems optional

Database software

Product: Bookends Extended
Company: Sensible Software, Inc.
Address: 210 South Woodward, Suite 229
    Birmingham, MI 48011
Phone: (313) 258-5566
List Price: $150
System Requirements: Apple II series computer, 128K RAM
Comments: Enters and prints information about user's magazines, scien-
    tific journals, newspapers, and books into electronic card catalog. Allows
    data to be printed in customized bibliographic and footnote form.

Product: dBASE II and III
Company: Ashton-Tate
Address: 10150 West Jefferson Blvd.
    Culver City, CA 90230
Phone: (213) 204-5570
List Price: dBASE II, $495; dBASE III, $695
System Requirements: IBM PC-series computer or compatible; dBASE II,
    128K RAM; dBASE III, 256K RAM

Product: Factfinder
Company: Forethought, Inc.
Address: 1973 Landings Drive
　　Mountain View, CA 94043
Phone: (800) MAC-WARE, (415) 961-4720
List Price: $150
System Requirements: Macintosh

Product: FileMaker
Company: Forethought, Inc.
Address: 1973 Landings Drive
　　Mountain View, CA 94043
Phone: (800) MAC-WARE, (415) 961-4720
List Price: $195
System Requirements: Macintosh

Product: Interlace
Company: Singular Software
Address: 5888 Castano Drive
　　San Jose, CA 95129
Phone: (408) 446-0207
List Price: $95
System Requirements: Macintosh

Product: MegaForm
Company: MegaHaus
Address: 5703 Oberlin Drive
　　San Diego, CA 92121
Phone: (619) 450-1230
List Price: $295
System Requirements: Macintosh 512 or Macintosh Plus

Product: Omnis 3
Company: Blyth Software
Address: 2655 Campus Drive, Suite 150
　　San Mateo, CA 94403
Phone: (415) 571-0222
List Price: $375
System Requirements: Macintosh

Display hardware

Product: IBM 5151 Monochrome Display
Company: IBM
Address: 1133 Westchester Avenue
　　White Plains, NY 10604

Phone: (914) 765-1900
System Requirements: Contact your local IBM Product Center for system
requirements and price

Product: IBM Color Display
Company: IBM
Address: 1133 Westchester Avenue
White Plains, NY 10604
Phone: (914) 765-1900
System Requirements: Contact your local IBM Product Center for system
requirements and price

Product: IBM Monochrome Display and Printer Adapter Board
Company: IBM
Address: 1133 Westchester Avenue
White Plains, NY 10604
Phone: (914) 765-1900
System Requirements: Contact your local IBM Product Center for system
requirements and price

Product: IBM Professional Graphics Display
Company: IBM
Address: 1133 Westchester Avenue
White Plains, NY 10604
Phone: (914) 765-1900
System Requirements: Contact your local IBM Product Center for system
requirements and price

Expansion hardware

Product: Graphics Memory Expansion Card
Company: IBM
Address: 1133 Westchester Avenue
White Plains, NY 10604
Phone: (914) 765-1900
System Requirements: Contact your local IBM Product Center for system
requirements and price

Product: Graphics Memory Module Kit
Company: IBM
Address: 1133 Westchester Avenue
White Plains, NY 10604
Phone: (914) 765-1900
System Requirements: Contact your local IBM Product Center for system
requirements and price

Product: Hercules Graphics Card
Company: Hercules Computer Technology
Address: 2550 Ninth Street, Suite 210
  Berkeley, CA 94710
Phone: (415) 540-6000
List Price: $499
System Requirements: IBM PC series computer

Font design software

Product: MF Medley Typefaces
Company: The Metafoundry
Address: 6565 Frantz Road
  Dublin, OH 43017
Phone: (614) 764-6482
Comments: TEX fonts optimized for laser printers.

Fonts

Product: Allotype Typographics PostScript Fonts
Company: Allotype Typographics
Address: 1600 Packard Road, Suite 5
  Ann Arbor, MI 48104
Phone: (313) 577-3035
List Price: $75–$125 each
System Requirements: LaserWriter or other PostScript printer
Comments: Eleven PostScript fonts.

Graphics hardware

Product: IBM Color/Graphics Adapter
Company: IBM
Address: 1133 Westchester Avenue
  White Plains, NY 10604
Phone: (914) 765-1900
System Requirements: Contact your local IBM Product Center for system
  requirements and price

Product: IBM PC Professional Graphics Controller
Company: IBM
Address: 1133 Westchester Avenue
  White Plains, NY 10604
Phone: (914) 765-1900
System Requirements: Contact your local IBM Product Center for system
  requirements and price

Graphics hardware/software system

Product: Concept 100 Publishing System
Company: Concept Technologies, Inc.
Address: P.O. Box 5277
Portland, OR 97208
Phone: (503) 222-7080
List Price: Concept 100, $2195; ConceptWriter, $5995
System Requirements: IBM PC, AT, XT, or compatible

Graphics software

Product: Chart
Company: Microsoft
Address: 16011 NE 36th Way, Box 97017
Redmond, WA 98073-9717
Phone: (800) 426-9400, (206) 882-8088
List Price: $295
System Requirements: Macintosh or IBM PC-series computer or compatible

Product: Harvard Presentation Graphics
Company: Software Publishing Corporation
Address: 1901 Landings Drive
Mountain View, CA 94043
Phone: (415) 962-8910
List Price: $395
System Requirements: IBM PC-series computer or compatible, 256K RAM

Product: MacDraft
Company: Innovative Data Design
Address: 1975 Willow Pass Road
Concord, CA 94520
Phone: (415) 680-6818
List Price: $239
System Requirements: Macintosh 512K or Macintosh Plus

Product: MacDraw
Company: Apple Computer, Inc.
Address: 20525 Mariani Avenue
Cupertino, CA 95014
Phone: (408) 996-1010
List Price: $195
System Requirements: Macintosh

Product: MacPaint
Company: Apple Computer, Inc.
Address: 20525 Mariani Avenue
  Cupertino, CA 95014
Phone: (408) 996-1010
List Price: Bundled with Macintosh
System Requirements: Macintosh

Product: PC Paint
Company: Mouse Systems Corporation
Address: 2336 H. Walsh Avenue
  Santa Clara, CA 95051
Phone: (408) 988-0211
List Price: $99
System Requirements: IBM PC-series computer or compatible, 256K RAM

Hard disk drives

Product: AST-4000
Company: AST Research, Inc.
Address: 2121 Alton Avenue
  Irvine, CA 92714
Phone: (714) 476-3866
List Price: $6995 (includes 60-megabyte tape backup)
System Requirements: Macintosh Plus
Comments: (74 megabytes); connects to the Macintosh Plus SCSI port.

Product: Hard Disk 20
Company: Apple Computer, Inc.
Address: 20525 Mariani Avenue
  Cupertino, CA 95014
Phone: (408) 996-1010
List Price: $1495
System Requirements: Macintosh

Indexing software

Product: Index Gen
Company: Electrosonics
Address: 38486 Cheldon
  Mt. Clemens, MI 48044-2312
Phone: (313) 286-6969
List Price: Contact company for price
System Requirements: IBM PC series computer or compatible, 128K RAM
Comments: Assists in production of table of contents or index for publication.

Product: Micro Indexing System, MIS Utilities Package
Company: Compugramma, Inc.
Address: P.O. Box 60
   Cranbury, NJ 08512
Phone: (609) 448-9152
List Price: Micro Indexing System, $600; MIS Utilities Package, $100
System Requirements: IBM PC series computer or compatible, 128K RAM
Comments: Prepares indexes for books, periodicals, and newspapers. Utilities package provides additional features and increases possible index size.

Integrated software

Product: Book Publisher's Business Data Processing
Company: Resource Publications, Inc., Resource Systems
Address: 160 East Virginia Street, Suite 290
   San Jose, CA 95112
Phone: (408) 286-8505
List Price: $10,000
System Requirements: IBM PC series computer or compatible
Comments: Integrated data processing system for book publishers.

Product: Jazz
Company: Lotus Development Corporation
Address: 161 First Street
   Cambridge, MA 02142
Phone: (617) 577-8500
List Price: $595
System Requirements: Macintosh 512K or Macintosh Plus

Product: Lotus 1-2-3
Company: Lotus Development Corporation
Address: 55 Wheeler Street
   Cambridge, MA 02138
Phone: (617) 492-7171
List Price: $495
System Requirements: IBM PC-series computer or compatible

Product: Magazine Business Data Processing
Company: Resource Publications, Resource Systems
Address: 160 East Virginia Street, Suite 290
   San Jose, CA 95112
Phone: (408) 286-8505
List Price: $10,000
System Requirements: IBM PC series computer or compatible
Comments: Integrated data processing system for magazines.

Product: Microsoft Works
Company: Microsoft Corporation
Address: 16011 NE 36th Way, Box 97017
   Redmond, WA 98073-9717
Phone: (800) 426-9400, (206) 882-8088
List Price: Contact company for price
System Requirements: Macintosh 512K or Macintosh Plus

Local area networks

Product: AppleTalk
Company: Apple Computer, Inc.
Address: 20525 Mariani Avenue
   Cupertino, CA 95014
Phone: (408) 996-1010
List Price: $50 per connection

Product: Ethernet
Company: Xerox Corporation
Address: 800 Long Ridge Road, P.O. Box 1600
   Stamford, CT 06904
Phone: (203) 329-8700
List Price: $750 per connection
System Requirements: RS-232 interface

Product: IBM RT PC Network
Company: IBM
Address: 1133 Westchester Avenue
   White Plains, NY 10604
Phone: (914) 765-1900
System Requirements: Contact your local IBM Product Center for system
   requirements and price

Product: IBM Token Ring Network
Company: IBM
Address: 1133 Westchester Avenue
   White Plains, NY 10604
Phone: (914) 765-1900
System Requirements: Contact your local IBM Product Center for system
   requirements and price

Product: Omninet
Company: Corvus Systems, Inc.
Address: 2100 Corvus Drive
   San Jose, CA 95124
Phone: (408) 559-7000

List Price: $495 per connection
System Requirements: IBM PC series computer or compatible; Apple II, III, or Macintosh

Local area network software

Product: Advanced NetWare
Company: Novell, Inc.
Address: 748 North 1340 West
   Orem, UT 84057
Phone: (801) 226-8202
List Price: $1595
System Requirements: IBM PC series computers or compatibles
Comments: Operating system for NetWare/G-net, NetWare/S-net, Net-Ware/ProNET, and NetWare/ARCNET. Supports multiple fileservers, bridges, gateways, remote workstations, and DOS 3.1.

Product: SFT NetWare 286
Company: Novell, Inc.
Address: 748 North 1340 West
   Orem, UT 84057
Phone: (801) 226-8202
List Price: $2495
System Requirements: IBM PC series computers or compatibles
Comments: Operating system for NetWare/G-net, NetWare/S-net, Net-Ware/ProNET, and NetWare/ARCNET. Supports multiple fileservers, bridges, gateways, remote workstations, and DOS 3.1. Features disk mirroring, media corrections, and transaction back out.

Local area network systems

Product: NetWare/ARCNET
Company: Novell, Inc.
Address: 1170 North Industrial Park Drive
   Orem, UT 84057
Phone: (801) 226-8202
List Price: $2595
System Requirements: IBM PC series computers or compatibles
Comments: Baseband, token-passing network that accommodates up to 50 stations.

Product: NetWare/G-Net
Company: Novell, Inc.
Address: 1170 North Industrial Park Drive
   Orem, UT 84057
Phone: (801) 226-8202
List Price: $2395

System Requirements: IBM PC series computers or compatibles
Comments: Baseband, CSMA/CD network that accommodates up to 50 stations covering a total distance of 7000 feet.

Product: NetWare/ProNET
Company: Novell, Inc.
Address: 1170 North Industrial Park Drive
Orem, UT 84057
Phone: (801) 226-8202
List Price: $3095
System Requirements: IBM PC series computers or compatibles
Comments: Baseband, twin-ax, twisted pair, fiber optic, token passing network that accommodates up to 50 stations over a total distance of 100 meters to 2.5 kilometers.

Modems

Product: 103/323 Smart-CAT
Company: Novation, Inc.
Address: 20409 Prairie Street, P.O. Box 2875
Chatsworth, CA 91311
Phone: (800) 423-5419, (818) 996-5060
List Price: $495
System Requirements: RS-232 interface

Product: Apple Personal Modem
Company: Apple Computer, Inc.
Address: 20525 Mariani Avenue
Cupertino, CA 95014
Phone: (408) 996-1010
List Price: $428.95
System Requirements: RS-232 interface

Product: Hayes Smartmodem 1200, Smartmodem 1200B
Company: Hayes Microcomputer Products
Address: P.O. Box 105203
Atlanta, GA 30348
Phone: (404) 449-8791
List Price: Smartmodem 1200, $599; Smartmodem 1200B, $549 (includes Smartcom II software)
System Requirements: Smartmodem 1200, RS-232 interface; Smartmodem 1200B, IBM interface

Newspaper accounting software

Product: Accounts Payable
Company: Whalen Computer Services, Inc.

Address: Bennett Complex
Millbrook, NY 12545
Phone: (914) 677-5025
List Price: $1500–$2750
System Requirements: IBM PC series computer or compatible, 128K RAM

Product: General Ledger
Company: Whalen Computer Services, Inc.
Address: Bennett Complex
Millbrook, NY 12545
Phone: (914) 677-5025
List Price: $1500–$2750
System Requirements: IBM PC series computer or compatible, 128K RAM

Product: Newspaper Accounts Receivable
Company: Whalen Computer Services, Inc.
Address: Bennett Complex
Millbrook, NY 12545
Phone: (914) 677-5025
List Price: $4000–$9000
System Requirements: IBM PC series computer or compatible, 128K RAM

Newspaper circulation and advertising management

Product: Sub-Tracker and Ad-Tracker
Company: Software World, Inc.
Address: 4750 N. Sheridan Road
Chicago, IL 60640
Phone: (312) 275-6611
List Price: $3495
System Requirements: IBM PC, XT, AT, or compatible, 256K RAM

Newspaper software

Product: Computrac
Company: Graphic Products Corporation
Address: 522 Cottage Grove Road
Bloomfield, CT 06002
Phone: (203) 243-0730
List Price: Contact company for price
System Requirements: IBM PC, XT, or compatible
Comments: Carries entries, results, and PR material on parimutuel industry directly to newspapers for publication.

Product: Newspaper Circulation
Company: Whalen Computer Services, Inc.

Address: Bennett Complex
  Millbrook, NY 12545
Phone: (914) 677-5025
List Price: $5000–$26000
System Requirements: IBM series computer or compatible
Comments: Modular system includes Basic Circulation, Carrier/Dealer, Mail Circulation, Customer Service, and Total Market Coverage. Generates press run and audit bureau reports, truck manifests, and bundle labels.

Product: Newspaper Classified Ad Billing
Company: Whalen Computer Services, Inc.
Address: Bennett Complex
  Millbrook, NY 12545
Phone: (914) 677-5025
List Price: $1500–$4000
System Requirements: IBM PC series computer or compatible
Comments: Open item billing for transient classified ads.

Product: Newspaper Total Market Coverage
Company: Whalen Computer Services, Inc.
Address: Bennett Complex
  Millbrook, NY 12545
Phone: (914) 677-5025
List Price: $3000–$8000
System Requirements: IBM PC series computer or compatible
Comments: Allows integration of newspaper circulation base with nonsubscriber base to accomplish total market coverage. Zone and demographic selection available.

Product: Newspaper Ad Production Manifest
Company: Whalen Computer Services, Inc.
Address: Bennett Complex
  Millbrook, NY 12545
Phone: (914) 677-5025
List Price: $3500–$6000
System Requirements: IBM PC series computer or compatible, 128K RAM
Comments: Stores ads to be run—for producing detailed production manifests.

Product: Payroll
Company: Whalen Computer Services, Inc.
Address: Bennett Complex
  Millbrook, NY 12545
Phone: (914) 677-5025
List Price: $1500–$2750

System Requirements: IBM PC series computer or compatible
Comments: Payroll package for newspaper industry.

On-line services

Product: Agnet
Company: University of Nebraska
Address: Lincoln, NE 68583
Phone: (402) 472-1892
List Price: Contact university for price
System Requirements: Modem
Comments: Offers a variety of agricultural marketing databases and dozens of computational agricultural management programs.

Product: AgriStar Network
Company: AgriData Resources, Inc.
Address: 205 West Highland Avenue
Milwaukee, WI 53203
Phone: (414) 273-0873
List Price: Contact company for price
System Requirements: Modem
Comments: Agriculture database with four categories: news, finances, agriculture, and weather.

Product: Billboard Information Network
Company: Billboard Publications
Address: 1515 Broadway
New York, NY 10036
Phone: (212) 764-7424
List Price: Contact company for price
System Requirements: Modem
Comments: Radio playlists from 700 U.S. stations.

Product: BRS
Company: BRS Information Technologies
Address: 1200 Route 7
Latham, NY 12110
Phone: (518) 783-1161
List Price: Contact company for price
System Requirements: Modem
Comments: Has more than 80 databases in the areas of business and finance, education, reference, science and medicine, and the social sciences. Offers electronic mail through MCI Mail. The bargain, non-prime-time version is called After Dark.

Product: CompuServe
Company: CompuServe Information Services

Address: 5000 Arlington Centre Blvd.
  Columbus, OH 43220
Phone: (614) 457-8600
List Price: Contact company for price
System Requirements: Modem

Product: Dialog
Company: Dialog Information Services, Inc.
Address: 3460 Hillview Avenue
  Palo Alto, CA 94304
Phone: (415) 858-3792
List Price: Contact company for price
System Requirements: Modem
Comments: Offers more than 200 databases that reference more than
  60,000 paper publications internationally in a variety of broad cate-
  gories. Includes numerous bibliographic databases. A scaled-down,
  less-expensive version that operates only during non-prime-time hours
  is Knowledge Index.

Product: Dow Jones News/Retrieval Service
Company: Dow Jones News/Retrieval Service
Address: P.O. Box 300
  Princeton, NJ 08540
Phone: (609) 452-2000
List Price: Contact company for price
System Requirements: Modem
Comments: Financial and general databases.

Product: Educom
Company: Educom
Address: P.O. Box 364
  Princeton, NJ 08540
Phone: (609) 734-1915
List Price: Free
System Requirements: Modem
Comments: Provides access to the computing facilities at 18 major univer-
  sities.

Product: Free-Text Search database
Company: Dow Jones News/Retrieval Service
Address: P.O. Box 300
  Princeton, NJ 08540
Phone: (609) 452-2000
List Price: Contact company for price

System Requirements: Modem

Comments: Database contains all the articles since June 1979 that have made a 90-day appearance in the Dow Jones News database (slightly condensed versions of articles in the *Wall Street Journal*, *Barron's*, and the Dow Jones wire service). Also has the full text of the *Wall Street Journal* since January 1984.

Product: GTE Minet (Medical Information Network)
Company: GTE Telenet Communications Company
Address: 8229 Boone Blvd.
Vienna, VA 22180
Phone: (703) 442-1934
List Price: Contact company for price
System Requirements: Modem
Comments: Offers a variety of medical reference databases and education and communications features.

Product: InfoLine
Company: Pergamon International Information Corporation
Address: 1340 Old Chain Bridge Road
McLean, VA 22101
Phone: (703) 442-0900
List Price: Contact company for price
System Requirements: Modem
Comments: British service offering about 30 databases on the sciences and business.

Product: InnerLine
Company: InnerLine
Address: 95 West Algonquin Road
Arlington Heights, IL 60005
Phone: (312) 364-8800
List Price: Contact company for price
System Requirements: Modem

Product: The Source
Company: Source Telecomputing Corporation
Address: 1616 Anderson Road
McLean, VA 22102
Phone: (703) 734-7500, (800) 336-3366
List Price: Contact company for price
System Requirements: Modem
Comments: Banking databases in nine categories.

Product: Insider Trading Monitor
Company: FCI-Invest/Net

Address: 99 Northwest 183rd Street
  North Miami, FL 33169
Phone: (305) 652-1710
List Price: Contact company for price
System Requirements: Modem
Comments: Stock market database.

Product: Instant Update
Company: Professional Farmers of America
Address: 219 Parkade
  Cedar Falls, IA 50613
Phone: (319) 277-1278
List Price: Contact company for price
System Requirements: Modem
Comments: Offers financial agricultural information.

Product: Legi-Slate
Company: Legi-Slate
Address: 444 North Capitol Street, N.W.
  Washington, DC 20001
Phone: (202) 737-1888
List Price: Contact company for price
System Requirements: Modem
Comments: Electronic legislative bill-tracking service.

Product: Lexis
Company: Mead Data Central
Address: 9393 Springboro Pike, P.O. Box 933
  Dayton, OH 45401
Phone: (513) 865-6800
List Price: Contact company for price
System Requirements: Modem
Comments: Legal database.

Product: Media General database
Company: Media General Financial Services
Address: P.O. Box C-323333
  Richmond, CA 23293
Phone: (804) 649-6739
List Price: Contact company for price
System Requirements: Modem
Comments: Financial database. You can access it on the Business Information Systems, Inc. service (747 Third Avenue, New York, NY 10010; (212) 752-0831).

Product: MJK database
Company: MJK Associates

Address: 122 Saratoga Avenue
Santa Clara, CA 95050
Phone: (408) 247-5102
List Price: Contact company for price
System Requirements: Modem
Comments: Offers daily and historical commodity prices from all major U.S. and Canadian exchanges.

Product: NewsNet
Company: NewsNet
Address: 945 Haverford Road
Bryn Mawr, PA 19010
Phone: (215) 527-8030
List Price: Contact company for price
System Requirements: Modem
Comments: Offers full text of more than 300 newsletters in 32 categories, in addition to numerous news wires.

Product: Nexis
Company: Mead Data Central
Address: 9393 Springboro Pike, P.O. Box 933
Dayton, OH 45401
Phone: (513) 865-6800
List Price: Contact company for price
System Requirements: Modem
Comments: Full text of more than 14 newspapers, 39 magazines, 12 wire services, 50 newsletters, the Encyclopædia Britannica, etc.

Product: Orbit
Company: Systems Development Corporation
Address: 2500 Colorado Avenue
Santa Monica, CA 94060
Phone: (213) 820-4111
List Price: Contact company for price
System Requirements: Modem
Comments: Offers more than 70 databases covering business, law, the social sciences, and science and technology (the largest category).

Product: Photonet
Company: Photonet Computer Corporation
Address: 250 West 57th Street
New York, NY 10019
Phone: (212) 307-6999
List Price: Contact company for price

System Requirements: Modem
Comments: Information for serious photographers and the organizations that need them. Features in six sections: photographic agencies, photo search, communications, marketplace, manufacturer-provided services, and news and information.

Product: Questel
Company: Questel, Inc.
Address: 1625 Eye Street, N.W., Suite 818
Washington, DC 20006
Phone: (202) 296-1604
List Price: Contact company for price
System Requirements: Modem
Comments: Offers more than 30 databases, a majority from French producers.

Product: Texline and Dataline
Company: U.S. Representative: Information Access Company
Address: 11 Davis Drive
Belmont, CA 94002
Phone: (415) 591-2333
List Price: Contact company for price
System Requirements: Modem
Comments: Texline: international bibliographic database. Dataline: offers financial profiles of companies in the United Kingdom and Western Europe.

Product: Vickers On-Line
Company: Vickers Stock Research Corporation
Address: 226 New York Avenue
Huntington, NY 11743
Phone: (516) 423-7710
List Price: Contact company for price
System Requirements: Modem
Comments: Stock market database.

Product: Vu/Text database
Company: Vu/Text Information Services
Address: 1211 Chestnut Street
Philadelphia, PA 19107
Phone: (215) 663-3300
List Price: Contact company for price
System Requirements: Modem
Comments: Full text of numerous newspapers for the current and previous year, Grolier Electronic Publishing's Academic America Encyclopedia, Mediawire wire service, and Predicast's Overview of Markets and Technology database of abstracts from business publications worldwide.

Product: Westlaw
Company: West Publishing Company
Address: 50 West Kellog Blvd., P.O. Box 3526
St. Paul, MN 55165
Phone: (612) 228-2500
List Price: Contact company for price
System Requirements: Modem
Comments: Electronic legal research service.

Optical character readers

Product: Kurzweil 4000
Company: Kurzweil Computer Products, Inc.
Address: 185 Albany Street
Cambridge, MA 02139
Phone: (800) 343-0311
List Price: $36,500
Comments: Reads 30-55 characters per second of typewritten or typeset material.

Product: Workless Station OCRs
Company: Dest Corporation
Address: 1201 Cadillac Court
Milpitas, CA 95035
Phone: (408) 946-7100
List Price: $5995–$9995
Comments: Reads 145-240 characters per second of specified fonts.

Outline-processing software

Product: ThinkTank
Company: Living Videotext, Inc.
Address: 2432 Charleston Road
Mountain View, CA 94043
Phone: (800) 822-3700, (415) 964-6300
List Price: $195
System Requirements: Apple II Plus, IIe, III, or Macintosh; IBM PC-series computer or compatible

Page description languages

Product: FTLTEX for the Macintosh
Company: FTL systems Inc.
Address: 234 Eglinton Avenue East, Suite 205
Toronto, Ontario, Canada M4P 1K5
Phone: (416) 487-2142

List Price: $750
System Requirements: Macintosh Plus, PostScript-compatible printer, hard-disk drive recommended

Product: MicroTEX
Company: Addison-Wesley Publishing Company, Educational and Professional
Address: Technologies Division
Reading, MA 01867
Phone: (617) 944-6795
List Price: $495; additional printer drivers increase the cost
System Requirements: IBM PC, XT, AT, or compatible; 512K RAM; 10-megabyte hard-disk drive

Product: PCTEX
Company: Personal TEX
Address: 20 Sunnyside, Suite H
Mill Valley, CA 94941
Phone: (415) 388-8853
List Price: PCTEX, $279; PCDOT, $100; PCLaser, $300; MF Medley, $100
System Requirements: IBM PC XT, AT, or compatible; DOS 2.0 or higher; 512K RAM; 10-megabyte hard disk drive

Product: SofType
Company: SofTest, Inc.
Address: 555 Goffle Road
Ridgewood, NJ 07450
Phone: (201) 447-3901
List Price: For single-user computers, $1000; for multiuser computers, $1500; extra font family, $400
System Requirements: IBM PC XT, AT, or compatible; word processing program

Product: TEX Preview
Company: Textset, Inc.
Address: Box 7993
Ann Arbor, MI 48107
Phone: (313) 996-3566
Comments: Screen preview for use with TEX.

Product: TEX Products and Services
Company: Textset, Inc.
Address: Box 7993
Ann Arbor, MI 48107

Phone: (313) 996-3566

Comments: TEX drivers for laser printers, phototypesetters, and other output devices; screen preview; custom output; assistance with TEX macros and book and document design.

Page layout software

Product: DO-IT
Company: Studio Software
Address: 17862-C Fitch
Irvine, CA 92714
Phone: (800) 437-4496
List Price: $1800
System Requirements: IBM PC XT or AT or exact compatible; 512K RAM minimum, 640K recommended; hard disk; laser printer or typesetter

Product: FACELIFT 2
Company: Companion Software, Inc.
Address: 7400 West Beverly Blvd.
Los Angeles, CA 90036
Phone: (213) 462-2759
List Price: $50
System Requirements: IBM PC series computer or compatible, 256K RAM
Comments: Accesses 96 typefaces, styles, and sizes on Epson printers and compatibles. Selects typeface, style, or size from menu.

Product: JustText 1.0
Company: Knowledge Engineering
Address: G.P.O. Box 2139
New York, NY 10116
Phone: (212) 473-0095
List Price: $130 (JustText 1.1, slated for release in August 1986, will be $195)
System Requirements: Macintosh; LaserWriter or Linotype Series 100 typesetter

Product: Lasersoft
Company: Business Systems International, Inc.
Address: 20942 Osborne Street
Canoga Park, CA 91304
Phone: (818) 998-7227
List Price: $995; multiuser system, $6300
System Requirements: IBM PC series computer or compatible, 128K RAM
Comments: Page composition and forms generation software for Xerox and Hewlett-Packard LaserJet laser printers. Performs data merging with electronically created forms.

Product: MacPublisher II
Company: Boston Software Publishers
Address: 1260 Boylston Street
  Boston, MA 02215
Phone: (617) 267-4747
List Price: $149.95
System Requirements: Macintosh; ImageWriter or LaserWriter

Product: MagnaType
Company: Magna Computer Systems, Inc.
Address: 14724 Ventura Blvd.
  Sherman Oaks, CA 91403
Phone: (818) 986-9233
List Price: $1000
System Requirements: IBM PC XT, AT, or other PC-DOS-compatible
  computer; 512K RAM; hard-disk drive

Product: Micro Print - X
Company: Composition Technology International (CTI)
Address: 209 East Alameda Avenue
  Burbank, CA 91502-1561
Phone: (818) 848-1010
List Price: $3995
System Requirements: IBM PC series computer or compatible, 256K RAM
Comments: Composition markup language that you can enter with any
  word processor or text editor that can create a pure ASCII file. The file
  is then processed by MP-X to produce an output file that can drive any
  of the Autologic family of typesetters.

Product: Page Descriptor Language
Company: Composition Technology International (CTI)
Address: 209 East Alameda Avenue
  Burbank, CA 91502-1561
Phone: (818) 848-1010
List Price: Contact company for price
System Requirements: IBM PC series computer or compatible; 512K RAM
Comments: Device-, resolution-, and pixel aspect ratio-independent raster
  image processor that drives preview terminals, page makeup stations,
  dot matrix printers, laser printers, typesetters—displays both text and
  graphics.

Product: PageMaker
Company: Aldus Corporation
Address: 411 First Avenue South, Suite 200
  Seattle, WA 98104
Phone: (206) 622-5500

List Price: $495
System Requirements: Macintosh 512K or Macintosh Plus; ImageWriter or LaserWriter

Product: PagePlanner
Company: PagePlanner Systems, Inc.
Address: 463 Barell Avenue
Carlstadt, NJ 07072
Phone: (201) 933-4700
List Price: $3995
System Requirements: IBM PC series computer with IBM Graphics Card or Hercules Graphics Card, or other MS-DOS or CP/M-based computer; 512K RAM; hard-disk drive recommended

Product: Page Planner
Company: Composition Technology International (CTI)
Address: 209 East Alameda Avenue
Burbank, CA 91502-1561
Phone: (818) 848-1010
List Price: $3995 and up
System Requirements: IBM PC series computer or compatible, 512K RAM
Comments: Composition and page makeup language that drives numerous typesetters. Features include 16 type display modes, mono and proportional spacing, interactive previewing and two hyphenation methods.

Product: PC Proof
Company: Composition Technology International (CTI)
Address: 209 East Alameda Avenue
Burbank, CA 91502-1561
Phone: (818) 848-1010
List Price: $995
System Requirements: IBM PC series computer or compatible, 256K RAM
Comments: Allows previewing of pages on a monochrome monitor with a Hercules card. Type and graphics are displayed in actual size and position.

Product: ReadySetGo
Company: Manhattan Graphics
Address: 163 Varick Street
New York, NY 10013
Phone: (212) 989-6442
List Price: $195
System Requirements: Macintosh, LaserWriter

Product: SuperPage
Company: Bestinfo

Address: 33 Chester Pike
Ridley Park, PA 19078
Phone: (215) 521-0757
List Price: SuperPage, $7000; lower-end version, $500–$700, depending on
options
System Requirements: IBM PC XT, AT, or compatible computer; PC-
DOS; 512K RAM; IBM monochrome monitor; large-option or Hercules
Graphics Card; LaserWriter or other laser printer; mouse or digitizing
tablet optional

Product: TypeSim
Company: Composition Technology International (CTI)
Address: 209 East Alameda Avenue
Burbank, CA 91502-1561
Phone: (818) 848-1010
List Price: $995
System Requirements: IBM PC series computer or compatible; CP/M-86-
compatible computer
Comments: Uses a generic algorithmic font. Shows roman, bold, italic,
bold italic, expanded, and condensed faces in any point size and set
width.

Plotters

Product: Hewlett-Packard 7470A
Company: Hewlett-Packard Company
Address: 8020 Foothills
Roseville, CA 95678
Phone: (800) FOR-HPPC
List Price: $1095
System Requirements: IBM PC Series computer or compatible; Apple IIe,
IIc, or III

Product: IBM XY/749
Company: IBM
Address: 1133 Westchester Avenue
White Plains, NY 10604
Phone: (914) 765-1900
List Price: $1995
System Requirements: IBM PC series computer

Product: PC 595, 695
Company: Houston Instrument
Address: 8500 Cameron Road
Austin, TX 78753
Phone: (800) 531-5205, (512) 835-0900

List Price: PC 595, $595; PC 695, $695
System Requirements: IBM PC series computer or Macintosh

Printers

Product: IBM Graphics Printer
Company: IBM
Address: 1133 Westchester Avenue
  White Plains, NY 10604
Phone: (914) 765-1900
System Requirements: Contact your local IBM Product Center for system requirements and price

Product: Vision System
Company: Anser Technology, Inc.
Address: 5535 Airport Freeway
  Fort Worth, TX 76117
Phone: (817) 831-4191
List Price: $155,000
System Requirements: IBM PC series computer or compatible; Macintosh
Comments: High-speed nonimpact printing system that combines electronic and ionographic technologies to print at speeds up to 125 pages per minute. 240 dpi.

Printers, dot-matrix

Product: ImageWriter II printer
Company: Apple Computer, Inc.
Address: 20525 Mariani Avenue
  Cupertino, CA 95014
Phone: (408) 996-1010
List Price: $599
System Requirements: Computer with an RS-232 interface

Printers, ink-jet

Product: Hewlett-Packard 2225 ThinkJet
Company: Hewlett-Packard Company
Address: 8020 Foothills
  Roseville, CA 95678
Phone: (800) FOR-HPPC
List Price: $495
System Requirements: Centronics parallel interface

Printers, laser

Product: Model 630/8
Company: BDS Corporation
Address: 800 Maude Avenue
  Mountain View, CA 94043
Phone: (415) 964-2115
List Price: $2995
System Requirements: IBM PC series computer or compatible; Macintosh
Comments: 300 dpi, 8.1 pages per minute.

Product: 8/300, 12/300, and 24/300 Printstations
Company: Imagen Corporation
Address: 2650 San Tomas Expressway, P.O. Box 58101
  Santa Clara, CA 95052
Phone: (408) 986-9400
List Price: 8/300, $8950; 12/300, $15,800; 24/300, $29,950
System Requirements: IBM PC series computer or compatible, Macintosh

Product: 2700 Distributed Electronic Printer
Company: Wang Laboratories, Inc.
Address: One Industrial Avenue, Mail Stop 1307B
  Lowell, MA 01851
Phone: (800) 225-9264, (617) 459-5000
List Price: $18,995
System Requirements: Macintosh; Centronics parallel or RS-232C interface
Comments: 300 dpi, 600 lines per minute, 12 pages per minute.

Product: Corona LP-300 Laser Printer
Company: Corona Data Systems, Inc.
Address: 275 East Hillcrest Drive
  Thousand Oaks, CA 91360
Phone: (800) 621-6746, (805) 495-5800
List Price: $2995
System Requirements: IBM PC series computer or compatible; MS-DOS;
  256K RAM (512K for best use of graphics)

Product: Daisylaser 1000
Company: Personal Computer Products, Inc. (PCPI)
Address: 11590 West Bernardo Court
  San Diego, CA 92127
Phone: (619) 485-8411
List Price: $3495–$3785
System Requirements: Macintosh; Centronics parallel or RS-232C interface
Comments: 300 dpi, 8 pages per minute.

Product: Domain/Laser

Company: Apollo Computer, Inc.
Address: 330 Billerica Road
  Chelmsford, MA 01824
Phone: (617) 256-6600
List Price: Contact company for price
System Requirements: Centronics parallel or RS-232C interface
Comments: 300 dpi, 26 pages per minute.

Product: Formwriter 2 Laser Printing System
Company: Computer Language Research, Inc., Sprinter Division
Address: 2395 Midway Road
  Carrollton, TX 75006
Phone: (214) 250-7083
List Price: Contact company for price
System Requirements: IBM PC series computer or compatible
Comments: 300 dpi, 500 lines per minute, 8 pages per minute.

Product: GBT 6620PC Laser Printer
Company: General Business Technology, Inc.
Address: 1891 MacGaw Avenue
  Irvine, CA 92714
Phone: (714) 261-1891
List Price: $9995
System Requirements: IBM PC series computer or compatible
Comments: 300 dpi, 12 pages per minute.

Product: GBT 6630PC Laser Printer
Company: General Business Technology, Inc.
Address: 1891 McGaw Avenue
  Irvine, CA 92714
Phone: (714) 261-1891
List Price: $3495
System Requirements: IBM PC series computer or compatible
Comments: 300 dpi, 8 pages per minute.

Product: Hewlett-Packard LaserJet and LaserJet PLUS
Company: Hewlett-Packard
Address: 8020 Foothills
  Roseville, CA 95678
Phone: (800) FOR-HPPC
List Price: LaserJet, $2995; LaserJet PLUS, $3995
System Requirements: RS-232 interface or HPIB interface; IBM PC series
  computer with JLASER board from Tall Tree Systems for full-page bit-
  mapped graphics

Product: ImageStation Printers
Company: Imagen Corporation

Address: 2650 San Tomas Expressway, P.O. Box 58101
  Santa Clara, CA 95052
Phone: (408) 986-9400
List Price: Priced according to memory
System Requirements: IBM PC series computer or compatible, Macintosh

Product: Laserprint 0870
Company: Advanced Technologies International
Address: 2041 Mission College Blvd., Suite 163
  Santa Clara, CA 95054
Phone: (408) 748-1688
List Price: $5500
System Requirements: IBM PC series computer or compatible
Comments: 300 dpi resolution, 528 lines per minute, 8 pages per minute.

Product: Laserprint 1270
Company: Advanced Technologies International
Address: 2041 Mission College Blvd., Suite 163
  Santa Clara, CA 95054
Phone: (408) 748-1688
List Price: $9500
System Requirements: IBM PC series computer or compatible
Comments: 300 dpi resolution, 800 lines per minute, 12 pages per minute.

Product: Laserprint 2670
Company: Advanced Technologies International
Address: 2041 Mission College Blvd., Suite 163
  Santa Clara, CA 95054
Phone: (408) 748-1688
List Price: $12,900
System Requirements: IBM PC series computer or compatible
Comments: 300 dpi, 1800 lines per minute, 26 pages per minute.

Product: LaserView 300
Company: Composition Technology International (CTI)
Address: 209 East Alameda Avenue
  Burbank, CA 91502-1561
Phone: (818) 848-1010
List Price: $7995
System Requirements: IBM PC series computer or compatible
Comments: 300 dpi, 8 pages per minute.

Product: LaserView 300 RX
Company: Composition Technology International (CTI)
Address: 209 East Alameda Avenue
  Burbank, CA 91502-1561
Phone: (818) 848-1010

List Price: $9995
System Requirements: IBM PC series computer or compatible
Comments: 8 pages per minute.

Product: LaserMaster's XT/m Laser
Company: LaserMaster, Ltd.
Address: 6111 Creek View Trail
Minnetonka, MN 55345
Phone: (612) 934-0680
List Price: $2490
System Requirements: IBM PC series computer or compatible
Comments: 800 dpi, 8 pages per minute.

Product: LaserWriter Plus
Company: Apple Computer, Inc.
Address: 20525 Mariani Avenue
Cupertino, CA 95014
Phone: (408) 996-1010
List Price: $6798

Product: LBP-200S
Company: Canon U.S.A., Inc.
Address: One Canon Plaza
Lake Success, NY 11042
Phone: (516) 488-6700
List Price: $3550
System Requirements: IBM PC series computer or compatible; Centronics
parallel interface
Comments: 8 pages per minute.

Product: LBP-8A1
Company: Canon U.S.A., Inc.
Address: One Canon Plaza
Lake Success, NY 11042
Phone: (516) 488-6700
List Price: $3500
System Requirements: IBM PC series computer or compatible; Centronics
parallel interface
Comments: 300 dpi, 8 pages per minute.

Product: LZR 2650
Company: Dataproducts Corporation, Customer Services Division
Address: 21300 Roscoe Blvd.
Canoga Park, CA 91304
Phone: (818) 887-8409
List Price: $17,900

System Requirements: Interleaf
Comments: 300 dpi, 26 pages per minute.

Product: LZR 2660
Company: Dataproducts Corporation, Customer Services Division
Address: 21300 Roscoe Blvd.
  Canoga Park, CA 91304
Phone: (818) 887-8409
List Price: $20,900
System Requirements: PostScript
Comments: 300 dpi, 26 pages per minute.

Product: M3071
Company: Fujitsu America, Inc., Storage & Peripheral Products Division
Address: 3055 Orchard Drive
  San Jose, CA 95134
Phone: (408) 946-8777, (408) 945-1318
List Price: $5100
System Requirements: IBM PC series computer or compatible
Comments: 300 dpi, 16-20 pages per minute.

Product: M 5211
Company: KEL, Inc.
Address: 400 West Cummings Park
  Woburn, MA 01801
Phone: (617) 933-7852
List Price: $17,500
System Requirements: Macintosh, RS-232C interface
Comments: 240 dpi, 20 pages per minute.

Product: Model 4580 (OPUS 1)
Company: Facit, Inc.
Address: 9 Executive Park Drive
  Merrimack, NH 03054
Phone: (603) 424-8000
List Price: $9500
System Requirements: Macintosh; Centronics parallel or RS-232C interface
Comments: 300 dpi, 12 pages per minute.

Product: QMS KISS Laser Printer
Company: Quality Micro Systems, Inc.
Address: P.O. Box 81250
  Mobile, AL 36689
Phone: (205) 633-4300
List Price: $2000
System Requirements: IBM PC series computer or compatible, Centronics
  parallel or RS-232C interface

Product: QMS Lasergrafix 800
Company: Quality Micro Systems, Inc.
Address: P.O. Box 81250
  Mobile, AL 36689
Phone: (205) 633-4300
List Price: $7995
System Requirements: Centronics parallel or RS-232C interface

Product: QMS Lasergrafix 1200
Company: Quality Micro Systems, Inc.
Address: P.O. Box 81250
  Mobile, AL 36689
Phone: (205) 633-4300
List Price: $19,995
System Requirements: Centronics parallel or RS-232C interface

Product: QMS Lasergrafix 2400
Company: Quality Micro Systems, Inc.
Address: P.O. Box 81250
  Mobile, AL 36689
Phone: (205) 633-4300
List Price: $29,995
System Requirements: User-defined

Product: QMS Smartwriter Laser Printer
Company: Quality Micro Systems, Inc.
Address: P.O. Box 81250
  Mobile, AL 36689
Phone: (205) 633-4300
List Price: $3850
System Requirements: Centronics parallel interface; RS-232C interface op-
  tional

Product: QMS PS 800
Company: Quality Micro Systems, Inc.
Address: P.O. Box 81250
  Mobile, AL 36689
Phone: (205) 633-4300
List Price: $7995
System Requirements: IBM PC series computer or compatible, Macintosh
Comments: PostScript-compatible

Product: Qume LaserTEN
Company: Qume Corporation
Address: 2350 Qume Drive
  San Jose, CA 95131
Phone: (408) 942-4000

List Price: 128K model, $2795; 512K model, $3395
System Requirements: IBM PC XT, AT, or compatible

Product: Talaris 810 Laser Printer
Company: Talaris Systems, Inc.
Address: P.O. Box 261580
   San Diego, CA 92126
Phone: (619) 587-0787
List Price: $3850
System Requirements: Centronics parallel or RS-232 interface

Product: Xerox 4045
Company: Xerox Corporation
Address: 800 Long Ridge Road, P.O. Box 1600
   Stamford, CT 06904
Phone: (203) 329-8700
List Price: $4995; copier option, $400; interface-sharing device, $1395; RS-232 interface, $250
System Requirements: Personal-computer interface

Printing software

Product: Silicon Press
Company: Silicon Beach Software
Address: P.O. Box 261430, 9580 Black Mountain Road, Suite E
   San Diego, CA 92126
Phone: (619) 695-6956
List Price: $79.95
System Requirements: Macintosh 512K or Macintosh Plus
Comments: For labels, tags, and other special purposes.

Scanners

Product: MS-200 and MS-300 Image Scanners
Company: Microtek Lab, Inc.
Address: 17221 South Western Avenue
   Gardena, CA 90247
Phone: (213) 538-5369
List Price: MS-200, $1700 with choice of EyeStar or VersaScan software; MS-300, $2300
System Requirements: Macintosh or IBM PC series computer

Product: Scan 300
Company: Abaton Technology Corporation
Address: 1526 Coverfield Boulevard
   Santa Monica, CA 90404
Phone: (808) 905-9399

List Price: $2495
System Requirements: Macintosh or IBM PC series computer and laser
   printer

Product: Spectrafax
Company: Spectrafax Corporation
Address: 2000 Palm Street South
   Naples, FL 33962
Phone: (813) 775-2737
List Price: $3995
System Requirements: Macintosh 512K or Macintosh Plus, hard-disk drive
   recommended

Product: ThunderScan
Company: ThunderWare, Inc.
Address: 21 Orinda Way
   Orinda, CA 94563
Phone: (415) 254-6581
List Price: $229
System Requirements: Macintosh, ImageWriter

Search software

Product: Microdisclosure
Company: Disclosure, Inc.
Address: 5161 River Road
   Bethesda, MD 10816
Phone: (301) 951-1300
List Price: $250
System Requirements: IBM PC series computer or compatible
Comments: Automates searches in the Disclosure II database within Dialog
   and helps analyze information.

Product: PC/Net-Link
Company: Informatics General Corporation, Library Service Division
Address: 6011 Executive Blvd.
   Rockville, MD 20852
Phone: (301) 770-3000
List Price: $550
System Requirements: IBM PC series computer or compatible
Comments: Automates on-line searches on Dialog, BRS, and Dow Jones
   News/Retrieval Service.

Product: SCI-Mate Universal Online Searcher
Company: Institute for Scientific Information
Address: 3501 Market Street
   Philadelphia, PA 19104

Phone: (215) 386-0100

List Price: Universal Online Searcher, $440; Personal Data Manager, $540; both, $880

System Requirements: IBM PC series computer or compatible

Comments: Automates use of Dialog, BRS, or Orbit databases. The adjunct Personal Data Manager lets you download information from these services.

Simulation (phototypesetter)

Product: Composition

Company: Resource Publications, Inc., Resource Systems

Address: 160 E. Virginia Street, Suite 220
San Jose, CA 95112

Phone: (408) 286-8505

List Price: $1500

System Requirements: IBM PC series computer or CP/M-based computer

Comments: Simulates phototype output, inputs an ordinary text file and generates output. Permits hyphenation and justification. Covers type sizes from 6 point to 72 in a variety of typespaces.

Spreadsheet software

Product: Excel

Company: Microsoft Corporation

Address: 16011 NE 36th Way, Box 97017
Redmond, WA 98073-9717

Phone: (800) 426-9400, (206) 882-8088

List Price: $395 with Macintosh Multiplan trade-up; $200 with Macintosh Multiplan and Chart trade-up

System Requirements: Macintosh

Stock market software

Product: Standard & Poor's StockPack II

Company: Standard & Poor's Corporation

Address: 25 Broadway
New York, NY 10004

Phone: (212) 208-8000

List Price: One-year subscription, $520; adjunct data disks, programs, and updates, $275 each

System Requirements: Apple II series computer; IBM PC series computer or compatible

Text-formatting/graphics hardware/software systems

Product: The DataCenter
Company: Corporate Data Sciences, Inc.
Address: 2560 Mission College Blvd., #102
Santa Clara, CA 95054
Phone: (213) 674-3117
List Price: $13,895 for the complete DataCenter; $7600 without laser printer; PC mouse, $150; VDRAW, $750; VESS, $590
System Requirements: IBM PC XT or AT, 512K RAM, 10-megabyte hard-disk drive, 8087 (XT) or 80287 (AT) coprocessor, serial port (for VDRAW), parallel port (for printer)

Translation software

Product: MacWrite Translator
Company: DCS
Address: 401 URIS Hall, Cornell University
Ithaca, NY 14853
List Price: Free (public domain)
System Requirements: Macintosh
Comments: Translation software from MacWrite into formats used by other software.

Typesetting machines

Product: Alphatype CRS 4900 and 9900; Work Station II
Company: Alphatype Corporation
Address: 7711 North Merrimac Avenue
Niles, IL 60648
Phone: (312) 965-8800
List Price: CRS 4900, $25,000; CRS 9900, $60,000; Work Station II package, $1900 (software available separately for $960); SoftVu full-page video display, $12,500
System Requirements: IBM PC series or compatible; 256K RAM, 10-megabyte or larger-capacity hard-disk drive
Comments: Typesetting machines; accompanying software/hardware package.

Product: Autologic
Company: Autologic, Inc.
Address: 1050 Rancho Conejo Blvd.
Newbury Park, CA 91320
Phone: (805) 498-9611
List Price: Various models, $18,500–$72,500
System Requirements: ICL (Input Command Language)

Product: Linotronic 100 and 300, Linotron 202
Company: Linotype Company, A Division of Allied-Signal
Address: 425 Oser Avenue
  Hauppauge, NY 11788
Phone: (516) 434-2000
Linotron 100, $29,950; Linotronic 202, $38,000–$59,000, depending on options; Linotronic 300, $57,900

Typesetting software

Product: DTI
Company: Digital Technology International
Address: 500 West 1200 South
  Orem, UT 84058
Phone: (801) 226-2984
List Price: $30
System Requirements: Macintosh

Product: Microcomposer Editwriter
Company: Cybertext Corporation
Address: 1695 10th Street, P.O. Box HH
  Arcata, CA 95521
Phone: (707) 822-7079
List Price: $1895
System Requirements: IBM PC series computer or compatible; CP/M-80-compatible computer
Comments: Interfaces CP/M, MS-DOS, and TRSDOS-based personal computers to the Editwriter.

Product: Microcomposer I, II, and IV
Company: Cybertext Corporation
Address: 1695 10th Street, P.O. Box HH
  Arcata, CA 95521
Phone: (707) 822-7079
List Price: $1495–$1895
System Requirements: IBM PC series computer or compatible; CP/M-80-compatible computer
Comments: Interfaces to various CompuWriter models. Microcomposer I upgrades the Compugraphic phototypesetter with editing and storage abilities. Allows computer to become keyboard for entering text with editing and updating. Microcomposer II and IV provide editing and storage, allowing CompuWriter to become keyboard for input and updating via word processing software.

Product: Microcomposer MCS 8400
Company: Cybertext Corporation

Address: 1695 10th Street, P.O. Box HH

Arcata, CA 95521

Phone: (707) 822-7079

List Price: $2395

System Requirements: IBM PC series computer or compatible

Comments: Interfaces to Compugraphic MCS 8200 and 8400. Provides editing and typesetting controls, including hyphenation and justification, ruling commands, user-defined keys and formats, up to 100 tab positions, hyphenation control, job control, and billing information.

Product: Microcomposer Unisetter

Company: Cybertext Corporation

Address: 1695 10th Street, P.O. Box HH

Arcata, CA 95521

Phone: (707) 822-7079

List Price: $1895

System Requirements: IBM PC series computer or compatible; CP/M-80-compatible computer

Comments: Furnishes Compugraphic phototypesetter with editing and storage capabilities. Allows computer to become keyboard for entering text; you edit and update in a word processing program.

Product: Qtroff

Company: Quality Micro Systems, Inc.

Address: P.O. Box 81250

Mobile, AL 36689

Phone: (205) 633-4300

List Price: $1500

System Requirements: UNIX-compatible computer

Comments: Support package for QMS's *troff* typesetting package. Prepares fonts, handles print spooling, and converts CAT typesetter output of *troff* to appropriate formats for the Lasergrafix family of printers. Fonts are loaded to the printer and managed by the software.

Product: TSI Editor

Company: Type-Share, Inc.

Address: 5952 N. Adenmoor Avenue

Lakewood, CA 90713

Phone: (213) 867-1751

List Price: $195

System Requirements: IBM PC series computer or compatible

Comments: Inputs files directly to Type-Share. Checks the integrity of the command and generates typeset work, which is returned via UPS and Express Mail. Lets you prepare material for printing.

Product: Type Faces

Company: Alpha Software Corporation

Address: 30 B Street
  Burlington, MA 01803
Phone: (800) 451-1018, (617) 229-2924
List Price: $95
System Requirements: IBM PC, XT, or compatible
Comments: Enables many printers to print large characters in 15 type-styles, including Greek, Roman, italic, script, and English character forms. You can mix different typestyles on the same page. Prints banners and edits fonts.

Product: Type Processor One
Company: Bestinfo, Inc.
Address: 33 Chester Pike
  Ridley Park, PA 19078
Phone: (215) 521-0757
List Price: $5000
System Requirements: IBM PC series computer or compatible, 256K RAM
Comments: Real-time interactive graphics for publishing and typesetting industry. Generates code for typesetter.

Product: XLATE
Company: Resource Publications, Inc., Resource Systems
Address: 160 East Virginia Street, Suite 290
  San Jose, CA 95112
Phone: (408) 286-8505
List Price: $400
System Requirements: IBM PC series computer or compatible
Comments: Copies text files, replacing identified strings with designated information. Converts WordStar document files into standard text files for input to typesetters. Builds reusable specification files for translation instructions.

Utility software

Product: Switcher Construction Kit
Company: Apple Computer, Inc.
Address: 20525 Mariani Avenue
  Cupertino, CA 95014
Phone: (408) 996-1010
List Price: $19.95
System Requirements: Macintosh

Video digitizers

Product: MacVision
Company: Koala Technologies Corporation

Address: 3100 Patrick Henry Drive
Santa Clara, CA 95052
Phone: (408) 986-8866
List Price: $399
System Requirements: Macintosh, printer

Product: Magic
Company: New Image Technologies, Inc.
Address: 10300 Greenbelt Road, #104
Seabrook, MD 20706
Phone: (301) 464-3100
List Price: $399 ($150 for black-and-white video camera)
System Requirements: Macintosh, printer

Product: MicronEye
Company: Micron Technology, Inc., Systems Group
Address: 1447 Tyrell Lane
Boise, ID 83706
Phone: (208) 386-3800
List Price: $395
System Requirements: Macintosh

Product: Micro-Imager
Company: Servidyne Systems, Inc.
Address: 1735 Defoor Place NW, Box 93846
Atlanta, GA 30377
Phone: (404) 352-2050
List Price: $350
System Requirements: Macintosh, video camera, video monitor

Word processing software

Product: IBM DisplayWrite Series
Company: IBM
Address: 1133 Westchester Avenue
White Plains, NY 10604
Phone: (914) 765-1900
List Price: $95–$299
System Requirements: IBM PC, XT, AT, Portable

Product: MacWrite
Company: Apple Computer, Inc.
Address: 20525 Mariani Avenue
Cupertino, CA 95014
Phone: (408) 996-1010
List Price: $125
System Requirements: Macintosh

Product: Multi-Lingual Scribe
Company: Gamma Productions, Inc.
Address: 710 Wilshire Blvd., Suite 609
  Santa Monica, CA 90401
Phone: (213) 394-8622
List Price: $349.95; demo, $15 plus $3 shipping ($15 applicable to purchase price)
System Requirements: IBM PC, XT, AT, or 100 percent graphics-compatible computer; DOS 2.0 or higher; 320K RAM; IBM or Hercules Color Graphics Card; black-and-white composite or color monitor

Product: Multimate Word Processor
Company: Multimate International Corporation
Address: 52 Oakland Avenue
  East Hartford, CT 06108-9911
Phone: (800) 842-8676, (203) 522-2116
List Price: $495
System Requirements: IBM PC, XT, or AT; 256K RAM

Product: PFS:Write
Company: Software Publishing Corporation
Address: 1901 Landings Drive
  Mountain View, CA 94043
Phone: (415) 962-8910
List Price: Apple version, $125; IBM version, $140
System Requirements: Apple IIe or IIc; IBM PC, XT, AT, Portable, or compatibles

Product: Spellbinder, Spellbinder Desktop Publisher
Company: Lexisoft
Address: P.O. Box 1950
  Davis, CA 95617
Phone: (916) 758-3630
List Price: $495
System Requirements: IBM PC-series computer or compatible

Product: Word
Company: Microsoft, Inc.
Address: 16011 NE 36th Way, Box 97017
  Redmond, WA 98073-9717
Phone: (800) 426-9400, (206) 882-8088
List Price: $375
System Requirements: Macintosh or IBM PC

Product: WordPerfect
Company: Satellite Software International

Address: 266 West Center
Orem, UT 84057
Phone: (801) 224-4000
List Price: $495
System Requirements: IBM PC, AT, XT, or compatible; or Apple IIe or IIc, 128K

Product: WordStar
Company: MicroPro International Corporation
Address: 33 San Pablo Avenue
San Rafael, CA 94903
Phone: (415) 499-1200
List Price: $350
System Requirements: Apple II Plus, IIe, or III with Z80 card; or IBM PC-series computer

Product: XyWrite
Company: XyQuest
Address: Box 372
Bedford, MA 01730
Phone: (617) 275-4439
List Price: Contact company for price
System Requirements: IBM PC, AT, XT, or compatible; DOS 2.1 or 3.0; 256K; one double- sided disk drive

Workstations

Product: CadMac
Company: Cadmus Computer Systems
Address: 500 Suffolk Street
Lowell, MA 01854
Phone: (800) 221-3384, (617) 453-2899
List Price: $25,000 with 2 megabytes of RAM, an 80-megabyte disk, and a 30-megabyte tape system (MC68020 microprocessor); system based on MC68010, $21,000
System Requirements: PostScript-compatible page printer

Product: IBM RT PC
Company: IBM
Address: 1133 Westchester Avenue
White Plains, NY 10604
Phone: (914) 765-1900
List Price: $12,000–$23,000

Workstation hardware/software system

Product: Electronic Publishing System
Company: Interleaf, Inc.
Address: 1100 Massachusetts Avenue
   Cambridge, MA 02138
Phone: (617) 497-5570
List Price: $100,000 +
System Requirements: Apollo, DEC, IBM, or Sun workstation

Workstation software

Product: Documentation Workstation
Company: Context Corporation
Address: 8285 S.W. Nimbus Avenue
   Beaverton, OR 97005
Phone: (503) 626-1173
List Price: $16,900–$28,900
System Requirements: Apollo workstation

Product: Workstation Publishing Software
Company: Interleaf, Inc.
Address: 1100 Massachusetts Avenue
   Cambridge, MA 02138
Phone: (617) 497-5570
List Price: $1995
System Requirements: IBM RT PC

Product: Technical Publishing System
Company: Caddex Corporation
Address: 18532 142nd NE
   Woodinville, WA 98072
Phone: (206) 481-7751
List Price: Contact company for price
Comments: Slated for release in mid-1986.

Appendix C

Selected Bibliography

BOOKS

InfoVision, publisher of the *CAP Report* sells, for $49.95, the *1986 Buyer's Guide to Computer Aided Publishing*—hundreds of pages of product, service, and supplier data, including sections on CAP workstations, PC-based CAP systems, illustrator and presentation workstations, PC-based illustration systems, laser printers, phototypesetters, CAD/CAM workstations, scanners, media conversion software, service bureaus, and consultants, with more than 350 companies represented. The book also includes articles and overviews by industry specialists. *CAP Report* is a monthly newsletter about computer-aided publishing. It describes new products (usually with one featured in detail), lists resources, and explains aspects of computer-aided publishing. A one-year subscription for $195 includes a free copy of the $14.95 book CAD/CAM with Personal Computers by Pat Carbery of the *CAP Report* editorial board.
52 Dragon Court
Woburn, MA 01801
(617) 935-5186

The Chicago Manual of Style, 13th edition
The University of Chicago Press, 1982
With a greatly improved index, the 13th edition of this authoritative style manual covers everything from the correct use of hyphens to book design and layout.

The Complete Handbook of Personal Computer Communications
Glossbrenner, Alfred
St. Martin's Press, 1985
A comprehensive guide.

The Complete IBM Personal Computer
Novogrodsky, Seth; Davis, Frederic E.
Simon and Schuster, 1985.
Guide to hardware expansion for the IBM PC, XT, AT, and compatibles.

Direct Mail and Mail Order Handbook
Hodgson, S. Richard
Dartnell Corporation, Chicago, 1981
Excellent reference book with well over 1000 pages.

Directory of Online Databases
Cuadra Associates, Inc.
2001 Wilshire Blvd., Suite 305
Santa Monica, CA 90403
(213) 764-5100

Editing by Design: Word-and-Picture Communication for Editors and Designers
White, Jan V.
R. R. Bowker Company,1984
A superb, must-read book for aspiring desktop publishers. Deals with many graphic and textual elements of design. By the same author: Designing for Magazines, R.R. Bowker, 1976.

The Elements of Style
Strunk, William, Jr., and White, E.B.
Macmillan, 1979
This is the classic little book about clean, crisp, clear writing.

Encyclopedia of Associations
Gale Research Company, 1986
A valuable reference work that contains summary information about thousands of nonprofit organizations and other associations.

Encyclopedia of Information Systems and Services
Gale Research Company
Book Tower
Detroit, MI 48226

The Federal Data Base Finder: A Dictionary of Free and Fee-Based Data Bases and Fields
Information USA, Inc.
12400 Beall Mountain Road
Potomac, MD 20854
(301) 983-8220

The Graphic Designers Handbook
Campbell, Alastair
QED Publishing, 1983
Good book for basic concepts of graphic design.

Infomania: The Guide to Essential Electronic Services
Ferrarini, Elizabeth M.
Houghton Mifflin Company, 1985
Survey of on-line databases.

Information Sources
The Annual Directory of the Information Industry Association (IIA)
316 Pennsylvania Avenue, SE, Suite 400
Washington, DC 20003
(202) 544-1969

Inside LaserWriter
Apple Computer, Inc., 1986
LaserWriter technical reference.

Inside Macintosh, vols. 1–4
Apple Computer, Inc.
Addison-Wesley Publishing Company, 1986
Macintosh technical reference.

MacGraphics for Business
Mar, Jerry
Scott, Foresman and Company, 1986
A good source for practical ideas.

Macintosh: A Concise Guide to Applications Software
van Nouhuys, Dirk
Wiley Press, 1985
How to use the most important Macintosh application programs.

North American Online Directory
R.R. Bowker and Company
1180 Sixth Avenue
New York, NY 10036
(212) 764-5100

PostScript Language Reference Manual
Adobe Systems, Inc.
Addison-Wesley Publishing Company, 1985
Comprehensive description of and reference to PostScript

PostScript Language Tutorial and Cookbook
Adobe Systems, Inc.
Addison-Wesley Publishing Company, 1985
Tutorial on programming in PostScript and a collection of useful programming procedures.

Publishing Newsletters
Hudson, Howard Penn
Charles Scribner's Sons, 1982
An excellent guide to the newsletter business.

Words into Type, 3rd edition
Prentice-Hall
Englewood Cliffs, NJ, 1974
Similar in scope and function to the *Chicago* manual. Both books are good, but we prefer The Chicago Manual of Style.

A REVIEW OF PERIODICAL LITERATURE

Design and Graphics

"Catalog Printing Market"
Toth, Debora
Graphic Arts Monthly, vol. 57 (Sept. 1985), 71
Discusses catalogs, advertising, direct-mail innovations, and advertising layout and typography.

"Combining the Verbal and the Visual"
Marrs, Rebecca
American Printer, vol. 194 (May 1985), 86
Graphic arts and electronic publishing.

"Corporate I.D.—Logo Logic"
New Englander, vol. 22, no. 12 (April 1976), 46–47
Advice on the development of corporate identification programs. Recommends that a logo should incorporate a symbol that conveys the essence of the company's operations. Suggests that a logo should be simple and reproduce in black and white or color, be adaptable to animation, and preferably be geometric.

"The Design of Indexes"
Ridehalgh, N.
Indexer (GB), vol. 14, no. 3 (April 1985), 165–74
Typography, layout, and design of indexes.

"Electronic Imaging Systems Offer Alternatives to Graphic Arts Users"
Fay, Thomas
Graphic Arts Monthly, vol. 57 (Oct. 1985), S58
Uses and costs of electronic publishing systems for graphic arts.

"Electronic Systems Targeted for Corporate Publishing Departments"
Benson, Roger R.
Graphic Arts Monthly, vol. 57 (April 1985), 142

"Graphic Design for Computer Graphics"
Marcus, Aaron
Computers in Industry, vol. 5, no. 1 (March 1984), 51–63
States that computer graphics specialists have the responsibility of modernizing communication between the display surface of a computer and the human viewer. Provides examples of how graphic design can improve three different types of computer graphics: outerfaces, interfaces, and innerfaces.

"How to Buy Design Services for Your Publications"
Association Management, vol. 34, no. 7 (July 1982), 85–87
How a talented designer can be as important as a talented researcher,
writer, or editor and why a contract is very important.

"Integrated Electronic System for Three Publishing Applications"
Graphic Arts Monthly, vol. 57 (Jan. 1985), 90

"Into the Electronic Age: A Lasers in Graphics Preview"
Dunn, S. Thomas
American Printer, vol. 194 (July 1985), 50
Technological innovations in laser printers.

"Merging Text and Graphics: The Good, the Bad"
Krummel, Larry
American Printer, vol. 192 (Oct. 1983), 216
Analysis of graphics arts in electronic publishing systems.

"Picking Type That Does the Job as to Fit, Message, Readability"
Haley, Allan
Printing Impressions vol. 20, no. 4 (Sept. 1977), 70, 71
Guidelines for selecting typefaces and typestyles for use in advertising,
menus, and invitations.

"Prospects for Artificial Intelligence in the Graphic Arts Industry"
Cheslow, Robert
Graphic Arts Monthly, vol. 57 (Oct. 1985), S46
How computer graphics equipment and artificial intelligence can be com-
bined in electronic publishing systems.

"The Storage, Retrieval and Display of Integrated Graphics and Text"
Earnshaw, R.A.
Computer Graphics '84. Proceedings of the International Conference
(1984), 53–62

"Technical Publishing System Adds Enhanced Graphics Capabilities"
Graphic Arts Monthly, vol. 57 (Feb. 1985), S70

"What Are the Purposes of an Advertisement?"
Industrial Marketing, vol. 64, no. 6 (June 1979), 130
Guidelines for creating effective advertising with typography, graphics, and
layout.

"What Is a Good Letterheading?"
Natal, Philip
Industrial Marketing Digest (UK), vol. 10, no. 4 (Fourth Quarter 1985),
33–38
Typographer Beatrice Warde discusses letterhead design

Electronic and Desktop Publishing

"Ad Agency Finds Automation Pays Off"
ComputerData (Canada), vol. 8, no. 12 (Dec. 1983), 12
How Cote Advertising Ltd. (Mississauga, Ontario) began automation with
a word processing system and a typography system.

"Authors Versus Producers: Narrowing the Gap with Computer-Aided
Publishing"
American Printer, vol. 194 (May 1985), 72

"Book Publishing: The Electronic Revolution"
Paul, Sandra K.
Videodisc/Videotex, vol. 2, no. 3 (Summer 1982), 206–211
How a combination of computer and computer-assisted technologies— in-
volving both electronic data input and paper hard copy—will probably
bring about revolutionary changes in books within the decade and that
publishers will have to develop a cooperative relationship with computers.

"Boosting Productivity through Timely, Tailored Documents"
Benson, Roger R.
Graphic Arts Monthly, vol. 57 (March 1985), 108
Analysis of electronic publishing with schematic of electronic publishing
system.

"Bring the Power of Publishing to Your PC: New Options Let You Produce
Professional-Looking Documents on Your Computer"
Simonsen, Redmond
Popular Computing, vol. 5 no. 1 (Nov. 1985), 56–59
Discusses laser printers, digitizers, page makeup programs, and typesetting
communication systems.

"The Business Behind the Book: Current Trends and Forecasts in
Publishing"
Neuman, Susan B.
English Journal, vol. 74 (Nov. 1985), 68
Makes predictions about publishers and publishing; booksellers and book-
selling, and electronic publishing.

"Capturing Keystrokes"
Remer, Daniel
PC, vol. 1 no. 7 (Nov. 1982), 232–236
Lists and recommends hardware and software needed by the IBM PC for
typesetting.

"Computer Publishing: Securing the Competitive Edge"
Dorman, William J.
American Printer, vol. 194 (Aug. 1985), 54
U.S. market estimates and market segmentation for computer publishing systems.

"Desktop Publishing: Apple's Macintosh Office Strategy Has Major Implications for the Publishing Industry"
Barry, John; Davis, Frederic E.; and Wiesenberg, Michael
A+, vol. 3 (May 1985), 119
Apple Macintosh, Apple LaserWriter, Allied-Mergenthaler typesetting machines, and technological innovations related to computer typography.

"Desktop Publishing: The One-Stop Type Shop"
Seymour, Jim
Today's Office, vol. 20, no. 3 (Aug. 1985), 23–25
How personal computers and inexpensive laser printers have converted secretarial workstations into typesetting and printing centers.

"Desktop Publishing Bandwagon Gaining Momentum with Dealers"
Chartock, D.S.
Computer & Software News, vol. 3, no. 37 (Sept. 16, 1985) 1, 16
Estimates that by 1989 the desktop publishing market will reach the $1 billion level.

"Desktop Publishing Comes of Age."
Sandberg-Diment, Erik
New York Times, vol. 135 (Nov. 26, 1985), 21(N), C4(L)
Commentary on the growing field of desktop publishing.

"Desktop Publishing Could Be Big Business: It Could Propel the Next Sales in Personal Computers"
Rose, Craig D.
Electronics, vol. 58 (Sept. 9, 1985), 30
Aldus Corporation's Pagemaker, the Apple Macintosh, and the Apple Laserwriter.

"Desktop Publishing Popularity Booms"
Forbes, Jim
InfoWorld, vol. 7 no. 37 (Sept. 16, 1985), 1

"Desktop Publishing with the Macintosh"
Markoff, J.; Robinson, P.; and Osgood, D.
Byte, vol. 10, no. 5 (May 1985) 371, 373, 375

"Developments in Electronic Publishing"
Borrell, Jerry
Bulletin of ASIS, vol. 8, no. 5 (June 1982), 11–15
How word processing, photocomposition and phototypesetting, computer graphics, laser scanning, communications, and information retrieval can be employed to assemble both graphics and text and to manipulate images. Speculates that as long as print and video media have different psycho-physiological effects, there will be demand for familiar print products.

"DRI's Latest Spinoff to Do Desktop Publishing"
Foster, E.
InfoWorld, vol. 7, no. 39 (Sept. 30, 1985) 3
Ventura Software is a new independent spinoff company from Digital Research, Inc., that will specialize in desktop publishing software for the IBM PC and compatibles.

"Electronic Pagination and Hard Work Produce Documentation 'Miracle.'"
Roth, Jill
American Printer, vol. 194 (Aug. 1985), 60
How electronic publishing increased quality control in documentation.

"Electronic Publishing—A Boon for Forms Management"
Office, vol. 102, no. 6 (Dec. 1985), 76–79
Interview with H. E. Benson, former purchasing and forms administration manager of Tenneco Corporation about how electronic publishing will make forms management a part of information management.

"Electronic Publishing—Are All the Pieces Together?"
Cunningham, Michael
Graphic Arts Monthly, vol. 57 (Sept. 1985), 100
Typical work flow and problems associated with publishing. The interpage approach to electronic publishing.

"Electronic Publishing: The Future Convergence of Many Disciplines"
Gibbins, Patrick
Journal of Information Science Principles & Practice (Netherlands), vol. 8, no. 3 (April 1984), 123–129
Identifies needs for the design of information products in a form independent of their ultimate form of delivery and discusses how repackaging information in many forms provides hope for the future development of the publishing industry.

"Electronic Publishing: The Predicament of Occasional Users in the Editorial Process"
Standera, O. L.
Journal of the ASIS, vol. 36, no. 4 (July 1985), 230–240
Study of problems created by the editorial process for occasional users of electronic publishing.

"Electronic Publishing Captures All Eyes"
Frank, Jerome P.
Publishers Weekly, vol. 226 (Nov. 2, 1984), 44

"Electronic Publishing for Policy Issuance"
Laufer, Mary E.
Best's Review (Life/Health), vol. 86, no. 4 (Aug. 1985), 98–102
Study of how the Hartford Insurance Group developed a system for printing
and distribution of various field insurance functions.

"Electronic Publishing Lands on the Desktop"
Borrell, Jerry
Mini-Micro Systems, vol. 18, no. 16 (Dec. 1985), 85–92
Discusses how electronic publishing is challenging traditional printing
methods by combining microcomputers, page scanners, and laser printers
with specialized software.

"Electronic Publishing System Helps Packaging Firm Chart Growth"
Computerworld, vol. 19, no. 45 (Nov. 11, 1985), 68
Discussion of how American Can Company (Greenwich, Connecticut) di-
rectors and executives obtained better trend analyses and forecasts by using
Interleaf Electronic Publishing System software with a Sun Microsystems
Sun 2/120 workstation and an Imagen 8/300 laser printer.

"Electronic Publishing System Manages Firm's 'Checklist'"
Computerworld, vol. 17, no. 30 (July 25, 1983), 38, 40
How Ace Hardware Corporation (Oak Brook, Illinois) benefited from the
installation of an electronic publishing system by getting better dealer service, faster turnaround on orders, and higher service quality.

"Electronic Technology Spawns Potential for Customized Documents"
Infosystems, vol. 32 (Feb. 1985), 20

"EPB: Electronic Publishing and Bookselling"
Katz, Bill
Library Journal, vol. 110 (July 1985), 50

"Fighting the Goliaths in Electronic Publishing"
Rose, Craig D.
Electronics, vol. 58 (Dec. 9, 1985), 54
Interleaf expects software- and hardware-independent strategy will give it
an edge over the giants. Predicts huge growth for electronic publishing
systems.

"Firm Claims Scanner Is First Step Toward Desktop Publishing"
Littmann, J.
PC Week, vol. 2, no. 46 (Nov. 19, 1985) 33–34
Microtek Labs' MS-300 document scanner can read detailed character bit patterns and is hailed by the firm as being the first step toward desktop publishing.

"Fit to Print"
Bernstein, Amy
Business Computer Systems, vol. 4, no. 1 (Jan. 1985), 48–55
How electronic publishing systems require fewer human and material resources and how project turnaround time is reduced. Prediction that electronic publishing will become a part of every U.S. business and that by 1990 more than 200,000 companies will use in-plant publishing systems.

"Future Trends in A&I Data-Base Publication"
Williams, Martha and Brandhorst, Ted
Bulletin of ASIS, vol. 5, no. 3 (Feb. 1979), 27–28
How electronic publishing will affect publishers of abstracts and indexes (A&I).

"A Generation of PC Publishing Software Emerges"
Greitzer, J.
PC Week, vol. 2, no. 7 (Feb. 19, 1985) 59–60

"Have You Taught Your PC to Paste-Up?/Computer Sense: Writer, Editor, Illustrator or Designer Becomes Publisher"
Gluck, Dale and Rosen, Sheri
Communication World, vol. 2, no. 3 (March 1985), 29–32, 39
How desktop publishing represents an efficiency breakthrough in the typesetting and assembly of publications. Mentions Interleaf's OPS-2000, Texet's Live Image System, and the ViewTech Computer-Aided Publishing System.

"IBM PCs Get Desktop Publishing"
Forbes, Jim
InfoWorld, vol. 7 no. 44 (Nov. 4, 1985), 11

"Implementing a Copier Program from Scratch"
Gardner, Barbara K.
Office, vol. 102, no. 4 (Oct. 1985), 202–203
How Pacific Mutual Life Insurance Company in Newport Beach, California, has been moving toward electronic publishing and distributed output.

"In-House Publishing Eases Printing Costs"
Forte, Joseph R.
Marketing News, vol. 19, no. 23 (Nov. 8, 1985), 25–26, 30
Discussion of how in-house electronic publishing aids efficient and rapid communications and makes marketing more efficient.

"In-House Publishing Set to Grow"
Haggerty, Steve
Electronics Week, vol. 57 (Nov. 26, 1984), 38

"In No Uncertain Terms: Defining Electronic Publishing Helps Clarify the Confusing Issues"
Klauber, James J.
American Printer, vol. 194 (Aug. 1985), 68
Business applications of electronic publishing and laser printers.

"Inhouse Publishing: From Concept to Print"
Allen, Robert
Modern Office Technology, vol. 30, no. 11 (Nov. 1985), 56–62
How distributed processing is affecting in-house printing by coupling personal computers to such devices as printers and digitizing scanners.

"Interleaf Aims at Office-Publications Market"
O'Reilly, Richard
Los Angeles Times, vol. 104 (June 10, 1985), Section IV, 3

"Interleaf Grows Apace"
Hamilton, Rosemary
Boston Business Journal (July 22, 1985), 1

"Laser Printing in Publishing"
McGauran, P.
Data Processing (GB), vol. 27, no. 3 (April 1985), 40, 41
How a UK publishing house has installed a desktop publishing system for short-run technical publications.

"Mac Business Appeal Pinned to Desktop Publishing"
Ranney, Elizabeth
InfoWorld, vol. 7, no. 46 (Nov. 18, 1985), 18
Predicts that sales of desktop publishing software and hardware will hit between $230 million and $280 million in 1986.

"New Power for the Printed Page; the Desktop Publishing Revolution"
Onosko, Timothy
Creative Computing, vol. 11 (Dec. 1985), 48
Includes information about PostScript, Apple Laserwriter, Apple Macintosh, ReadySetGo, MacPublisher, PageMaker.

"OCR in the Office of the Future"
Avedon, Don M.
Information & Records Management, vol. 15, no. 2 (Feb. 1981), 12, 40
How optical character recognition (OCR) can convert typewritten copy into digital form suitable for entry into other office machines. Mentions in-house typography.

"QMS Joins the Battle of Desktop Publishing"
Gantz, John
InfoWorld, vol. 8, no. 2 (Jan. 13, 1986), 19

"PC Based Publishing: Opportunity for Office Information Processing"
Kapoor, Ajit and Steiner, Peter
Graphic Arts Monthly, vol. 57 (Nov. 1985), 78
Explores the role of microcomputers in electronic publishing and computerized typesetting.

"A PC in the Type Shop: Better Than Dedicated"
Wolbart, Susan
PC, vol. 3 (Jan. 24, 1984), 214
IBM PCs used in electronic publishing system.

"Photocomposition: Its Technology Advances"
Kellner, Mark A.
Office, vol. 102, no. 4 (Oct. 1985), 18, 120
How typesetting is now available in offices at prices far more reasonable than in the past.

"Printers with Page-Description Languages Due"
Sorensen, Karen
InfoWorld, vol. 7, no. 51 (Dec. 23, 1985) 5

"Printing and Its New Love" [electronic publishing]
Ewer, William H.
Graphic Arts Monthly, vol. 57 (July 1985), S60

"Product Line Requires Electronic Publishing for Documentation"
Graphic Arts Monthly, vol. 57 (Sept. 1985), 105
How Texet's Live Image Publishing System is used by Transcom Electronics for publishing technical literature.

"Program Gives Mac Publishing Features to PC"
Edelhart, Mike
PC Week, vol. 2, no. 48 (Dec. 3, 1985) 4
T/Maker's ClickArt Personal Publisher.

"Relief Is on the Way for Documentation Headaches—Electronic Publishing Systems Automate the Chore"
Iversen, Wesley R.
Electronics, vol. 59, no. 8 (Feb. 1986), 76–78
How computer aided design (CAD) and electronic technical publishing systems are merging to provide better ways to produce product documentation.

"A Revolution Is Coming in In-House Printing"
Ruderman, Gary S. and Hendrickson, Bill
Purchasing, vol. 98 (June 27, 1985), 82
Corporate electronic publishing systems using Interleaf OPS-2000 Office
Publishing System and Interleaf TPS-2000 Technical Publishing System.

"Software for Desktop Publishing"
A+, vol. 3 (May 1985), 124
Computer page layout programs for Apple Macintosh.

"Still a Need for Paper"
Myers, Edith
Datamation, vol. 30, no. 2 (Feb. 1984), 91–94
How Ace Hardware Company produces ten different versions of its cata-
log, each about 4400 pages long and has realized cost savings, speed, and
accuracy as a result of implementing electronic publishing.

"Successful EP (Electronic Publishing) Transition"
Graphic Arts Monthly, vol. 57 (Oct. 1985), S56
Making a smooth transition from manual systems to electronic publishing
systems.

"Vendors Plan Joint Demos of Desktop Publishing"
Sorensen, Karen
InfoWorld, vol. 7 no. 46 (Nov. 18, 1985), 18

"Workstation at Hub of Corporate Publishing System"
Graphic Arts Monthly, vol. 57 (April 1985), 136
Interleaf's electronic publishing system.

Newspapers and Newsletters

"Computers Rapidly Replacing Graphic Artists' Mechanical Tools"
Editor & Publisher, vol. 118 (Nov. 9, 1985), 19
How computer graphics can be used in newspaper publishing.

"Corporate Publishing: PCs Are Giving Businesses More Freedom of the
Press"
Greitzer, John
PC Week, vol. 2 (Feb. 19, 1985), 55
Business publishing, newsletters, newspapers.

"Front Page Still Off-Limits to Art Departments."
Fitzgerald, Mark
Editor & Publisher, vol. 118 (Nov. 9, 1985), 19
Discussion of graphic arts, layout, and typography for newspapers.

"High-Speed Newspaper"
Cornez, Marie C.
Graphic Arts Monthly, vol. 57 (Oct. 1985), S36
How electronic equipment allows the *Investor's Daily* to stay on top of the
world of investment and finance.

"The Mac Makes News in the Newsroom"
Webb, Craig
A+, vol. 4, no. 3 (March 1986), 118–124
More and more newspapers are using Macintoshes in their graphics depart-
ments.

"More Newspaper Art Departments Using Computers for Graphics"
Editor & Publisher, vol. 118 (Sept. 28, 1985), 28
Survey of computer graphics usage in newspaper layout and typography
by the Society of Newspaper Design.

"Newspaper Firms Involved in Electronic Publishing"
Miller, Tim
Editor & Publisher, vol. 118 (March 9, 1985), 28

"PCs Help the Fourth Estate Stay State-of-the-Art"
PC Week, vol. 2 (Feb. 19, 1985), 58
Newspaper layout and typography at the Providence Journal-Bulletin.

"The Perception of Graphics"
Fitzgerald, Mark
Editor & Publisher, vol. 117 (Nov. 3, 1984), 14
Influenced by *USA Today*, newspapers are packed with more graphic in-
formation than ever before.

"Promotional Newsletters May Be on the Decline: Those with Helpful
Features and Interesting Articles Are Still Making the Grade"
Behrens, John C.
American Printer, vol. 194 (June 1985), 138
Newsletter publishing, typography, advertising, and direct-mail.

"Tabloids—Ugly Ducklings No Longer"
Fitzgerald, Mark
Editor & Publisher, vol. 117 (Nov. 3, 1984), 16
Newspaper layout and typography.

Page Description Languages

"Adding Page Description Languages"
Murphy, D.
Computer Systems News, No. 221 (July 22, 1985), 26
Interpress, PostScript, and Riprint.

"Adobe Systems' PostScript"
Raskin, Robin
PC, vol. 5, no. 1 (Jan. 14, 1986), 108–109

"Data Interchange: The Industry Desperately Needs Standards"
Fastie, Will
PC Tech Journal, vol. 3 no. 10 (Oct. 1985), 9–10
Suggests that IBM's Document Content Architecture (DCA) and Post-Script can provide initial standards for text processing systems.

"The Design of a Device Independent Print File Format"
Brotz, D.K.; Geschke, C.M.; Warnock, J.E.
Digest of Papers, COMPCON Spring '84. Twenty-eighth IEEE Computer Society International Conference (IEEE Cat. No. 84CH2017-2) (1984), 108
Early paper on PostScript.

"Digitized Fonts in PostScript"
Cavuoto, J.
Computer Graphics World, vol. 8, no. 9 (Sept. 1985), 27–30
PostScript's strength in type fonts has achieved a satisfactory compromise among speed, memory, and quality considerations.

"From Text Formatter to Printer"
Brown, H.
PROTEXT I. Proceedings of the First International Conference on Text Processing Systems (1984), 98–107
Device-independent text formatters such as TEX and *troff*.

"An Important PostScript"
Jeffries, Ron
PC, vol. 4, no. 19 (Sept. 17, 1985), 77–80
Quantum Leap column presents an overview of PostScript.

"Interpress and PostScript compared"
Mendelson, Jerry
Graphic Arts Monthly, vol. 57 (Sept. 1985), 90
Comparison of Adobe's PostScript and Xerox's Interpress page description languages.

"Introduction to the TEX Language"
Bemer, R.W.
Interface Age, vol. 3, no. 8 (Aug. 1978), 144–47

"Knuth Makes Mathematical Typography an Art"
Swaine, Michael
InfoWorld, vol. 5 no. 11 (March 14, 1983), 25–28
Science column examines TEX and Metafont.

"The Language That Talks to Your Printer"
Sprague, Richard
MacWorld, vol. 2 no. 2 (Feb. 1985), 106–115
Discusses PostScript.

"PostScript: Master of the Raster"
Nace, Ted
PC World, vol. 3, no. 8 (Aug. 1985), 257–262

"PostScript: The Medium and the Message"
Rosenthal, Steve
A+, vol. 3, no. 9 (Sept. 1985), 81–84
Fourth and last part of a series on PostScript.

"The PostScript Horizon"
Stahr, Lisa B
MacWorld, vol. 2, no. 2 (Feb. 1985), 111

"Shaping PostScript to Do Your Bidding"
Rosenthal, Steve
A+, vol. 3, no. 7 (July 1985), 61–66
Second part of a tutorial on using PostScript.

"Softer Tools for Graphic Arts: Matching the Ambidexterity of the Quill
Challenges Electronic Page Description Languages"
Warnock, John; Nace, Ted
Graphic Arts Monthly, vol. 57 (Oct. 1985), S20
Discussion of PostScript.

"Standards Battle Brews over Page-Description Language"
Schneiderman, R.
Systems & Software, vol. 4, no. 9 (Sept. 1985), 22, 24
Interpress vs. PostScript.

"TEX on the Mac"
A+, vol. 3, no. 5 (May 1985), 128

"TEX Must Eventually Replace *nroff/troff*"
Murphy, T. Proceedings of the EUUG Conference. European UNIX Systems User Group Spring Meeting (1985), 94

"TEX's Coming of Age"
MacKay, P.A. PROTEXT I. Proceedings of the First International Conference on Text Processing Systems (1984), 26–34

"Text Presentation with PostScript"
Rosenthal, Steve
A+, vol. 3, no. 8 (Aug. 1985), 73–77
Third part of a four-part tutorial on using PostScript.

"Two TEX Implementations for the IBM PC"
Furuta, Richard and MacKay, Pierre A.
Dr. Dobb's Journal, vol. 10, no. 9 (Sept. 1985), 80–91

Typography

"The Computer in Typography: Challenges and Opportunities"
Higgins, Jay and Higgins, James I., Jr.
Graphic Arts Monthly, vol. 55 (April 1983), 46

"Computers, Bibliography, and Foreign Language Typography"
Hewitt, H.-J.J.
Computers & Humanities, vol. 19, no. 2 (April–June 1985), 89–95
Compiling bibliographies with the assistance of a computer.

"Considerate Typography"
White, Jan V.
Folio, vol. 13 (March 1984), 97
Magazine and periodical design techniques.

"The Delicate Art of Digital Type: Classical Typographers Juggle Pixels
to Increase Readability"
Stewart, Doug
Popular Computing vol. 4, no. 3 (Jan. 1985), 99–102

"Digital Typography"
Day, Donald and Bigelow, Charles
Scientific American, vol. 249 (Aug. 1983), 106
Technological innovations in typesetting.

"Effective Direct Response Typography"
Hauptman, Don
Direct Marketing, vol. 42, no. 8 (Dec. 1979), 24–28
Guidelines for freelance or production people in how to turn manuscripts
into effective space ads, brochures, or self-mailers, coupons, and order
forms.

"Font Center Brings Typography to Electronic Printing"
Shanks, Lorna
Graphic Arts Monthly, vol. 57 (May 1985), 74

"Font Design for Personal Workstations"
Bigelow, C.
Byte, vol. 10, no. 1 (Jan. 1985), 255–70

"Publisher-Quality Typography Is Here"
Sargent, J.H.
MIS Week, vol. 5, no. 11 (March 14, 1984) 47
How typography is a practical tool that can highlight key sentences, sort information into categories, and make information more readable.

"Size Measures and National Characters in Computer Generated Text with Typography"
PROTEXT I. Proceedings of the First International Conference on Text Processing Systems (1984), 222–226

"Typographic Quality Printing on Plain Paper: Filling a Product Gap in Output Systems"
Spencer, David R.
Graphic Arts Monthly, vol. 57 (April 1985), 110
Discussion of quality of various output devices. Includes schematic of thin diagonal line that shows how resolution and associated dot size affect thickness and jaggedness of lines (also includes related article on defining elements of electronic publishing).

"Type and Letterform in Presentation Graphics"
Mathews, E.
Computer Graphics World, vol. 8, no. 9 (Sept. 1985), 15–24
How recognizing the principles of readability and aesthetics in type and building on that knowledge of form and function will hasten the evolution of automated presentation graphics systems.

"Typography Gets Down to Business"
Roe-Hafer, Ann
Graphic Arts Monthly, vol. 57 (July 1985), S46

"Using Electronic Typography to Enhance Visual Communications"
Boucher, Bert
Office, vol. 98, no. 4 (Oct. 1983), 39–40
How computers can simplify and enhance the creation of illustrative and phototypeset materials.

"Zapf on Tomorrow's Type"
Anonymous
Communication World, vol. 1, no. 1 (Nov. 1983), 20–21
Hermann Zapf, the creator of the Palatino, Melior, and Optima typefaces, discusses some pitfalls of computer typography.

Glossary

These definitions are associated with desktop publishing. Many of these definitions have other meanings in other disciplines and other areas.

*   *   *

air—unused space on a page; also called white space.

American National Standards Institute (ANSI)—the group that gives official sanction to programming languages.

art—for the purpose of page layout, everything that is not text.

ascender—the part of a letter that extends above the *x-height*, as the upper half of the vertical stroke of a *d*.

ASCII—American Standard Code for Information Exchange. A method of encoding alphanumeric and symbolic characters in a format that is convenient for electronic storage and data communication.

back matter—any part of a book or manual, such as an index, that comes after the *body* text.

banner—a heading or title that extends the width of a page; any large heading or title.

baseline—the line on which uppercase letters, and lowercase letters exclusive of their descenders, sit; used as a reference point for vertical alignment of letters and for interline spacing.

baud—the rate at which electronic transmissions take place, usually between computers, generally representing bits per second; named after J. M. E. Baudot (1845-1903), a French inventor; often used to refer to the transmission speed of data by modem; common modem ratings are 300, 1200, and 2400.

bit map—a computerized dot-by-dot description of an image, with each dot represented by a bit (binary digit) 0 (off) or 1 (on).

bleed—printing or illustrations that run off a page.

block diagram—a chartlike representation of the steps in a process, or a set of interconnected, labeled boxes representing the elements of a group of related processes, components of a system, manuals, etc.

block text—paragraphs with no indents.

body—in page layout, the primary area of text on a page; in editing, the complete text of a document.

bold[face]—type that has thicker, heavier lines than roman type; usually used for special emphasis, headings, etc. Extra bold is heavier still.

box—a rectangular section of text and/or graphics, usually delimited by printed rules. A large box of text is often called a *sidebar*.

byte—eight bits.

CAD/CAM—computer-aided design and manufacturing.

callout—text that identifies elements of an illustration, usually a few words next to the illustration with a line or an arrow running from the text to the element being described; or any material, such as a *pull quote*, that is called out of text.

camera-ready—finished material that is ready to be reproduced or printed.

caps—capital letters; uppercase letters.

caption—text that accompanies an illustration.

Centronics—a form of *parallel* output; so called because the Centronics Corporation, a pioneer in the computer printer field, used this protocol for the interfaces on its early printer models.

cold type—type produced electronically or photographically, as opposed to *hot type*.

column—a vertical area of running text on a page.

column inch—an area one column wide by one inch tall. Publishers use this measurement to determine advertising costs in a publication.

commands—formatting instructions in a document that determine how the text will print; interactive instructions such as search-and-replace, cut-and-paste, or delete.

composition—laying out pages, usually with respect to the type; also, setting type.

composition and markup—laying out and marking up pages (see *markup*).

computer typography—the process of using computers to create typeset materials.

condensed—a font whose letters are narrower than the corresponding standard font.

continuous tone—*gray scale*.

controller—a microprocessor, or several of them, that directs the operations of a printer or disk drive.

copyfit—to estimate the amount of copy, or text, that will fit and how it will fit into a publication.

CPM—critical path management.

crop—to select, using crop marks, a region of a graphic image for use as an illustration.

CRT—cathode ray tube, as in a television or computer display.

cursor—a sometimes blinking marker on a display screen that indicates where in a document you are working.

cutline—*caption.*

cut and paste—to move blocks of text from one place in a document to another; originally a manual task but now usually performed electronically within a word processing program or editor.

daisywheel printer—a computer printer or electronic typewriter that has a spinning wheel with spokes that vaguely resembles a daisy. Each spoke contains one raised character; when the desired spoke is properly positioned in the printhead, a hammer presses the spoke against the ribbon, which is between the printhead and the paper.

dash—in typesetting or printing, a character consisting of a horizontal line sitting at about half the *x-height*; usually an en dash or an em dash. Hyphens are often mistakenly referred to as dashes.

descender—the part of a lowercase letter that extends below the baseline, as the tail of a *y*.

desktop publishing—the use of personal computers, page layout software, page printers, and typesetters to produce corporate documents, periodicals, books, or other materials.

desktop publishing system—a combination of hardware and software products used for desktop publishing, including a computer, page layout or page formatting software, and a high-resolution output device such as a laser printer.

digitize—transform an image into a dot pattern so that it can be printed by a dot matrix or laser printer.

digitized type—type stored in a computer in dot patterns rather than as strokes.

digitizer—an optical device that transforms an image into a dot pattern.

display—a CRT or monitor screen; sometimes the entire CRT unit or monitor; also, what you see on the screen.

display type—a typeface used for display purposes—that is, one not meant for ordinary text, but for advertisements, signs, headlines, and so on.

dot commands—nonprinting formatting commands that specify how a document prints, sometimes on a given printer, sometimes on more than one printer; so called because such commands are usually preceded by a period.

dot matrix printer—a printer that forms characters and graphics by the arrangement of dots.

dots per inch (dpi)—an expression of the resolution of a CRT screen or laser or dot matrix printer.

download—receive information from another computer; load a complete description of a font into the memory of a printer, enough to permit printing characters with that font.

downloadable font—a printer (usually laser printer) font that is stored on disk and that can be loaded into the printer's memory, as opposed to within a cartridge that must be plugged in.

draft quality—low-resolution output from a dot matrix printer; usually the result of the high-speed mode of a dot matrix printer with more than one mode, the slower speed of which produces letter-quality or near-letter-quality output, which is between the other two in quality.

driver—a program that controls a printer; short for *printer driver*.

dummy—a mockup of a typesetting job, usually showing locations of textual elements and illustrations.

duty cycle—the durability of a printer, usually expressed in terms of how many pages per month the manufacturer recommends printing.

dvi file—stands for *device-independent file*, a file produced by a formatting language and containing information that can be translated into a form that can print a document on any printer.

editor—a computer program that manipulates text on a CRT screen but usually does not have formatting capabilities for printing out documents. Compare with *word-processing program*, which usually has more capabilities. Also, a person who edits.

electronic publishing system—any computer system (micro, mini, or mainframe) that can assist with typography and/or page layout. A desktop publishing system is a type of electronic publishing system that is centered on personal computer technology.

em—originally the width of the letter *M* in a given font but now generally equivalent to the *point* size of the font; this measure is relative, since it changes with the font and the point size of the font, as opposed to pica and point, which are absolute measures.

em dash—a dash one em long.

em space—space one em wide.

emulate—one device performing like another.

en—usually half the width of an em.

en dash—a dash one en long.

en space—a space one en wide.

engine—the printing components of a laser printer, as opposed to the packaging and the extra memory usually installed by the company that markets the printer; Apple's LaserWriter and Hewlett-Packard's LaserJet printers, for example, use the Canon engine. Other engines are made by Ricoh, Hitachi, and Xerox.

expanded characters—extra-wide characters, particularly as produced on a dot matrix printer.

face—typeface.

family—a group of related fonts, as, for example, all of the fonts that make up Computer Modern.

figure space—in typesetting, a space used in setting numerals, usually equal to an en space.

file—a document as stored in a computer, either in its memory, where it can be edited, or in a storage unit such as a floppy disk drive or a hard disk.

fileserver—a computer storage device that stores computer files to which users on a network have equal access.

filler—a short piece of text or graphics that fills space in a periodical.

flag—the name and identifying marks of a publication, which are reproduced on the cover page.

float—let a piece of a document move on a page to where space is optimal. Some electronic formatting packages let various elements of a document float to where they fit best.

floppy disk—an electronic storage medium for computers, consisting of a thin, magnetic mylar sheet that revolves within a jacket and from which a floppy disk drive reads data, and to which it writes data.

flush left—aligned at the left margin.

flush right—aligned at the right margin.

folio—the page number, usually as printed in the *header* or *footer*; sometimes refers to an entire footer. In book production, a sheet of paper folded once to make two leaves (that is, four pages).

font—a group of type of one style and size.

font cartridge—a plug-in cartridge for a laser printer (sometimes also for a phototypestter) with one or more fonts.

foot—the bottom of a page.

footer—a running line of text at the bottom of a page that can include the page number, title of the document, the author's name, or other information.

format—the layout specifications of a printed document; to specify the format of a document.

formatting—arranging text on a page; the embedded commands that arrange text.

front end—the editing and formatting device that works with a typesetting machine.

front matter—title page, printing history, copyright page, table of contents, etc., as opposed to *body text*.

galley—A continuous column of typeset text not made up into pages; a copy of a galley supplied to a proofreader or to the author of an article or book for proofreading and last-minute changes.

gothic—any of a group of square-cut *sans serif* typefaces.

gray scale—different light intensities in an image or picture, representing a continuous spectrum from blackest black to whitest white; a simulation of this on a computer screen such that the gradations appear continuous (sometimes called *continuous gray scale* or *continuous tone*).

gutter—the area in the center of a two-page spread where the pages are connected to the spine of the publication.

hairline—in type design, the thinnest possible stroke; an extremely thin rule.

halftone—representation of *gray scale* by the use of dot patterns. Usually the darker the tone, the denser the dot pattern.

hanging indentation—type set such that the first one or more lines meet the left margin, but succeeding lines are indented a fixed distance (as in this glossary).

hard disk—a high-capacity storage medium for computers. Also called rigid disk or Winchester disk. Unlike *floppy disks*, hard disks are usually fixed in place, although some have removable cartridges.

head—a title at the top of a page or a section of text, usually set in larger type or in a different font or both to distinguish it from the main text.

header—a running line of text at the top of a page that can include the page number, title of the document, the author, or other information.

Helvetica—a popular *sans serif* typeface; depending on the manufacturer, also known as Geneva.

hot type—metal type in mechanical typesetting machines.

hyphen—a punctuation mark that divides words or other textual elements.

imaging area—the portion of a page that contains images, photos, text, illustrations, etc.; also called *live area*. This area is generally smaller than the actual size of the page.

impact printer—a printer that strikes the surface of the paper, usually with an inked ribbon between the actual striker and the paper; a dot matrix or daisywheel printer, as opposed to a laser printer or ink jet printer.

initial—a letter larger than normal that starts a chapter, or, less commonly, a section or paragraph; if the initial extends above the line, it is termed raised; if below, dropped.

ink jet printer—a form of dot matrix printer with an ink reservoir, instead of a ribbon, at the printhead position that sprays superheated ink in the dot patterns that make up characters onto the paper through miniature jets.

interface—the point at which two entities meet; usually refers to the method of interaction between people and computers or the connection between a computer and its peripheral devices.

interletter spacing—increasing or decreasing the spaces between letters, in addition to interword spacing, to justify text; sometimes called letterspacing.

interword spacing—increasing or decreasing the spaces between words to justify text.

italic—a slanted version of the roman font of the same name, and, particularly for electronically produced fonts, often derived from that font; for example, Computer Modern Italic is derived from Computer Modern Roman.

italics—an italic typestyle.

justification—alignment of a column of type at both the right and left margins.

kerning—placing letters relatively closer to or further from each other; adjusting textual elements minutely with respect to each other.

kerning pairs—letter combinations that look better closer to each other than proportional printing would normally place them. For example an *i* and an *l* should in some fonts be placed closer to each other than an *i* and an *a*.

landscape—printed page or screen orientation such that the shorter dimension of the rectangle is vertical.

laser printer—a printer that works on the same principle as a photocopy machine; it uses a laser beam to "etch" page images onto a photoelectric drum.

layout—the planning, design, and arranging of text and graphics on a page.

leader—regularly spaced intervals of the same character, usually to lead the eye across the line, as the dots in a table of contents between the end of a title and the page number.

leading—the extra space between lines of printed text (rhymes with *heading*).

letter quality—printer output, as from a daisywheel printer, that resembles typewriter type and is suitable for correspondence.

ligature—a special letter combination treated by some typesetters as a unit and often joined together when printed, as the Æ in *Æsop*, or *fi* in *finger*.

lightface—a typeface with thinner lines than roman type.

line art—art with no continuous tones.

Linotype—a trademark for a typesetting machine that makes lead casts of a solid line of type using dies that are selected automatically from a keyboard.

local-area network—a combination of computer hardware and software that interconnects numerous computers and peripherals to provide communications and access to shared data.

logo—an identifying symbol.

loose—having liberal amounts of space between letters, words, or lines; as opposed to *tight*.

lowercase—letters that are not capitals.

macro—a prewritten set of instructions that you can invoke to automate a particular computing task.

mainframe—a large computer, serving scores or even hundreds of users simultaneously; the larger computers made by IBM, Burroughs, Data General, etc., are mainframes; although a mainframe is usually considerably more powerful than a minicomputer, the distinction between a low-end mainframe and high-end minicomputer has of late become blurred.

makeup—the construction of a page.

marking engine—the part of a page printer that creates the image; in a laser printer the marking engine uses light from a laser to create the image.

markup—specifications, usually on the hard copy of a manuscript, of formatting instructions for the text, with indications of point sizes, typefaces, fonts, leading, etc.; analogous instructions in the form of formatting commands; to mark up.

markup language—a set of formatting commands that identify textual elements as opposed to giving specific formatting instructions.

masthead—a listing of personnel and business information related to a publication that is usually presented at the beginning of a periodical or editorial page of a newspaper.

mechanical—a completely constructed page or group of pages ready for reproduction.

minicomputer—a computer, typically the heart of a multiuser system with 6–20 users, considerably more powerful than the average personal computer, but not as powerful as the average mainframe, although both distinctions have of late become somewhat blurred; Hewlett-Packard and Digital Equipment Corporation are two of the better-known makers of minicomputers.

modem—a device with which you can send computer data over telephone lines.

modern—a typestyle, often one designed in the last century.

monospacing—allotting the same spacing for all characters, regardless of width, as opposed to *proportional spacing*.

mouse—a device with which you perform actions on a computer screen by moving the device on a surface, which causes an arrow or cursor on the screen to move correspondingly, and clicking a button on the device to activate a command or select an area on the screen for some action. So called because it vaguely resembles the animal.

multiuser—a computer system with more than one terminal, so several users can use the computer simultaneously.

near-typeset quality—the term applied by many manufacturers of computer equipment to the output of page printers that print at a resolution of 300 dots per inch or greater on plain paper. This is to differentiate them from typesetting devices that print on photographic film at resolutions of about 1200 dots per inch or greater.

newsletter—a publication aimed at a select group, such as investors in a particular kind of stock, or published by a users' group for its members; a subscription to the former sort of newsletter is usually expensive, but the latter is often inexpensive or free with membership.

nonprinting—characters, often formatting commands, that do not appear when the document prints and sometimes do not appear on the screen.

oblique—a slanted typestyle, as italic.

OEM—original equipment manufacturer; as a noun, a company that manufactures and sells a component to another company that then often repackages the component, usually adding certain enhancements, under the latter company's brand name; as a verb, to so supply components; Canon *OEM*s its LBP-CX laser printer engine to Hewlett-Packard for the LaserJet and LaserJet PLUS printers, and to Apple for the LaserWriter.

on—in typesetting, a way of expressing the *point* size of type plus leading; for example, 11 *on* 13 is 11-point type set with two points of leading between each line.

operating system—software that controls the operations of a computer system.

optical character reader—a form of optical *scanner* that "reads" letters on a printed page and translates them into the form used in a computer; often known as an *OCR*.

optical scanner—a device that "reads" flat art and digitizes the image.

output—as a noun, informally, information printed or plotted on paper or other flat medium; as a verb, to send information from a computer to the printed page.

output device—usually a printer or a *plotter*.

page composition—layout.

page makeup—the process with which you can lay out final output, whether by hand or electronically, with *page makeup software*.

page makeup software—a program with which you lay out pages on a *CRT*, to be printed later as they appear on the screen.

page proof—also called proof. An impression of typography after it has been put into page form.

paper sizes—letter: $8\frac{1}{2} \times 11$ inches, legal: $8\frac{1}{2} \times 14$ inches, A4: $11\frac{3}{4} \times 8\frac{1}{4}$ inches, B5: $10 \times 7\frac{3}{4}$ inches, mini; $8\frac{1}{2} \times 5\frac{1}{2}$ inches.

parallel—one of the output ports of a computer.

parallel printer—a printer that connects to a parallel port.

paste up—lay down on a board blocks of typeset text together with illustrations, headers, footers, and page numbers.

pasteup—the result of *pasting up*.

periodical publishing—the distribution of printed or reproduced materials of a similar theme or format at regular intervals.

personal computer—a computer used by one person and usually small enough to fit on top of a desk, often in a business setting.

personal publishing—the distribution of printed or reproduced materials for personal gain or self-satisfaction.

PERT—program evaluation and review technique.

phototypesetter—a typesetter that produces images directly on photographic film.

pica—a measure used in layout, typesetting, and printing; a pica is 12 *points*, or about one-sixth of an inch.

pitch—the number of characters per inch a printer produces; 10-pitch, for example, means 10 characters per inch.

pi font—a font consisting mostly or entirely of symbols, such as mathematical symbols, Greek letters, or logos.

pixel—picture element; in a *CRT*, one of the phosphor elements coating the inside of the picture tube that, when struck by an electron beam, glows; on a page printed by a laser printer or dot matrix printer, one of the dots that constitute the visible part of the image.

plate—a sheet of metal, plastic, glass, or other hard material on which images are photographically developed, engraved, etched, molded, drawn, etc., to be inked and placed in a printing press to produce impressions on other surfaces, often paper.

plotter—a device that draws lines on a piece of paper, or other flat medium, by moving one or more pens across the surface of the medium; with more than one pen, multiple colors are possible. A plotter is a *vector device*, as opposed to a *raster device* such as a dot-matrix or laser printer.

point—a unit of measurement equivalent to about $\frac{1}{72}$ inch, or $\frac{1}{12}$ *pica*.

port—a channel through which data leaves or enters a computer.

portrait—printed page or screen orientation in which the longer dimension of the rectangle is vertical.

postprocessor—a program that translates one set of usually high-level formatting commands into lower-level formatting commands. Same as a *translation program*.

PostScript—a de facto standard page description language from Adobe Systems, Inc.

print engine—the part of a page printer that performs the physical printing functions, as opposed to the *RIP*, which creates the image and controls the printing process.

printer—a person or company that produces printed matter, usually using a printing press; a device that produces printed output on paper or other flat medium, usually a dot matrix, daisywheel, laser, ink jet, or heat transfer printer.

printhead—the portion of a printer mechanism that brings the spokes of a daisywheel into contact with the paper, impresses the dot matrix pattern on the paper, forces the ink of an ink jet printer onto the paper, etc.

printer paper—special paper with removable perforations on the sides to accommodate the spokes of a tractor-feed mechanism; many sheets are linked together end to end, with perforations at the junctions for ease of separation.

proportional spacing—the allocation of proportionately more spacing for wider characters and less for narrower characters—for example, the *l* takes up less space than does the *m*; cf. *monospacing.*

protocol—any standard system for defining or controlling data communications.

pull quote—a small piece of text pulled from an article and set off in larger type or boxed for emphasis.

publishing—making information publicly available, usually through print media.

quad—in typesetting, spacing added to align an element in the center (*quad center*), to the left (*quad left*), or to the right (*quad right*) of a given space.

ragged—lines that do not align at a margin, usually the right margin; such an instance is called *ragged right.* If a column of type is aligned at the right margin (*flush right*) but not the left, the left margin is *ragged left.*

RIP—stands for raster image processor. A combination of computer software and hardware that controls the printing process by calculating the *bit maps* of images and instructing a printing device to create the images.

roman—the upright style of type most common in Western literature, as, for example, most of the type in this book, as opposed to italics or boldface.

RAM—random-access memory; memory whose contents you can alter and that vanishes when you turn off power.

raster device—a device that produces an image by turning dots on or off, such as a CRT screen with its pixels, or a laser printer, which deposits tiny dots of toner at thousands of predetermined points.

repro—finished reproduction, that is, *camera-ready* copy.

resident—held within memory; a resident font in a printer is permanently available within the printer's memory.

resolution—absolute or relative density of pixels on a CRT screen or dots on a page; usually expressed as *pixels* per inch for a screen and *dots per inch* for a page.

ROM—read-only memory; memory whose contents you cannot alter.

RS-232, RS-232C—one of the ports of a computer, often called the *serial* port; the protocol of data transfer through this port.

rule—a line, often one that extends the width of a column or page; sometimes the vertical line surrounding a box or separating one column from another.

sans serif—a font designed without *serifs*.

scanner—a device that *digitizes* images it picks up with some light-gathering device.

screening—converting a continuous *gray-scale* image into dot patterns; see *halftone*.

script font—a font that looks like handwriting.

SCSI—Small Computer System Interface.

serial—an output port of a computer.

serif—a font with embellishments on letters; such an embellishment. The small bars at the top and bottom of a capital are serifs.

service bureau—an establishment that sells a service, such as the use of its laser printer at a certain cost per page.

sidebar—text and/or graphics separated from the main document by rules or white space. Small sidebars are often called *boxes*.

slant—the orientation of a typestyle, whether *roman*, *italic*, or *slanted*.

slanted—a typestyle that is merely an angled version of the *roman* typestyle, as opposed to *italic*, in which the letters belong to the same *family* but are differently shaped.

slug line—a line of text identifying the content of a story.

small caps—capital letters in a font that are smaller than the regular capital letters in the font. The lowercase letters in the word CAPS in this sentence are small caps.

space—that portion of a layout that has nothing on it; the space character.

spread—two facing pages, particularly when treated as a unit.

spreadsheet—a paper or electronic grid of rows and columns on which you can do numerical projections, keep financial records, etc.

stem—the main stroke of a letter, as the vertical stroke of a *T*.

streaming tape—a device that dumps (or backs up) the contents of a *hard disk* onto magnetic tape, often a cassette.

tail—the lower portion of a letter, as the descender of a *y* or the curlicue of a *Q*.

TEX—a typesetting language devised by Stanford professor Donald Knuth.

text—type, as opposed to *art*.

thin space—a space smaller than a normal space.

translation program—a program that translates one set of formatting commands into another, usually higher-level formatting commands into lower.

troff—a *UNIX* typesetting language.

typeface—the design of a set of characters.

typesetter—a machine that produces typeset output, usually on photographic paper; a person who sets type.

typestyle—a style uniformly imposed on a typeface; e.g., italic, bold, outline.

UNIX—the operating system that controls most workstations.

uppercase—capital letters.

VDT—video display terminal.

vector device—an output device that prints by drawing lines, as opposed to a *raster device*; an example is a *plotter*.

weight—the relative thickness of the strokes of the characters in a particular font, usually describing whether a font is light, normal, or bold.

workstation—a computer system that usually consists of a large high-resolution display, is based on UNIX, and can function as a node in a network.

word processing program—a program with which you write, edit, and, to some extent, format text.

word processor—a person who enters text into a word processing system and sometimes formats it; also a computer system dedicated to word processing.

word wrap—a feature of word processing programs and text editors that moves a word to the next line as it is being typed if the word would otherwise extend beyond the right boundary of the screen or the right margin of the text area.

WYSIWYG—"what you see is what you get"; that is, what appears on a screen is similar to what will appear when the page is printed.

x-height—the measure, in a given *font*, of the height of the lowercase *x*.

Index